ALIENS AND STRANGERS?

Aliens and Strangers?

The Struggle for Coherence in the Everyday Lives of Evangelicals

ANNA STRHAN

OXFORD
UNIVERSITY PRESS

UNIVERSITY PRESS

Great Clarendon Street, Oxford, OX2 6DP,
United Kingdom

Oxford University Press is a department of the University of Oxford.
It furthers the University's objective of excellence in research, scholarship,
and education by publishing worldwide. Oxford is a registered trade mark of
Oxford University Press in the UK and in certain other countries

© Anna Strhan 2015

The moral rights of the author have been asserted

First Edition published in 2015

Impression: 1

Published in the United States of America by Oxford University Press
198 Madison Avenue, New York, NY 10016, United States of America

British Library Cataloguing in Publication Data
Data available

Library of Congress Control Number: 2014954694

ISBN 978-0-19-872446-9

Printed and bound by
CPI Group (UK) Ltd, Croydon, CR0 4YY

Acknowledgements

As this study examines how a religious world is made and sustained through forms of speaking and listening, so this book is also the product of my conversations with many people to whom I owe a great debt of gratitude. First and foremost, this research was made possible by the generosity and hospitality of members of 'St John's', whom I cannot thank by name. The leaders of the church didn't need to open up their congregation to my study. I am very grateful to them that they did, and to all the many individuals who participated in this research, for their kindness and gracious reception of me as a researcher.

This book took shape while I was a graduate student at the University of Kent, and I am enormously grateful to Gordon Lynch and Chris Shilling, my doctoral supervisors. Their example as sociologists and scholars has been a profound influence and inspiration. Gordon deserves special thanks for helping crystallize my initial interest in this field of study and helping me situate my work within the sociology of religion. He and Chris have been outstanding mentors and interlocutors, and their critical comments and ongoing questions provoked, challenged, pushed me to write more clearly, and opened up new avenues in my thinking. Simon Coleman and Linda Woodhead examined my doctoral thesis, and I am very grateful to have had the opportunity of ongoing discussions with them. The Religious Studies Department at Kent provided a stimulating and supportive environment to develop this work. My doctoral cohort at Kent—Ruth Sheldon, Sarah Harvey, and Steph Berns—have been a huge support and inspiring fellow researchers throughout: many thanks to them. As the text progressed from PhD thesis to monograph, the Leverhulme Trust has funded my research, through an Early Career Fellowship. The Bloomsbury Consortium funded the first year of my doctoral research while I was based at Birkbeck College, and the latter two years of my doctoral research were funded by the University of Kent.

Throughout this research, I have benefited enormously from the mentorship of Matthew Engelke, who has helped put my work in conversation with anthropology. Andrew McKinnon's generous comments and advice on an early draft chapter provided important insights that helped clarify my argument. Lois Lee, Ruth Sheldon, Dawn Llewellyn, and Paul-François Tremlett read and provided really helpful comments on an earlier draft of the whole text. Conversations with many others along the way have also encouraged and shaped the development of this work and suggested new possibilities, and among these I would especially like to thank: Jeremy Carrette, Abby Day, Mat

Francis, Cosimo Zene, Mat Guest, Jessica Frazier, Joanne McKenzie, Tom Boylston, Jon Bialecki, Meadhbh McIvor, Katharine Fletcher, Timothy Carroll, Sasha Antohin, Chris Deacy, Alan Le Grys, Stephen Laird, Lisa Baraitser, Jolyon Mitchell, Terhi Utriainen, Chris Baker, John Reader, James Bielo, Rachel Hanemann, and Melissa Caldwell. Thanks also to Tom Perridge, Lizzie Robottom, Karen Raith, and Alexander Johnson at Oxford University Press, to the two anonymous reviewers for their insightful readings and suggestions, and to Elizabeth Stone and Gayathri Manoharan in the final stages of preparing the manuscript.

The research has benefited from the opportunities I have had to present papers at symposia and research seminars: thanks are due to audiences at Goldsmiths College, the London School of Economics, Birkbeck College, the University of Chester, the University of Roehampton, and King's College, London, as well as at several conferences. Material from some of these chapters has appeared in different forms elsewhere, although substantially revised here. An earlier version of Chapter 3 appears as 'The Metropolis and Evangelical Life: Coherence and Fragmentation in the "lost city of London"', *Religion* 43:3 (2013). Other sections from this chapter and from the Introduction appear in 'English Evangelicals, Equality, and the City', in *Globalized Religion and Sexuality*, ed. Heather Shipley (Leiden: Brill, 2014), 'Negotiating the Public and Private in Everyday Evangelicalism', in *Is God Back?*, ed. Titus Hjelm (London: Bloomsbury, 2015), and 'English Evangelicals and the Claims of Equality', in *Religion, Equalities and Inequalities*, ed. Dawn Llewellyn and Sonya Sharma (Aldershot: Ashgate, 2015). Small sections of Chapters 4 and 6 appear in 'Practising the Space Between: Embodying Belief as an Evangelical Anglican Student', in *Journal of Contemporary Religion* 28:2 (2013), and of Chapter 4 in 'Listening Subjects, Rationality, and Modernity', in *Sociological Theory and The Question of Religion*, ed. Andrew McKinnon and Marta Trzebiatowska (Aldershot: Ashgate, 2014). A section of Chapter 2 appears in 'Latour, Prepositions and the Instauration of Secularism', in *Political Theology* 13:2 (2012), and sections of Chapter 1 in 'Christianity and the City: Simmel, Space, and Urban Subjectivities', *Religion and Society* 4 (2013).

Family and friends have been supportive throughout: special thanks to Petra and Lou Strhan, Lorna Houseman, Phil and Lesley Block, Suzy Mangion, Anthony Braithwaite, Philip Kidson, Vian Sharif, Sophie Cubbon, Kate McCullagh, Priya Devaraj, Vicki Smith, Tania Rocha, and Tom Dorman. Thanks also to the staff at the British Library, and for ongoing inspiration and conversation over coffees and lunches there to Ruth Sheldon, Lois Lee, Charlotte Faircloth, Amit Desai, Carrie Heitmeyer, Hettie Malcomson, Steven Poole, and Paul-François Tremlett. Martin Block has given time and space for this work, and been a constant source of comfort, encouragement, and inspiration throughout. This book is dedicated to him.

The author and publisher gratefully acknowledge the permission granted to reproduce copyrighted material in this book:

Excerpt from David Frisby and Mike Featherstone (eds), *Simmel on Culture*, reprinted with permission from SAGE.

Excerpt from Donald N. Levine (ed.), *Georg Simmel On Individuality and Social Forms*. Copyright 1971 The University of Chicago, reprinted with permission of the University of Chicago Press.

Excerpt from Maurice Merleau-Ponty, *The Phenomenology of Perception*, reprinted with permission from Taylor and Francis.

Excerpt from Marshall Berman, *All That is Solid Melts into Air*, reprinted with permission from Verso.

Excerpt from 'Burnt Norton' from *Four Quartets* by T. S. Eliot. Copyright 1936 by Houghton Mifflin Harcourt Publishing; Copyright (c) renewed 1964 by T. S. Eliot. Reprinted by permission of Houghton Mifflin Harcourt Publishing Company and by permission of Faber & Faber. All rights reserved.

Excerpt from *Waiting for Godot*, by Samuel Beckett, copyright (c) 1954 by Grove Press, Inc.; Copyright (c) renewed 1982 by Samuel Beckett. Used by permission of Grove/Atlantic, Inc. and by permission of Faber & Faber. Any third party use of this material, outside of this publication, is prohibited.

'Invited' image reprinted with permission from Matthew Varah Wilson, <http://mattvarahwilson.co.uk/>.

Contents

Even if Protestantism was not the true solution, it did pose the problem correctly. It was now no longer a question of the struggle of the layman with the priest outside himself, but rather of his struggle with his own inner priest, with his priestly nature.

Karl Marx

Introduction

> [T]he human being is the connecting creature who must always separate
> and cannot connect without separating ... And the human being is like-
> wise the bordering creature who has no border.
>
> (Simmel 1997a: 174)

In April 2012, during the run-up to the London mayoral election, Tory mayor
Boris Johnson intervened to stop a planned series of posters on London buses
which were due to proclaim: 'Not gay! Post-gay, ex-gay and proud! Get over
it!' The adverts had been produced by a conservative Christian group, the Core
Issues Trust, and were booked to appear on the buses by Anglican Mainstream
together with the Core Issues Trust, both organizations teaching that homosexuality is curable through therapy and religious teaching. The posters were
part of a campaign responding to the gay rights group Stonewall, which had
recently run posters on London buses stating: 'Some people are gay. Get over
it!' with the Core Issues Trust ads designed in the same red and white colour
scheme. Johnson contacted *The Guardian* to announce that he was banning
the adverts within an hour of their contents becoming public, and the story
ran on the front page, quoting Johnson as saying: 'London is one of the most
tolerant cities in the world and intolerant of intolerance. It is clearly offensive
to suggest that being gay is an illness that someone recovers from and I am not
prepared to have that suggestion driven around London on our buses' (*Guardian* 2012a).[1] His main rival in the mayoral election, Ken Livingstone, said the
posters were 'damaging for anyone who believes that London is the greatest
city in the world because of its tolerance' (*Guardian* 2012a), and a spokes-
person for Transport for London said 'we do not believe that these specific ads
are consistent with TfL's commitment to a tolerant and inclusive London'
(BBC News 2012). *The Guardian* featured a longer article in addition to the

---

[1] The Core Issues Trust afterwards sought a judicial review of the ban. The High Court ruled
that whilst the process for introducing the ban had been unfair, Transport for London acted
lawfully in banning the advert, because it would cause 'grave offence' to those who were gay. Core
Issues Trust v. Transport for London, High Court, 22 March 2013. Accessed 27 March 2013.
<http://www.judiciary.gov.uk/media/judgments/2013/core-issues-trust-v-tfl.>

cover story, framing this in terms of an increasing mobilization of conservative Christian groups in Britain, headlined 'Conservative Christians are becoming more confident in the political arena. The anti-gay bus ads are the latest move by Christian groups hoping to replicate US politics, where religion is centre stage' (Guardian 2012b). Positioning this as part of an attempt by conservative Christian groups to bring to Britain the religio-political mix of the US culture wars, *The Guardian* linked the attempted bus campaign with anti-abortion campaigners 'taking their fight into the public arena in the UK, buying in American expertise'.

This incident and responses to it reveal the interweaving of contemporary ideals about public religion, difference, tolerance, equality, sexual morality, and cities. Johnson's comments frame London as intolerant of religious expressions that transgress principles of equality and are felt as polluting ideals of inclusivity. London here seems to stand as a paradigmatic site of modernity: the ideal of tolerance has played an important part in imaginings of cities as complex, pluralist settlements, patterned on an interplay of social distance and proximity that does not interfere but allows the other the freedom to be other. As spaces where strangers are most likely to meet, so cities can be understood as sites of civility where social lives are forged through maintaining distance, where people live with others rather than feeling the need to get close to them (Sennett 2002a: 264–5).

But this story of cities as shaped by an ethics of tolerance is bound up with a more melancholy narrative. Drawing on Baudelaire as flâneur, Richard Sennett notes that while walking in the middle of New York, 'one is immersed in the differences of this most diverse of cities', but because these scenes are disengaged, there is little vivid human encounter—'a telling moment of talking or touching or connection'. Instead, 'A walk in New York reveals . . . that difference from and indifference to others are a related, unhappy pair' (1990: 128–9). While social distance in cities may promote the freedom not to be interfered with, it can also be seen in terms of a lonely individualism. As Alexis de Tocqueville wrote, characterizing the nineteenth century as the 'Age of Individualism', each individual 'behaves as though he is a stranger to the destiny of all the others . . . As for his transactions with his fellow citizens, he may mix among them, but he sees them not; he touches them, but does not feel them; he exists only in himself and for himself alone. And if on these terms there remains in his mind a sense of family, there is no longer a sense of society' (cited in Sennett 2002b: 323). Cities are sites that heighten the complexities of social life and raise central sociological questions about plurality, tolerance, and relations with others: how do people engage with those who are different from them and what conditions of possibility does this create? How do we separate from and connect with others through the creation of physical, emotional, and imagined boundaries?

These questions are central to the story of religion and secularity in modernity, and are particularly pertinent to understanding conservative evangelicalism. The etymology of 'tolerance' derives from 'to endure' and raises the fundamental social question of how we get along with others whose views and lifestyles we disagree with. This is an issue underlying contemporary controversies about conservative forms of religion in secular modern contexts, and the evangelical movement has been a particular focus of such debates in Britain and elsewhere.[2] In a speech in August 2013 at the Evangelical Alliance headquarters in London, the Archbishop of Canterbury, Justin Welby, argued that it was a problem for the Church in Britain that it is defined by what it is against and 'comes across too easily as negative' (cited in *Church Times* 2013). As society has become more tolerant in relation to issues such as homosexuality, this has increasingly shaped perceptions of evangelicals as not only intolerant in their responses to others. Welby stated: 'We have seen changes in the ideas about sexuality, sexual behaviour, which quite simply [mean that] we have to face the fact that the vast majority of people under 35 think not only that what we are saying [in opposing the Marriage (Same Sex Couples) Bill] is incomprehensible, but also think that we are plain wrong and wicked and equate it to racism and other forms of gross and atrocious injustice' (*Church Times* 2013). Throughout the movement's history however, evangelicals have made large claims, drawn boundaries, and erected barriers against 'worldliness', and labelling of evangelicals as intolerant is not a distinctively contemporary phenomenon. The Conservative Prime Minister at the end of the nineteenth century, Lord Salisbury, expressed distaste for the movement, describing its 'reign of rant' and as an 'incubus of narrow-mindedness . . . brooding over English society' (cited in Bebbington 1989: 276).

Conservative evangelicals' positions on a range of issues in recent years—from opposition to same sex marriage and to leadership roles for women and gay clergy in the Church, to arguments that religious freedoms are increasingly under threat—have frequently made headline news. In a de-Christianizing British context, the media increasingly present polarizing narratives of conservative evangelicals either as marginalized as their lifestyles come into conflict with universalizing processes of modernization—most often symbolized in conflicts with gay rights groups and antagonistic relations with equalities legislation—or as developing into a rising new Christian Right, seeking to

---

[2] I use the term 'evangelical' to refer to the broader tradition that has existed in Britain since the 1730s, marked, as David Bebbington summarizes, by characteristics of conversionism, Biblicism, activism, and crucicentrism (1989: 3). I use 'conservative evangelical' to refer to the tradition emerging within British evangelicalism following a rift with liberal evangelicals in the 1920s, with differing estimates of the Bible a central point of tension (pp. 181–228). Warner (2007) contextualizes tensions between charismatics and conservatives within post-war British evangelicalism, arguing that charismatics are defined by an orientation towards conversionism and activism, while conservatives tend to be shaped by Biblicism and crucicentrism (p. 240). These distinctions broadly characterize the lifeworld I describe here.

mobilize to defend established practices and extend their political influence. This book aims to move beyond stereotypical portraits perpetuated by head-line-grabbing stories that largely focus on the actions of publicity-seeking campaign groups and the statements of a small number of media-savvy evangelical leaders. I address instead what it is actually like to be a member of a conservative evangelical church in a largely secular metropolitan context in which their teachings are increasingly at odds with broader cultural norms, and to explore what matters to its members. As evangelicals' moral viewpoints are frequently stigmatized by those outside the Church, exploring evangelicals' lived religion opens up what it means to try to hold on to a strong religious identity in a secular modern context and the tensions this can generate. What are the ordinary comforts, tensions, experiences, and concerns of conservative evangelicals as they negotiate their everyday lives? How do they engage with the fact that their teachings on gender, sexuality, and other religions lead to their being labelled 'intolerant' by 'tolerant' liberals?

This book takes as its subject the lives of a congregation of mostly white middle-class conservative evangelicals in London, and as such is situated in relation to, investigates, and mediates different understandings of the rela-tionship between religion and modernity. Much existing sociological literature about evangelicals has portrayed evangelicalism as a unified culture that is *either* a reactionary protest against aspects of modernity, seeking to sustain traditionalist moral teachings and religious authority, *or* an accommodation to and reshaping *by* modernity, so that evangelicalism flourishes to the extent that it has affinities with processes such as globalization, individualization, and rationalization. However, to deepen understanding of what it is to be and to become an evangelical in modern, secular contexts we need to move beyond understandings of evangelical culture as a coherent, unified phenomenon that is either protest against or accommodation to modernity. This book develops such an approach through focusing on evangelicals' material practices and everyday interactions in a cosmopolitan, global city. Through examining relations between evangelicalism and urban sociality, my aim is to open up how the interplays between religion and secularism take place in everyday experience, both in the world around us *and* inside our heads, in the ways we experience ourselves.

Deepening understanding of the complexities of evangelical subjectivities, this book is a story of how a struggle for coherence becomes a central defining task of evangelical life. My central argument is that conservative evangelicals develop a response to the fluidity and fragmentation of late modernity that is shaped by their focus on the personality of God as coherent, which leads them both to desire coherence and to become conscious of subjective fragmentation within themselves. This response reflects a specific kind of cultural and moral fragmentation that is inherent to conservative evangelicalism, in their seeking to become 'aliens and strangers' in the immanent city and citizens instead of a heavenly City of God. Identifying and examining the aesthetics of evangelicals' alienation, I describe the material processes through which evangelicals learn to understand themselves as 'aliens and strangers' and demonstrate the precariousness of their projects of staking out boundaries of moral distinctiveness from others. Through focusing on their interactions in church and in spaces outside the church and by examining the place of doubt in evangelical life, I show that evangelicals' subjectivities are simultaneously shaped through both secular norms and by moral sensibilities of their faith that rub against these. Thus I argue that their self-identification as 'aliens and strangers in this world' both articulates and constructs an ambition to be different from others within the contexts they inhabit, rooted in a consciousness of the extent to which their habituated modes of practice, hopes, and longings are simultaneously shaped by their being in the world.

I wanted to move beyond concentrating solely on issues that typically dominate public debates about conservative evangelicals—for example, debates about their opposition to same sex marriage and women bishops—and consider instead the *relative* importance of these issues in individuals' everyday lives. I therefore focus on what I found that most ordinary conservative evangelicals saw as the most significant elements of their faith: their desire for a relationship with God, and their sense of themselves as becoming 'disciples' and therefore distinctive from others. Reports of evangelicals' sense of themselves as marginalized are widely reported. I found however that while the subjects of this book *sometimes* spoke of themselves in these terms, they placed greater emphasis on their being 'distinctive' from those around them, as 'aliens and strangers'. They articulated this sense of being out of step and 'different' as related to their sense of relationship with God, which they saw as central to both their individual and communal identities. The central narrative of this book focuses on how this sense of relationship with God and related sense of their distinctiveness were formed through practices of listening and speaking, and how these interrelated in everyday experience with broader norms of interaction in urban life. Through exploring how evangelicals' sense of relationship with God, their relations with 'others' outside the Church and their subjectivities were interrelated, I develop a new approach to religious intersubjectivity that shows how conservative evangelicals' experience of the personality of God leads them to work to form themselves as 'aliens and strangers' and their ongoing struggles with this task.

My hope is to paint a more nuanced portrait than standard stereotypes of conservative evangelicals as reactionary fundamentalists, drawing out how features of their critiques of and uncertainties about aspects of late modernity—such as individualism, consumerism, and materialism—resonate (albeit in a different register) with concerns expressed by liberals who are most likely to feel themselves at odds with them. The point of this is not to reach for a facile moral consensus where none exists, but rather to explore how the issues that typically dominate contemporary debates on conservative evangelicalism are woven into broader moral landscapes of modernity and thereby deepen awareness of the complex textures of these. There were other stories I could have told. In this introduction, I will describe how and why I ended up telling *this* story.

EVANGELICAL ANGLICANS, MODERNITY, AND MORAL FRAGMENTATION

Ethnographies inevitably end up exploring different questions from those you set out with. When I began this project, I had intended to study a GAFCON-supporting evangelical church. The Global Anglican Future Conference (GAFCON) took place in June 2008, when 1,200 Anglican bishops, clergy, and laity met in Jerusalem, many boycotting the Lambeth Conference of that year. The event grew out of transnational alliances that had developed since the mid-1990s in opposition to the growing acceptance of homosexual relationships in some Anglican provinces, most prominently in the Episcopal Church in the United States (GAFCON 2009; Sadgrove et al. 2010; McKinnon et al. 2011: 364). As GAFCON and other ecclesiastical clashes over issues of equality have generated media attention, I wanted to explore how tensions related to disagreements over gender and sexuality in the Anglican Communion were experienced by members of a GAFCON-supporting church, and, at the start of my study, I visited a number of such churches. I chose to base my fieldwork at a large conservative evangelical Anglican church in London, 'St John's', because this church is considered by other British evangelicals, both conservative and charismatic, to be an important and influential representative of contemporary conservative evangelicalism, with links to other prominent conservative evangelical churches in the USA, Australia, Nigeria, and other global contexts. As is typical of a GAFCON-supporting church, St John's teaches that homosexuality and all sexual relationships outside marriage are sinful, and opposes the ordination of gay bishops in the Global Anglican Communion. It is also representative of the conservative evangelical movement within the Church of England in opposing women bishops, and does not accept the ordained ministry of women in the Church: all the ordained ministers and elders in St John's were men.[3]

When I began fieldwork, however, I soon discovered that many members of the congregation didn't know what GAFCON was, and were generally—especially the younger members—uninterested in Church politics. As one

---

[3] Women who had responsibilities for ministry with women in the congregation were on the senior leadership team.

man in his twenties put it, 'we leave it to our leaders to deal with things like that, and trust that they have wisdom to make right decisions on our behalf'. Therefore, as one of the unintended consequences of my asking people about GAFCON was to raise its profile, I changed tack to focus on what appeared to be more significant concerns for members of the church. Yet although GAFCON as a specific focus dropped out of my analysis, the disagreements on sexuality, gender, and equality it indexes relate to wider themes that did concern church members. Current schisms in the Anglican Communion exemplify tensions between forms of religion that hold onto traditionalist differentiated under-standings of gender and heteronormativity and universalizing tendencies asso-ciated with modernization that challenge this. José Casanova's pioneering work on public religion argues that such tensions can lead to the deprivatization of religion as groups whose lifestyles and values are disrupted by universalizing processes seek to mobilize and enter the public sphere to 'defend their trad-itional turf' (1994: 6) in response, for example, the Religious Right in the United States.

It is possible to see these logics in play in GAFCON. However, they are more evident in calls by some socially conservative British Christian groups for the 'public' articulation of faith, particularly since the introduction of the Equality Acts of 2006 and 2010. The 'Not Ashamed' campaign by the pressure group Christian Concern, launched in December 2010, exemplifies this. The website of this group states:

> More than any other person, Jesus Christ has shaped our society, for the good of all. The values and freedoms that flow from Him have been embedded in our culture and laws, bringing great benefit to our nation . . .
>
> Yet the truths, values and behaviour consistent with that foundation are under attack, to the detriment of the whole of society. There is mounting pressure to exclude Jesus Christ from public life, consigning Him instead to the realm of the 'private and personal'. Increasingly, Christians are encountering attempts to restrict their freedom to speak and live in accordance with biblical teaching in the workplace and in public life . . .
>
> In these challenging times Christians need to stand together and speak clearly of Jesus Christ as 'good news' not only for individuals but for society as a whole.
>
> (Christian Concern, not dated a)

Christian Concern's 'Equalities and Conscience' petition, the Coalition for Marriage,[4] the Core Issues Trust bus campaign, and the Christian Legal Centre's appeals to the European Court of Human Rights to 'protect the freedom of Christians to live in accordance with their Christian beliefs'[5] are all situated in a broader narrative of Christians being marginalized and

---

[4] See Christian Concern 2011 and Coalition for Marriage 2012.
[5] See Christian Legal Centre 2014.

increasingly persecuted as Britain becomes progressively de-Christianized.[6] The former Archbishop of Canterbury, George Carey, for example, was quoted in the *Daily Mail* (2012) saying that Christians are now 'persecuted', being 'sought out and framed by homosexual activists', and he argued that people of faith are treated as 'bigots'.

When I first began fieldwork, I found this desire for the 'public' articulation of faith articulated together with a sense of conservative teachings on issues such as gender, sexuality, and other faiths rubbing up against wider norms of equality strikingly evident in what the church leaders were saying. The rector of St John's, David, preached in a Sunday morning sermon, for example, that Christian fellowship should be 'energetic and corporate, public and unpopular, and selfless and sacrificial'. He stated: 'We contend publicly for the objective truth of the gospel that God has done in and through Jesus, hence the unpopularity of this ... Wherever the gospel is proclaimed publicly by gospel partners, we find them engaged in conflict, as in Acts ... As this country careers away from its Christian heritage, we will increasingly be considered immoral, bigoted, out of date.' This idea that Christianity will be considered 'bigoted' and 'out of date' suggests a sense of temporality that is shaped through moral teachings being experienced as in tension with universalizing modern norms of equality. Judith Butler has argued that liberal freedoms, particularly in relation to sexual freedoms, are now 'understood to rely upon a hegemonic culture, one that is called "modernity" and that relies on a certain progressive account of increasing freedoms' (2009: 109). An uneasy relationship between evangelicalism and modernity in this sense was also implied when David preached in another sermon: 'the culture wars of the '60s and '70s were fought about freedom, in which sexual freedom, equality and choice were seen as inextricably linked ... But are we *less* free today?'

Religious responses that oppose universalizing processes are often described as a resistance to and protest against modernity, and the global strength of evangelicalism has often been explained in this sense. Conservative evangelicals' re-inscription of gender differences and insistence on revelation as an event that establishes certain truths have been interpreted as responses to the fluidity of meaning and existential anxieties, as other sources of security and authority are eroded through globalization and the extension of impersonal market forces. Much recent scholarship has also explored how evangelicalism has adapted to and thrived within the conditions of modernity and postmodernity,

---

[6] The description of England as de-Christianizing is accurate in relation to indicators such as church attendance. The 2005 English Church Census shows that since 1998 there has been an overall decline in regular church attendance of 15 per cent, from 3,714,700 to 3,166,200. Of these regular churchgoers, 40 per cent attend evangelical churches. This represents a rise from 37 per cent in the same survey in 1998, and means that in 2005, in an average week, 2.5 per cent of the English population attended an evangelical church (Brierley 2006a, 2006b).

arguing that its use of new media forms and the portability of its practices mean that evangelicals 'belong to the present age – and almost certainly the future, as well' (Coleman 2000: 3).

At the start of my fieldwork, the prominence of the language of being 'exiles' and 'aliens and strangers in this world', and of countercultural teachings on gender, sexuality, and the exclusivity of salvation in Jesus seemed to fit with interpretations of conservative evangelicalism as an anachronistic re-inscription of traditionalist values. Yet, as I spent time with members of the church, observed what they did in different places, and listened to what they said and noted what they did not say, the neatness of this narrative began to unravel. I began to understand the logic of their faith as patterned through their simultaneously being shaped as modern, urban subjects according to ethical norms internalized outside the church *and* their development through participation in the church of moral and temporal orientations that rubbed up against these.

In his influential work on US evangelicals, Christian Smith highlights the regular portrayal of evangelicals as either demons—'an ominous resurgence of religious oppression, a movement of radical, intolerant, and coercive zealots determined to undermine American freedoms'—or angels, a myth 'fostered by many religio-political conservative activists who posture American evangelicals as the country's last bastion of righteousness in a decaying society' (2000: 193). Smith points out that such mythologies offer entertaining stories for journalists to appeal to the reading public and aid political fundraising, and continue to exert a powerful hold on both secular and religious imaginations. Phil Zuckerman's writing on evangelicals is an example of this kind of sociological mythologizing. In an article for *The Huffington Post* entitled 'Why Evangelicals Hate Jesus', Zuckerman cites statistics published by the Pew Forum on Religion and Public Life and argues that these show that white evangelicals are the group 'least likely to support politicians or policies that reflect the actual teachings of Jesus' and 'the very people most likely to reject his teachings and despise his radical message' (2011). Yet my informants' reaction to Zuckerman's depiction suggests a more complicated picture than his narrative, based on survey data, allows. During my fieldwork, Freddie, a floppy-haired curate, read a long section of Zuckerman's article aloud in a sermon, and said: 'the uncomfortable things that those outside Christianity have to say often have some truth in them', and he challenged the congregation: '*are* we concerned with living in a way that saves your brother, or just with being happy in your own salvation?'. Freddie's agreement with Zuckerman's critique of evangelicalism indicates the complexity of the moral landscape evangelicals inhabit, how their ideals are formed both through their participation in the church, *and* wider cultural norms that lead them to simultaneously stand in critical relationship with these.

There is a growing ethnographic literature on evangelicalism within sociology and anthropology, advancing understanding of evangelicals across

diverse global contexts beyond the simplistic portraits Smith criticizes.[7] Within this body of work, the contribution of this book is twofold. First, in focusing
on how evangelicals' sense of relationship with God has particular social and
subjective effects in their lives, leading to experiences of cultural and moral
fragmentation, I develop a new approach to religious intersubjectivity that
opens up the complexity of evangelical subjectivities. Second, in examining the
everyday ethics shaping middle-class conservative evangelicals' lives in an
urban context, my aim is to deepen understanding of the interrelations of
Christianity, 'the urban', ethics, and modernity. Through this, I develop an
anthropology of shame, guilt, and doubt that shows the work that is required
to maintain evangelical subjectivity in a context such as London.

My attention to questions of fragmentation, shame, and subject formation
draws on Joel Robbins's work on these themes in his magisterial study (2004) of
Pentecostal conversion among the Urapmin of Papua New Guinea. Robbins's
narrative of cultural change describes the moral struggles the Urapmin experienced through tensions between the communal forms of their traditional
religion and the individualistic Protestantism to which they converted. The
interrelations between community, individual, morality, and modernity are,
however, differently located in my study. British evangelicals, like Robbins's
Urapmin converts, learn to think of themselves as 'sinful' in a narrative
conveying the tension of experiencing contradictory norms of practice. However in a de-Christianizing Northern European setting, my informants
expressed a sense of disjunction between a broader 'post-Christian', 'secular'
individualism and *their* ideal of a social life together. By studying evangelicals'
lives across the spaces of church, home, and workplace, this book identifies and
describes the processes by which they try to shape their thoughts, bodies, and
emotions according to a unified Christian ideal, and the continuing difficulty of
managing this in a secular, pluralist context.

The central narratives of Christianity, in which the exile of Israel is re-echoed
in the early Christians striving to turn away from the world and towards the
City of God, articulate a desire and a demand for Christians to be 'exiles', out of
step with 'the world', leading to what one of my informants described as 'the
tensions of ordinary Christian experience'. This book explores how conservative evangelicals' self-identification as 'aliens and strangers in the world' and
their desire for coherence demonstrates the cultural and moral fragmentation
they experience. As reflexively self-aware of the precariousness of their faith
and the extent to which they as subjects are also shaped through wider cultural
practices, I describe how routinized interactions in the church knot individuals
together in forms of interdependence that enable them to keep going in their

---

[7] See, for example, Bialecki 2008, 2009; Bielo 2009, 2011a, 2011b; Coleman 1996, 2000, 2006,
2011; Elisha 2008, 2011; Engelke 2010a, 2011, 2012, 2013; Erzen 2006; Frykholm 2004; Griffith
2004; Guest 2007; Harding 2000; Luhrmann 2004, 2012; Luhrmann et al. 2010; Wilkins 2008.

practice of faith. Evangelicalism is often described as individualistic. Yet these habituated rituals form members of St John's as subjects orientated outwards towards each other, towards others in the city, and towards God, with a strong sense of their individual insufficiency. While previous research concerning evangelicals has often shown them as dogmatically certain of their beliefs and experiencing very little doubt,[8] I show how my informants regularly acknowledged experiences of doubt and struggle, and were self-conscious about how their everyday practices of sociability with each other helped maintain their faith.

The complex intersection of values and meanings formed through evangelicals being both rooted in the world and developing an orientation towards the Kingdom of God is part of a 'distinctive Christian tension derived from simultaneous acceptance and rejection of the world, the goodness of creation and the demanding presence of an alternative kingdom' (Martin 2005: 186). Examining the forms of sociality experienced as members of St John's learn to direct themselves towards the transcendent orientation of Christianity penetrating into mundane time and space, this book contributes to understanding the lived textures of evangelicals' faith and their religious formation in the secular times and places of the metropolis.

DOING FIELD- AND BODY-WORK WITH CONSERVATIVE EVANGELICALS

The urban thoroughfare off which St John's is located is always far quieter on Sundays than on weekdays, yet on arriving before the 6 p.m. evening service, a steady stream of casually dressed people are walking towards the church from several surrounding tube stations, most having taken public transport to get there, with a few arriving on bicycles. Off the main road, in the shadow not only of glass-fronted commercial buildings but also of an oak tree pre-dating but dwarfed by these, small groups of young people stand in the stone-paved square in front of the church, waiting to meet friends before the service. Coming in from the cold, dark London streets, the inside of the church is warm and light, with conversation humming around the high-ceilinged, stone-floored room. The large space feels clean and bright, with utilitarian modern chairs arranged in rows facing a low stage and prominent wooden pulpit, but medieval history still tangibly present in the carved stone memorials and font. People hang their coats and scarves on rails by the door and chat in groups by the bookstall or over tea and biscuits in a side chapel. When there are lots of newcomers to the church—for example, in September, when new

---

[8] See, for example, Bialecki 2008: 379; Smith 1998: 29.

students and graduates starting work in the city arrive—there is often a sign put up over this side chapel, 'Arrivals Lounge', so that if new visitors don't know anyone, someone in the church will chat to them over warm drinks before the service.

When I first visited the church, the individuals I sat next to were encouraging about the possibility of my conducting research there, and offered to put me in touch with church leaders or to meet me before the service if I wanted to visit again. Because St John's is a large church—the three Sunday services each averaging about five hundred in attendance—various methods of welcoming newcomers are encouraged. In each service there is a five minute break to chat with neighbours, and ministers regularly remind the congregation to invite newcomers to coffee or supper after the service. Whenever I arrived early for a service and sat by myself, someone would inevitably come over to chat within a couple of minutes, and this culture of speaking to new people helped me get to know a range of individuals in the church.

I was fortunate in the welcoming attitude that David, the rector of St John's, took towards my research from the outset. He is interested in both sociology of religion—citing sociologists such as Peter Berger and Rodney Stark in his sermons—and wider social theory, although he characterized my study as more anthropological than sociological. About halfway through my fieldwork, noting that I was not especially interested in gathering statistics, he said: 'I have a friend who used to study a tribe in Kenya somewhere. I see now, *that's* what you're doing; *we're* your tribe. I quite like that idea.' At our initial meeting, he said the church had often received negative publicity, so was happy that I planned to anonymize the name of the church, and the name of the church and all individuals here are pseudonyms, although many said they would have been happy to be named.

I conducted fieldwork at St John's from February 2010 to August 2011. During this time, I attended two of the three Sunday services the church holds, one each Sunday morning and evening. Most members of the church participate in weekly Bible study groups during academic term times, and from April 2010 to July 2011, I attended one of these, which I call the 'Rooted' group, intended for individuals who have already attended the more introductory Bible study courses the church also offers. In addition I attended a student Bible study group for one term and during the holidays following this. I decided to concentrate on these two groups to observe differences and similarities between the practices of relative newcomers and those who had been at St John's some time, and to get a sense of the habitus the church was trying to encourage and the means of its formation over time.[9] It would have

---

[9] My use of the term 'habitus' follows Marcel Mauss's definition, denoting the '*exis*, the "acquired ability" and "faculty" of Aristotle', formed through particular techniques of the body that 'vary especially between societies, educations, proprieties and fashions' (2006: 74–5).

been interesting to explore the church's methods of childhood socialization, but since most of those I got to know described university as particularly formative in their faith—and with British evangelicals devoting significant attention and resources to students—focusing on the student groups and the Rooted group provided more insight into the means through which individuals were incorporated into this culture. The prominence of students (and relative paucity of children) at St John's was also down to its central London location: many middle-class members of the church moved out to the suburbs when having children in their late twenties and early thirties, because of high property prices in inner London. The specific demographic composition of the congregation was therefore shaped by a high percentage of students and twenty-something and older individuals (many of whom were single) working in London, many of these travelling up to half an hour and sometimes longer to get to the church, and a smaller number of (mostly relatively affluent) families with children living closer to the church.

When soliciting consent for researching these groups, I asked one of the student leaders which student group might be open to my joining. She placed me with a group of fifteen members, whom I spoke to about my project, explaining my research questions and methods, and asking whether they were happy for me to join as a participant observer. I think the fact that I was also a student and willing to participate in discussions contributed to their openness to my presence. Bible study groups at St John's are used to being observed: group leaders are regularly observed by other leaders who give feedback on their teaching styles, and some of the students initially interpreted my role in this way. Several of the students who were writing dissertations were interested in my methods, and we chatted about the kinds of question they thought would work for interviews.

When seeking consent to join the Rooted group, the curate in charge of this stream of groups recommended a particular group for me to join. As I had got to know a member of this group, Lucy, at the Sunday services I had been to, she emailed the information sheet about my project to the group, and they discussed whether they were happy for me to observe their meetings. I was informed that one member of the group had reservations. I discussed this with Hannah, one of the group's leaders, the following Sunday, and emphasized I did not want to be part of the group if it made anyone uncomfortable. By this point, the individual concerned had already changed her mind and told Hannah that I was welcome. Having got to know her subsequently, I am comfortable she would not have been easily coerced into this if she hadn't wanted me there, and she turned out to be especially friendly to me. Through these meetings, I was able to see and talk to individuals from these groups twice a week at church and in the small group (more frequently than I see most of my friends and family in London), and sometimes more often than this if we met up additionally during the week.

I also helped at other events to get a sense of the different kinds of 'serving', as it is called at St John's, expected of church members. So I was on the coffee rota, helped prepare and serve food at 'guest events', and helped steward at national evangelical events hosted at St John's. I also attended mid-week lunchtime services aimed at those working nearby, and went on a weekend away with all the Rooted groups to a conference centre outside London. As I got to know church members, they invited me—and often my husband too—to their homes, for suppers and Sunday lunches, and I met up with people for tea and coffee, in cafés or at their workplaces. When it felt appropriate, I made notes during interactions. There is a culture of note-taking in conservative evangelicalism, and informants sometimes joked that my prolific note-taking would lead the casual observer to see me as an especially keen evangelical, although one curate commented that seeing me writing notes while he was preaching made him nervous.

My observations of informants' modes of practice inside and outside the church and the interactions and conversations we had in these different spaces were my primary source of data. Yet although data from these different settings informed my analysis throughout, I have chosen to write here only about interactions that I felt would not compromise the privacy of individuals involved. Although I use pseudonyms, because of the possibility of members of the church being able to determine each others' identities, I chose not to include sensitive details of their lives that might make them feel compromised. Although everyone I spoke to understood that I was there for research and that I was making fieldnotes about our interactions, in some settings I felt conscious that individuals I had got to know well tended to forget this. Therefore my decisions about which details of people's lives I have included here were determined by how conscious I perceived they were that I might use data from particular interactions in my writing.

As well as recording what others said and did, I also noted my own participation and emotional reactions in services, small group meetings, and other settings. Doing preparation work for Bible studies, clearing up dirty dishes when it was our group's turn on the rota, developing friendships with members of the congregation, and other experiences from fieldwork I take as data indicative of the kinds of sociality developed through participation at St John's. Loïc Wacquant describes how, to understand boxing culture, the researcher needs 'to follow the unknown footsoldiers of the manly art in the accomplishment of their daily chores and to submit oneself along with them to their rigorous regimen, at once both corporeal and mental, that defines their state and stamps their identity' (2004a: 15). Given the military imagery conservative evangelical leaders use to describe the life of faith, this is not an inappropriate metaphor to describe how the body-work involved in doing Bible studies, going to services every Sunday, and forming relationships with members of St John's was an important part of understanding this lifeworld.

As I came to learn what was expected in a Bible study group, got used to the pattern of mid-week meetings, Sunday services, and forms of conversations over supper afterwards, I experienced something of how participation in the life of this church related to the rhythms of life outside the church. As a native Londoner, having grown up in the suburbs and living during my fieldwork in an urban neighbourhood around ten minutes' train journey from St John's, where several members of the congregation also live, I also tried to look on my city as strange. As I moved between church, home, university, and other social spaces, and reflected on the experiences, emotions, and meanings afforded by these, I tried to notice mundane urban interactions and physical structures I might otherwise have taken for granted because of their familiarity.

In the final months of fieldwork, I conducted more formal, open-ended interviews with thirty-one church members. Although almost everyone I asked was happy to oblige, it was easier to gain access to women than men, as women volunteered other women as potential interviewees. Developing friendships with individuals of the same gender plays an important role in conservative evangelical culture, and this was then reflected in my interviews, as I ended up chatting to comparatively more women than men during and after services. Although members of the Rooted group feature most significantly in the ethnographic descriptions of this book, my analysis was based on my interactions with *all* these many others I got to know through fieldwork, including more peripheral members of the church, and it was especially helpful to be able to discuss my developing analysis with church members who were not part of the Rooted or the student group.

The cultural capital of my own middle-class identity doubtless eased access,[10] and this seemed a more significant category of my identity than, for example, my whiteness. While St John's is a white-majority church, there are a significant number of individuals from (mostly middle-class, professional) Asian and African backgrounds. Not everyone at St John's is middle class, but this is the majority culture of the church, representative of conservative evangelical culture nationally.[11] This was exemplified one Sunday evening when one of the curates, Jon, said in a sermon:

> I wonder what names we use for other people at [St John's]. Obviously, in our minds, because we're polite. Posh. Formal. Cerebral. Rich. Busy. Emotionally constipated. City. Studenty. Socially awkward. Hardline. Dull. Young. Academic.

---

[10] My experience was in contrast with researchers who have experienced difficulties in negotiating access to conservative evangelicals (for example, Wilkins 2008: 19ff.). Specific cultural markers of my identity, for example, the fact I had been an undergraduate at Cambridge, were shared with several of the church's leaders.

[11] For discussion of the historical background to the middle-class culture of British evangelicalism, see Bebbington 1989: 110–11; McLeod 1974: 151ff; Ward 1997: 35–44.

But for those who belong to Jesus, the first name that should come to mind is
brother or sister. Whatever our cultural backgrounds, through the cross, in Christ
we are family.

Jon was intending to challenge the labels people at St John's might use to
describe themselves and others, but his words have the performative effect of
constructing the sense that this *is* the church's culture.

As well as indicating the church's cultural milieu, Jon's words also point
towards the complexity of evangelical subject formation. George Herbert
Mead describes an individual's sense of 'me' as coming from how she understands society as seeing her: we learn to see ourselves through the eyes of a
'generalized other' (1962: 154). Included in this 'generalized other' is a mental
personification of the feeling we have of what 'society says', the 'collective
conscious'. Jon's sermon signifies the 'generalized other' through which
members of St John's recognize themselves and form their sense of 'me',
and the performance of the sermon then further reinforces their collective
self-identification as 'posh', 'formal', 'cerebral', and so on. But his words also
express dissatisfaction with this, created through engagement with the Bible
and here articulated in the performance of the sermon form, through which
members of the church develop a desire to relate to each other in ways that
transcend social stratifications.

Other incidents also demonstrated that acquiring the 'me' and the 'generalized other' are complicated, uneven processes, and these helped shape my
focus on the formation of evangelical subjectivities as a means of opening up
their navigation of the complex cultural landscapes of pluralist modernity. My
conversations with Sam, a researcher in evolutionary biology in his early
thirties, are one example. Although most members of the church seemed
open to my presence, Sam initially responded with suspicion, asking when
I first spoke to him, where my research would end up: 'Will it be published in
some double-page spread in a Sunday supplement?' I replied that it was
directed towards a PhD thesis, but that hopefully some academic articles
would emerge from it. He then asked whether I thought their faith was totally
irrational. When I responded that this wasn't my primary characterization, he
gave me some credit: 'so you're more enlightened than Richard Dawkins'.
When I pointed out that Richard Dawkins isn't a sociologist, and that sociologists don't necessarily share his views, he said, 'so I'm curious what you *do*
think about us. Do you think faith makes no difference in our lives? Or do you
think we're just a bunch of well-meaning but misguided people? Or do
you think we're dangerous fundamentalists?' These three options Sam gave
me for how he saw social scientists' views of evangelicalism are indicative of
the kind of images that participate in constructions of the 'generalized other'
as it forms the evangelical 'me'. Several months later, his initial suspicion of me
having passed, we chatted about what ethnographic writing involved, and he

recommended a book called *The Unlikely Disciple* (Roose 2009), which he had read while a postdoctoral researcher in Texas, as a model of an outsider's perspective on US fundamentalism. He told me that the author was a 'liberal, secular student' who had gone undercover to spend a term at Jerry Falwell's Liberty University. Sam said he identified with both Roose's 'liberal, secular' judgements and the fundamentalists Roose depicts, demonstrating both his own distance from and proximity to Texan conservative evangelical culture.

Sam's statements indicate that evangelical subjectivities are not formed through a straightforward internalization of what the 'generalized other' thinks, but also imply the internalization of norms of interaction that can appear contradictory, shaped through participation in different social and moral spaces. Working in evolutionary biology, he is acutely conscious of how the judgements of those such as Dawkins mark him as 'other' through a perceived 'irrationality' of religious faith. Yet at the same time, he articulates a sense of connection with the 'secular' sensibilities of *The Unlikely Disciple*'s author. As I observed how participation in the church developed particular behavioural norms and how these intersected with individuals' sense of broader public perceptions of their faith, I came to explore how relations with many different others—inside and outside the church, with God and other sacred figures—became sources of the self and how individuals learnt to negotiate the (often conflicting) demands of these. The narrative that developed from this focus centres on a story of how evangelical subjectivities are formed through the interplay of an experience of cultural and moral fragmentation and particular embodied practices that lead to a desire for coherence and wholehearted service of God. To contextualize how this took shape, I will sketch three incidents that helped clarify my thinking.

Equality, Integrity, and Evangelical Identities

Rooted Bible study groups took place after work on Tuesday evenings in St John's. In one meeting, the group discussed how they would respond to a non-Christian friend who asked them what would happen after death to those who had never heard of Jesus. Emily, a tall, slim teacher in her early forties, responded that people who asked that kind of question were probably uninterested in the answer. Others in the group said they were less sure about this and that they wanted to discuss it. Alistair, the group's leader, an erudite lawyer in his late forties, said, 'I think there are at least three people around this table who are interested in the answer.'

'I have *often* thought about it,' Lucy said.

Alan, an insurance broker in his fifties, who had originally raised the question for discussion, said, after a pause, 'I think it's a question about the integrity of God. Can we rest in the sovereignty of God, that He will have his people?'

'Yes. It's a question about theodicy,' Alistair said.

The group spent time discussing biblical passages they could take as evidence of God's integrity and justice in relation to what happens to non-Christians after death, showing considerable knowledge of particular passages in which God's justice is foregrounded, so they could be assured that God would act according to principles of fairness towards those who have never heard of Jesus. As Alistair tried to summarize the discussion before moving onto the next question the group had been asked to talk about, Lorna, a woman in her early sixties, added, 'I wish people *would* ask me questions like this. Most of my friends are just so uninterested. Most non-Christians just think we're barmy. Going to church is just so alien to most people. I'd be really happy if they did ask me something like that.'

'I find people are just so not bothered, they're so blasé; they couldn't give a stuff about religion,' Emily said. Janet, a barrister in her forties, replied, 'And yet, on the BBC website, you can see what the top ten most viewed pages are, and when there's a story about religion, it's often one of the most viewed.'

'Even if people are saying negative things,' Hannah said.

'I think Christianity's hated, but there are very few negative comments about other religions,' Emily said. 'People are happy to slate Christianity, but wouldn't dare say anything negative about other religions.'

'They're afraid of offending people,' Lucy said.

'I don't know,' Edward, a blond banker in his thirties, countered, 'I think it's probably the same with Islam.'

'But most of the stories about Christianity all seem to be really negative, about things like women bishops, or homosexuality. They're all so *Anglican*,' Emily continued. 'I'd find it really hard to have a conversation about any of those issues. I would just find it really hard.' The group talked briefly about how boring they find the General Synod, and Hannah added, sensitively, how grateful she is for people like Lorna's late husband who have been on Synod. Alistair, who is involved in local diocesan politics, said, 'Actually, I could imagine a conversation about women bishops leading onto a discussion about the fact that actually the Bible does teach that everyone is created equal.' Emily reiterated her reluctance to engage in conversation with non-Christians on any of these issues: 'I just really wouldn't want to have a conversation about anything to do with women bishops, or any of those things.'

Here we see individuals acutely aware of which of their teachings rub up against contemporary cultural norms, and we see that they want to discuss with each other teachings about non-Christians going to hell, on which the ethical grounds of their faith are felt as in tension with broader cultural understandings of morality, suggesting that they are themselves affected by broader norms. But we also see their reserve inhibiting their discussion of these issues outside the church. Although Lorna said she would like it if non-Christian friends were to ask about her faith, this implies she would prefer to discuss it only if specifically asked, while Emily wanted to avoid conversations on issues where evangelical teachings are in tension with universalizing modern values. Emily's framing of discussions about women bishops and homosexuality as 'negative' seems in direct tension with how organizations such as Christian Concern seek to promote public discussion of these issues, following on from their conviction that 'biblical teaching' and values are 'good for society as a whole'. The group's comments about media portrayals of Christianity indicate how the 'generalized other' shaping their identities is an object for their reflection, and that they are sensitive to the kinds of conversation that would reinforce negative stereotypes. We also see how their discussions develop consciousness of the values constructing the symbolic boundaries separating them from their non-Christian friends and colleagues. Yet at the same time, they are formed as subjects within the same social structures that frame these values as countercultural, and want to discuss issues where the integrity and justice of God seem in question, so they can be reassured that they can trust in Him.

As noted earlier, the tension experienced between universalizing, de-differentiating processes of modernization mean that when religious teachings are felt to transgress broader norms of equality, this can lead groups to mobilize and enter the public sphere to defend their established ways of life. In the British media, this public defence is most often evident in relation to differing stances on gender and sexuality. This conversation amongst the Rooted group. however. challenges straightforward narratives of conservative evangelical mobilization. We see here a complex interweaving of differing norms conservative evangelicals negotiate in their everyday lives, opening onto questions of ethics, tolerance, and public space, and how these relate to speaking about faith. This and other similar incidents shaped my focus on how differing modes of talking (and not talking) with others—inside and outside the church—form particular kinds of subject.

Embodying the Word

Listening and speaking were central to how members of St John's understood themselves as standing in intimate relationship with God and as distinctive from others in the city, and embodied practice is the lens through which I examine the formation of evangelical subjects. My interest in how my informants embodied their faith was shaped through both the centrality accorded in the church to specific practices and wider academic conversations about embodiment and materiality. There has been a tendency in writing about Protestantism to portray this tradition sometimes somewhat monolithically as uneasy with the mediating role of bodies and material objects (e.g. Keane 2006, 2007; Meyer 2010). When I started my fieldwork, the critique leaders of St John's expressed for forms of Christianity they described as 'ritualistic' or 'emotional' led me at first to interpret the culture of St John's as likewise marked by an ambivalence towards the body and objects. Yet as I focused more closely on the habitus formed through participation at St John's, I began to understand individuals' engagement with materiality and embodiment as more subtle than I had first assumed. Certainly there were traces of a dematerializing Reformist orientation, which would lead ministers to state explicitly during rituals such as infant baptism that 'nothing magic is happening here'. Their stated reasons for the stance they took against, for example, charismatic worship as mediating the Holy Spirit were articulated both in terms of a theology that did not see God as present only in particular moments of emotional intensity and because of their concern at the agency accorded in rituals to humans as the actors performing rituals, undermining emphasis on God's grace.

Yet at the same time as church members articulated a critique of 'ritualistic' religion, they also demonstrated concern about how broader cultural modes of embodiment impacted on their desire to be formed as listening subjects who learn to hear God speak in the words of the Bible. I became more attuned to their consciousness of how media consumption shaped their practices when members of the church staff read Neil Postman's *Amusing Ourselves to Death* (1985) to consider how changes in media technologies affected practices the church privileged as the means of forming a sense of relationship with God; for example, how shortened attention spans determined people's ability to listen to sermons. Their reading of Postman to think about how people are shaped by media use, and their desire to think about how they might develop practices that resist these shifts, implies a complicated relationship between modernity, agency, and subjectivity. The mythological 'modern' Bruno Latour depicts in *We Have Never Been Modern* (1993) desires a purely human autonomy, uneasy about the agency objects have on us. But these evangelicals were conscious of the agency media objects have. They therefore wanted to develop alternative forms of practice through their relations with other objects—most prominently, the Bible—that would give them greater consciousness of a sense of God's agency over them, understanding this simultaneously as a process that they seek to develop their own and communal discipline in. Robert Orsi describes religions as practices of 'concretizing the order of the universe, the nature of human life and its destiny, and the various dimensions and possibilities of human interiority itself' (2005: 73). We might interpret the concerns articulated at St John's about the agency of God, objects, society, and themselves as a means of narrativizing questions and uncertainties about the nature of human power and powerlessness—similar questions, albeit formulated in a very different register, to those expressed in social scientific debates about structure and agency. In my analysis, I explored how these engagements with different forms of media and embodied practice situate conservative evangelicals' sense of relationship to 'modernity' and the ideas of human subjectivity, submission, autonomy, and agency these imply.

Shame and the People of God

In a sermon series on the letter to the Hebrews at the start of my fieldwork, David preached a sermon in which he described the difficulty members of the church experience about speaking about their faith publicly as an 'internal battle'. Inviting the congregation to identify with Moses and the original recipients of the letter, he said Moses chose 'rather to be mistreated with the people of God than to enjoy the fleeting pleasures of sin' and then stated how this applied to the Hebrews in the letter:

> Nothing could be more appropriate for the Hebrews . . . We've already identified at least part of the reason for their stepping back from the gospel was their social shame at associating with the people of God. There was no social status involved in being Christian. It was not cool to be Christian and part of that funny little group at work that meets to pray, or that strange little group that calls itself 'the Christian Union' in the hospital or the university.

He went on to give an example of how he saw this 'social shame' of being a Christian expressed in the lives of members of the congregation:

> Nothing has changed, has it? I remember talking about this to a group of Christian business people, and I said to them, 'what is the most costly aspect of being an out-and-out Christian to you at the moment in the office?' And they said, 'oh the ridicule, my reputation is at stake, I might be known as a Bible-basher'.

He stated that the author of Hebrews 'lines up shame and the social distance that might be placed between an individual and the people of God with sin and the moral battle that's going on in the individual's life' and said, 'it's my experience that that battle goes on right in the heart of every Christian believer, as the battle is raging morally, simultaneously as the battle is raging socially'.

The term 'shame' reverberated in many contexts in my fieldwork, and the 'Not Ashamed' campaign suggests its wider circulation in British evangelical culture. David's words here indicate that outside the church, members of St John's sometimes experience their evangelical identities with some ambivalence, and learn to narrate the subjective tensions this creates through the language of sin, internal struggle, and idolatry. This acknowledgement of shame points towards issues of human vulnerability and honour, and opens up questions about the structuring force of wider social hierarchies shaping evangelicals' actions and self-understanding.

In an article discussing Pierre Bourdieu's methods of fieldwork, Wacquant talks about how Bourdieu spotlighted the role of shame, 'that self-defeating emotion that arises when the dominated come to perceive themselves through the eyes of the dominant, that is, are made to experience their own ways of thinking, feeling, and behaving as degraded and degrading' (2004b: 393). The fission of subjectivity implied in the emotion of shame is, Wacquant argues, both determined by and expresses wider diminishing social cohesion. The shame felt by members of St John's about their faith outside the church leads us to see how their subjectivities can be understood as the interstitial, fractured space of their being addressed as different kinds of subject in different places. I explore how this subjective fragmentation is formed and experienced by church members, and how their habituated practices lead them to articulate and become conscious of this fission while developing their desire for a transcendent coherence and unity in which such tensions are reconciled.

The fracture of subjectivity is by no means particular to conservative evangelicals. However, their articulated consciousness of subjective division, formed through their focus on God as coherent and their reflexive technologies of the self, brings the specific forms of cultural fragmentation they experience within the conditions of urban modernity into clear relief. Yet it is also the experience of ethnographers, as we, like evangelicals, move between differing lifeworlds, and are likewise often aware of the disjunctures this can create through the academic practice of reflexivity. Bourdieu's multi-sited ethnographic approach, with paired field studies of Kabylia in Algeria and his childhood community of Béarn in the Pyrenees, aimed to draw attention to how the researcher is 'caught at the intersection of systems of difference' (Abu-Lughod, cited in Wacquant 2004b: 398). Simon Coleman describes how his fieldwork with Pentecostals and the Word of Life movement in Sweden, while living among students at Uppsala University, led to a 'somewhat schizophrenic existence' as he moved between these (2000: 14). He states that this was further complicated by discussing his work in the university's anthropology and theology departments: these contexts were not separate from 'the field', as 'local scholars (particularly theologians) helped to define the context in which the Word of Life was interpreted in Uppsala and Sweden as a whole' (p. 15). As well as being attentive to evangelical reflexivity, we should, as he argues, 'also reflect upon our own assumptions in the analysis of a religious group whose ideology appears to contradict many of the cherished principles of academic life' (p. 15). My fieldwork led me to move between comparable systems of difference, and Coleman's caveat about the need to reflect on our own assumptions is important. Bourdieu's reflexive sociology invites us to objectivize our relations with what we study, attending to the social construction of 'our' knowledge about 'others'. Taking up this invitation, I will outline how my personal and academic history play a role in this story, and how this reflexive knowledge might deepen our understanding of evangelicals.

ON BEING REFLEXIVE

Reflexive practices play an important role in the formation of conservative evangelical subjectivities, but reflexivity is also enshrined across the social sciences as a virtue, helping researchers establish the truthfulness of the accounts they offer (Lynch 2000). Reflexivity is seen as enabling a more objective understanding through bringing the researcher's subjective positions to the reader's attention, to consider how these affect their interpretations. It is also seen as a moral duty, problematizing operations of power at play in the social construction of knowledge. Yet the precise meaning and desirability of different forms of reflexivity is disputed (Lynch 2000). In *Invitation to Reflexive Sociology*, Bourdieu describes how reflexivity has mostly been understood in terms of researchers' objectivizing of their background, class location, gender, and so on to take account of how these can 'blur the sociological gaze' (Bourdieu and Wacquant 1992: 39). Bourdieu and Wacquant argue that what is *also* needed, but is often neglected, is a form of reflexivity that inscribes 'into the theory we build of the social world the fact that it is the product of a theoretical gaze, a "contemplative eye"' (p. 70). Wacquant describes Bourdieu as critical of 'the "textual reflexiveness" advocated by those anthropologists who have recently grown infatuated with the hermeneutic process of cultural interpretation in the world and with the (re)making of reality through ethnographic inscription' (p. 41). He notes that, for Bourdieu, reflexivity is not produced through 'engaging in *post festum* "Reflections on Fieldwork" à la Rabinow', and 'nor does it require the use of the first person to emphasize empathy, "difference" (or *différance*) or the elaboration of texts that situate the individual observer in the act of observation' (p. 41). It is rather 'achieved by subjecting the *position* of the observer to the same critical analysis as that of the constructed object at hand' (p. 41).

The importance of reflexivity for Bourdieu and Wacquant is related to—but not primarily directed towards—virtues of humility, sensitivity, and credibility that are privileged in the 'confessional' reflexivity practised in some anthropological ethnographies (Webster 2008). The importance of what they term 'epistemic reflexivity' is focused on strengthening the epistemological moorings of research through encouraging recognition of how specific social and academic practices shape researchers' analyses and their 'innermost thoughts' (Bourdieu and Wacquant 1992: 46). In this view, reflexivity is not so much about intimist confession as about 'uncovering the social at the heart of the individual, the impersonal beneath the intimate, the universal buried deep within the most particular' (p. 44). Participant observation then enables analysis of the conditions of possibility of the act of observation, aiming at 'objectivizing the subjective relation to the object which, far from leading to a relativistic and more or less anti-scientific subjectivism, is one of the conditions of genuine scientific objectivity' (Bourdieu, cited in Wacquant 2004b: 398).

The study of religion has increasingly practised both epistemic and confessional modes of reflexivity. One form has been the critique offered by post-structuralist scholars such as Talal Asad (1993), Russell McCutcheon (1997), and Timothy Fitzgerald (2000) of how what is termed 'religion' is formed through contingent historical discourses. Another form is practised by scholars in the 'lived religion' approach, who have reflected on how the sociological lens through which 'religion' has been studied has primarily focused, through its preference for quantitative methods, on affiliation to institutions and statements of beliefs as measures of 'religiosity'. Within this approach, Robert Orsi's work powerfully demonstrates how epistemic reflexivity enables richer understanding of the interrelationship of the worlds we study and our own places within these, troubling the inscription of distance that academic practice can produce. In *Between Heaven and Earth* (2005), Orsi argues that the history of the study of religion constructed 'religion' according to liberal, Protestant, modernist ideals, and conceptualized religious lifeworlds that differed from these as 'unhealthy' or 'deviant'. He argues against this moralistic urge to construct figures of otherness in the study of religion, and calls instead for attention to the common humanity that researcher and informant share as a third way between confessional theology and radically secular scholarship: 'an in-between orientation, located at the intersection of self and other, at the boundary between one's own moral universe and the moral world of the other' (2005: 198). This 'entails disciplining one's mind and heart to stay in this in-between place', as we learn to recognize ourselves in the stranger and the stranger in ourselves (p. 198).

Orsi proposes that autobiographical methods can help move beyond moralizing judgements in the study of religion through helping us objectify our subjective relations to our objects of study and thereby interrogate what is at stake in the (perhaps unavoidable) process of academic objectification. The conversation between researcher and participants will always take place, as Orsi highlights, on a stage established by the networks of relationships brought to the conversation by the participant and the researcher, and is addressed to specific audiences. Attending to the ghosts—personal and academic—that haunt the researcher's religious imagination should be part of an academic commitment to scientific objectivity, enabling us to offer accounts that attend to the conditions of the production of knowledge.

Complex autobiographical relationships with communities and individuals being studied reconfigure the relationship between self and other, near and far. Undertaking any form of ethnographic study places the researcher in this position of stranger within a spatial field. This is so even when writing about a lifeworld with which we are intimately familiar: the act of writing, objectivizing those close to us in the pursuit of establishing knowledge of social reality, establishes a distance between the researcher as 'subject' and the 'object' of knowledge; in the act of observing (*theorein*) a social world, the researcher must retire from it more or less completely (Bourdieu and Wacquant 1992: 70). But this process of objectivization can, when researching traditions close to us, reveal how those 'objects' of knowledge that shape the subjectivities of our participants also play a role in forming us as subjects. Sociological attentiveness to what had seemed in close proximity to the researcher's own experience can be an interpretive device that enables her to move beyond navel-gazing reflexivity to address what connects us with and separates us from what is near at hand.

My decision to research Anglican evangelicals can be partly linked to the intimacy of my knowledge of this lifeworld, through my own teenage involvement with the charismatic evangelical movement. I grew up attending the local liberal, Anglo-Catholic parish church with my parents and brothers in a leafy suburb of south-west London. But in addition to this, as a teenager I regularly attended a charismatic evangelical Anglican church and youth group, after a schoolfriend invited me to a Christmas 'guest event' at her church, and so, across these different kinds of religious space, secular school, home, friendship, and family groups, I, like my informants, negotiated the meaning and performance of my faith. My intense involvement with this thriving church—at the time very influenced by the then-recent Toronto Blessing—and desire to probe the history and teachings of Christianity motivated my decision to study theology as an undergraduate. At university, beginning with my engagement with the 'masters of suspicion'—Freud, Marx, Nietzsche et al.—in my first term, through to my embracing Don Cupitt's atheist Christianity during my Master's degree, I moved away from evangelicalism, while retaining a commitment to my Christian identity.

My teenage involvement with and gradual path away from evangelicalism shaped some of the prejudices I came to hold against the movement, while also motivating my desire to understand its social effects better. These judgements I came to hold—for example, that evangelicals' attitudes towards other faiths are intolerant, their teachings on gender roles misogynistic, their views on homosexuality homophobic—should be seen as related to how social scientific knowledge of evangelicals has often been inscribed. My judgements were in part developed through my formation in a liberal humanities department as an undergraduate, and indicate how the liberal, academic gaze comes to construct conservative evangelicals as 'other', albeit mundane and familiar. But these judgements are also instructive as data relevant to understanding the lived realities of evangelical experience. While studying in a liberal theology department played a part in shaping how I came to objectify the movement

I parted company with, my value judgements were also formed through my participation in broader social structures, friendships, and relationships, in which evangelical teachings on a variety of issues were countercultural in the late 1990s, and today are even more so.

Labels given to evangelicalism by those outside the movement constitute important data for understanding its contemporary formation: evangelicals participate in many of the same structures—for example, studying and work-ing in liberal universities, or consuming mass media—in which this labelling process takes place. It is, however, not only the case that these structures form a background context framing evangelicalism. To understand conservative evangelicals' lived experience, we need to understand the force of these structures in shaping subjectivities. The same cultural structures that led Boris Johnson to label the Core Issues Trust bus adverts as 'intolerant' also affect evangelicals' practices and how they come to understand others' views of their faith. My informants frequently reiterated that evangelicals are stereo-typed in the media and in the popular imagination as intolerant, judgemental, sexist, homophobic, and Islamophobic, and sermons also reflect this con-sciousness. George, one of the curates, stated in a sermon that evangelical teachings on sexuality and other moral issues would lead 'the world' to 'hate' them:

> You will be hated if you stick with the words of the Bible. Because many of the things that the New Testament writers said are very, very unpopular today. They're unpopular morally because they have all kinds of things to say about sexual ethics. They're unpopular because they're narrow, exclusive: Jesus is the *only* way, this is the *only* truth. They're unpopular because they're just out of chime with our society, on various different topics, from work, to the place of men and women in marriage, just doesn't say the same as what our society says. And people will hate you if you stick with some of the things that the Bible says.

We see here that the sorts of judgement I came to make against evangelicalism as a student in the 1990s, and that have helped focus the liberal lens by which academic knowledge of evangelicals has been constructed, are those that evangelicals also see as projected onto them by broader society. These flash-points gesture towards different sources of cultural authority that are in tension with conservative evangelicals' sources of moral authority, which individuals have to negotiate their responses to in their everyday lives.

Focusing on my own experiences of evangelicalism, both personal and academic (not that the two can be neatly separated), and how these relate to my fieldsite, troubles simplistic constructions of otherness. The distance between 'us' and 'them', created by the objectifying gaze as it has often been directed at evangelicals, is too simplistic: members of St John's inhabit similar social locations to sociologists, anthropologists, and religious studies scholars, and have been shaped by their formation in, for example, universities where liberal political ideals are the norm. In the small group I spent longest with, half the group had, like me, an undergraduate degree in a humanities subject from either Oxford or Cambridge. The narrative I develop therefore seeks to move beyond constructions of evangelical 'others' and depict the everyday realities of how conservative evangelicals experience and find ways of negotiating anxieties, concerns, sensitivities, vulnerabilities, and human frailties that characterize social life more broadly, and consider how this shapes and is shaped by their modes of urban dwelling.

ORDER OF CHAPTERS

The first two chapters situate the analysis of the following chapters in relation to debates on modernity, cities, and the study of religion. Chapter 1 examines the growing scholarly interest in urban religion, situating this in relation to the contemporary analytical significance of cities as sites where processes of social change, such as globalization, transnationalism, and the influence of new media technologies, materialize in interrelated ways. I argue that Georg Simmel's writing on cities offers resources to draw out further the significance of 'the urban' in this emerging field. I bring together Simmel's urban analysis with his approach to religion, focusing on Christianities and individuals' relations with sacred figures, and suggest this opens up a new approach to how forms of religious practice respond to experiences of cultural fragmentation in complex urban environments. This provides a lens through which to analyse the extent to which conservative evangelical faith offers a creative response to conditions of cultural fragmentation in an urban context. In Chapter 2, I draw together the concepts of body pedagogics, interrelationality, and ethical subjectivity to develop an approach to examining questions of coherence and fragmentation and the formation of 'religious' subjects in 'secular' times and places. I argue that to understand evangelicals' lived experience requires attending to their sense of relationship with God, and following Simmel, I argue that the personality of God exerts agency in shaping and dividing their subjectivities, and that their learnt orientation to His transcendence locates immanent/transcendent tensions within their bodies as they seek to internalize His voice and shape their thoughts and practices according to His desires.[12]

---

[12] I use the gendered 'Him', 'He', and so on when referring to God, as this was how members of St John's referred to God, although during one talk on the doctrine of God, the minister described God as 'neither masculine nor feminine'. I will explore the significance of these masculine idioms further in Chapter 5.

The remaining chapters describe the everyday practices of members of St John's, moving through Simmel's narrative of religion and modernity and focusing on the specificities of their word-based practices. I begin, in Chapter 3, with their speaking practices, and explore how these point towards conservative evangelicals' cultural and subjective fragmentation as they move across different city spaces. In Chapter 4, I address their listening, and consider how this shapes their distinctive sense of relationship with God and their subjectivities in relation to modern ideals of autonomy and rationality. In both these chapters, I consider how the ideals for speaking and listening in public and private spaces articulated by the leadership of St John's are experienced in the lives of its members.

Central to conservative evangelicals' listening practices and desire to speak is their sense of relationship with God. In Chapter 5, I show that the personality of God, mediated through their listening as coherent and requiring their coherence, increases their consciousness of their moral fragmentation, a tension they narrate through specific idioms of sin and idolatry. I argue that this awareness of subjective division increases their desire for God, and I describe how the ways they understand themselves as relating to Jesus's death provides an emotional release from these tensions. I suggest that their learnt sense of guilt serves to bind them more closely in their sense of relationship with God in an ongoing process as they seek to understand themselves as forgiven and these tensions as ultimately reconciled by God, while simultaneously identifying themselves as sinful. Chapter 6 addresses how this orientation towards the coherence of God's character is bound up with a sense of His transcendence, which leads to a consciousness of His absence. I argue that conservative evangelicals' focus on word-based practices in a busy metropolitan context, in which it is easy to lose focus on the transcendent, can generate experiences of uncertainty and doubt and a sense that their becoming disciples requires hard work and struggle. This final chapter describes how individuals develop relationships of accountability with each other that encourage them to keep going in their faith. I show how through individual and communal practices, members of St John's work to incorporate themselves into a wandering body that is in the process of turning away from the immanent city and seeking to make a passage through time to the City of God beyond time, a turning away that is, however, often interrupted and difficult.

1

Modernity, Faith, and the City

> We are constantly circulating over a number of different planes, each of which presents the world-totality according to a different formula; but from each our life takes only a fragment along at any given time.
>
> (Simmel, cited in Levine 1971: xxxviii)

In January 2011, the London branch of the University and Colleges Christian Fellowship (UCCF) held a week-long mission, entitled 'Invited', which several members of St John's were involved with. The week involved speakers giving talks over lunch at different campuses of the University of London colleges, and each evening there was an event at a church located off a busy commercial street in central London that was easy for students from the different colleges to get to. When I arrived for one of these evening events, the furniture had been rearranged so that chairs were gathered in groups of seven or eight around coffee tables, each with a candle, bowls of nuts, and neon-bright strawberry sweets. The room had dimmed lighting filtered in soft blue and pink hues, and cardboard figures of line-drawn cartoon pigeons on the church's central stage. These pigeons were a prominent motif that evening: the covers of the small copies of Luke's Gospel placed on all the chairs featured an image of pigeons gathered around an open door, as in Figure 1.1, and this formed the background to the slides that the speakers from UCCF used. I asked a student I was sitting with why there were these images of pigeons everywhere. He replied that they been planning the mission in a room in the Royal Festival Hall, 'when this pigeon flew in, and everyone was trying to get it out. In London, pigeons are unwanted . . . nobody wants them.' He said one of the students was a designer, and they took this idea of pigeons as symbolizing people in London who are excluded, and the open door conveying the idea 'that they are invited in'.

In his 1909 essay 'Bridge and Door', Georg Simmel describes human beings as making sense of the world through our capacity to connect and separate

Figure 1.1. Invited
(Courtesy of Matthew Varah Wilson)

things: this, he argues, guides all human activity.[1] This process of ordering and distinguishing our sensory experiences shapes physical, emotional, and imagined space, leaving material marks in the world around us: 'In the immediate as well as the symbolic sense, in the physical as well as the intellectual, we are at any moment those who separate the connected or connect the separate' (Simmel 1997a: 171). Bridges and doors are material and social facts that

---

[1] Fran Tonkiss's insightful discussion of this essay by Simmel and his 'The Metropolis and Mental Life', in *Space, The City and Social Theory* (2005, Chapters 2 and 6) informs my analysis here.

emerge from the human will to connect and to separate, confronting us as objective conditions that then direct our actions. Simmel describes how bridges place an emphasis on connection, whereas doors represent more clearly 'how separating and connecting are only two sides of precisely the same act' (p. 172). As a door forms 'a linkage between the space of human beings and everything that remains outside it, it transcends the separation between the inner and the outer' (p. 172). Because it can be opened, the act of shutting it provides a more decisive sense of isolation from what is outside than the unstructured wall. 'The latter is mute, but the door speaks' (p. 172).

Simmel's reflections on bridges and doors draw our attention to the doubled nature of lines of division: 'the separation of objects, people or places is always shadowed by the idea—the "fantasy" or the danger—of their connection' (Tonkiss 2005: 31). Throughout its history, urban analysis has explored the boundaries that run through cities and the relation between physical, imagined, and moral lines of division, and the rhythms emerging from tensions between these. The image of the door and pigeons used in the Invited mission symbolizes a line dividing Christians from non-Christians, who are imagined as the unwanted and unloved for whom Christian students should feel compassion and invite through the door that separates them. This is suggestive of the place cities have often occupied within evangelical imaginations: here we see an idea of London as a lost city in need of redemption, within which the Church is a community of belonging and salvation. But this boundary of separation is understood as porous, enabling connection and movement across it, as the city is also imagined as presenting particular opportunities for the circulation of the gospel through which others will be incorporated into the Church.

Questions about modes of separation and connection in cities open onto broader issues about interrelations between evangelicalism, the wider social order, and modernity, and how practices of 'othering' shape evangelicals' social interactions and subjectivities. A sense of separation between 'the Church' and 'the city' was frequently articulated at St John's in the moral register of differing values, with London described as being lured by the twin idols of money and sex, and simultaneously shaped by an individualistic dream of self-determining autonomy. Yet this articulated distinction from the perceived values of the non-Christian metropolis at the same time demonstrated the shadow idea of Christians as also connected with and affected by the dominant moral milieu they desired to be separate from.

This understanding of the city as a space of moral disorder resonates in biblical narratives, beginning in Genesis with Cain's building of the first city after killing Abel and the dream of building the city of Babel into the heavens. Yet at the same time, hopes for the city as a space of righteous order are symbolized in the building of Zion and the desire for a City of God, hopes that have also shaped the contours of Christian imaginings of the city. The earliest beginnings of Christianity took place in the cities of the Mediterranean, with Acts telling the story of the birth of the church beginning in Jerusalem with the ascent of Christ and moving to its conclusion in Rome, the urban centre of power and empire, with St Paul 'proclaiming the kingdom of God and teaching about the Lord Jesus Christ' (Acts 28: 31, ESV).[2] The urban St Paul played an important role in establishing Christian emphasis on the universality of the gospel message, and this dimension of his biography is not insignificant. Alain Badiou argues that Paul's particular emphasis on the truth of the Christ event as addressed to *all*, irrespective of markers of social difference, was affected by his encounter with cultural plurality as he travelled amongst the cities of the Mediterranean:

> Recall that Paul was born into a well-off family in Tarsus, that he is a man of the city rather than a man of the country...His style owes nothing to those rural images and metaphors that, on the contrary, abound in the parables of Christ. If his vision of things fervently embraces the dimension of the world and extends to the extreme limits of the empire...it is because urban cosmopolitanism and lengthy voyages have shaped its amplitude. Paul's universalism comprises an internal geography, which is not that of a perennial little landowner.
>
> (2003: 21)

Cities within the lives and imaginations of Christians have been crossed by lines of separation, both moral and physical, as they have sought to be different from the moral disorder the city represents, while themselves affected by boundaries, concrete and symbolic, already marked out. Their urban imaginings have also been shot through with a desire to speak across lines of cultural difference 'to proclaim the kingdom of God' to all, potently symbolized in Paul preaching the gospel in public city spaces of the Roman Empire.

The complex interweaving of desires, dreams, hopes, and fears about cities in the Bible runs through the lives of conservative evangelicals as they draw on these narratives in forming their understandings of the social order and their moral aspirations and identities, and those of others. Evangelicalism has historically thrived in towns and cities under conditions of capitalist industrialization while often simultaneously articulating an understanding of the city as a space of moral depravity, exemplified by the Congregationalist John Blackburn's words to a mechanics' institute class in London in 1827:

> The metropolis of a great empire must necessarily be, in the present state of human society, the focus of vice. Such was Ninevah, such was Babylon, such was Rome—SUCH IS LONDON. Here, therefore, is to be found in every district, the theatre, the masquerade, the gaming-table, the brothel. Here are to be purchased,

---

[2] The translation of the Bible I use is the English Standard Version, the version used at St John's.

in every street, books that . . . tend to weaken all moral restraints, and to hurry the excited but unhappy youth who is charmed by them into the snares of pollution, dishonesty, and ruin.

(cited in Brown 2009: 19)

In contemporary British evangelicalism, cities are imagined as both sites of disorder and as presenting opportunities for the spread of faith. An article on the website of the conservative evangelical network 'Reaching the Unreached', which works 'to make Jesus famous in the tough areas of the UK', articulates such ambitions: 'Cities are places of influence . . . If Christians want to reach the world and transform culture, we need to focus on cities' (Chester 2010a). The author writes that the disorder of cities makes them spaces especially receptive to the gospel: 'Most Christians think of the city as a hard place or a dark place. But the *opposite* is true . . . Always, always, *the more urban a place is, the more troubled and the more plural—the more people have responded to the message of Jesus*' (Chester 2010a, emphasis in original). He contrasts contemporary cities, spoiled by 'rejection of God', with a future city: 'the Bible's vision of the future, of God's future, is a vision of a new city, a renewed city, God's city. Jesus died outside the city so that we can be welcomed into God's city.' He argues that 'In the meantime, the Christian community is a city within the city. We are an outpost, a glimpse, a foretaste of God's new city . . . a place of welcome for outsiders.' Christians are, he writes, themselves outsiders within the city: 'Christians belong to God's city so we don't quite fit in—we're like temporary residents' (Chester 2010a).

In this chapter, I argue that micro-level analysis of the everyday *urban* manoeuvres of members of St John's provides a means of opening up questions about the location and experience of conservative evangelicalism in secular modern contexts. I begin by tracing the contemporary analytical significance of cities in social theory for understanding the nature of social change. I then consider the historic neglect of research on urban religion, and how perceptions of urbanization as equating to secularization have shaped broader understandings of evangelicalism. I suggest that the brilliant and prescient analysis of Georg Simmel provides resources for both exploring the formation of evangelical subjectivities and drawing out questions about 'the urban' within the emerging field of 'urban religion' that open onto broader themes about the nature of social and personal order in modernity. I outline the central themes of his 1903 essay 'The Metropolis and Mental Life', which considers the social and subjective effects of the cultural plurality of cities. Simmel argues that the overwhelming quantity of stimulations in cities leads to a retreat into the self in public spaces, as the urban dweller learns to interact with others in rationalized, impersonal ways. This logic of detachment and instrumentalization runs in tension with the evangelical norm—symbolized in Paul's preaching in Rome—of declaring the gospel to all, seeking to address the lost with a proclamation of the kingdom of God, a tension I take up in later chapters. I then draw on Simmel's conceptualization of urban subjectivity together with his work on religion to develop an approach that focuses on how particular practices can both respond to *and* intensify experiences of fragmentation in modern pluralistic contexts, deepening understanding of the complex interplay of modes of connection, separation, and interaction shaping everyday religious lives.

CITIES, SECULARIZATION, AND THE STUDY OF RELIGION

With half of humanity now living in urban areas, growing to two-thirds in the next fifty years, it is not surprising that there is growing interest in urban religious life emerging as part of a broader interest in cities across different disciplines. While the city has long been a significant site for exploring major questions about the nature of social and cultural life, it has not always been, as Saskia Sassen notes, a heuristic space with the potential for producing understanding of major social changes (2010: 3). The study of cities was central to the work of sociology's founding thinkers and throughout the early twentieth century, for example, in the work of Weber, Lefebvre, and the Chicago School. As these sociologists sought to understand the massive social upheavals associated with industrial capitalism across Europe and North America, studying the city was not just about understanding 'the urban': the city represented the paradigmatic site for examining processes of modernization, and produced key analytical categories for the discipline of sociology. The study of cities lost this privileged role following this period, in part, as Sassen describes, because the city ceased to be so central for epochal social transformations, and urban sociology became increasingly focused on examining 'social problems' (p. 3).

In the early twenty-first century, the city is again becoming an important lens for understanding processes of social change, as the city and the urban region emerge as key sites where macro-level social trends materialize and can be constituted as objects for research (Sassen 2010: 3). These trends include globalization, the development of new information technologies, the intensification of transnational and translocal dynamics, and the heightened visibility and voice of particular kinds of sociocultural diversity, and cities are where these processes are often intricately interrelated in complex formations (p. 3). Studying forms of social and cultural life in cities also offers a means of overcoming sociology's statist focus, opening up flows of power at subnational and transnational levels and the ways in which urban centres are defined through specific 'relationships with their hinterlands, and with the nation', while also emplacing macro-level processes of social change in individuals' everyday lives (Burchardt and Becci 2013: 14). Urban anthropology is a growing area for similar reasons. Historically, social and cultural anthropologists mostly neglected the study of cities, especially western urban fields, owing to concerns about losing their disciplinary distinctiveness from sociology and a sense that the discipline's methodological fieldwork toolkit developed in studying village and tribal communities could not be used with more complex, unbounded, urban spaces (Pardo and Prato 2012: 9). However, varying and rapid processes of urbanization, together with post-colonial disciplinary reflexivity, increasingly led anthropologists to explore industrialized urban settings, and has encouraged discussion about multi-sited ethnographic approaches.

As cities are increasingly located as strategic areas of study, there is also growing scholarly interest in urban religion as a field with the potential to deepen understanding of the interrelations between religion, secularity and macro-level social changes.[3] This follows a historical lack of interest. While cities played a crucial analytical role in early twentieth-century sociology, religion did not figure in such research. Sociology's neglect of urban religion was shaped by the early history of the discipline. The founders of this discipline were concerned with the consequences of the social upheavals associated with industrial capitalism, and mostly theorized the changing social location of religion they saw around them in terms of urbanization equating to secularization. Classical sociological approaches to the link between religion and cities were developed during a period of mass urbanization in Europe, with the nineteenth century having seen the growth of London, for example, from one million to six million (McLeod 1996: xx). Patterns of church decline during this period were explained as inextricably linked with urbanization and this shaped the significance of the city within secularization theories, most memorably expressed by the French sociologist Gabriel Le Bras in his statement that the moment a French peasant arrives in Paris's *Gare de Montparnasse*, he stops going to church (cited in Casanova 2013: 114).

The argument that urbanization leads to secularization is part of a broader narrative that equated 'the urban' with 'the modern' and has played an important role in the (increasingly problematized) broader linear narrative of a secularizing modernity. This narrative shaped scholarly approaches to evangelicalism, which sought to explain its ongoing resilience as either resistance or accommodation to an increasingly secular modernity. The theory that urbanization leads to secularization has been developed in various forms, with

---

[3] See, for example, volumes edited by AlSayyad and Massoumi (2011); Beaumont and Baker (2011); Becci, Burchardt, and Casanova (2013); Orsi (1999); Pinxten and Dikomitis (2009); and journal special issues in *Culture and Religion* 13(4) and *Religion* 43(3).

three main forms of the argument.[4] The first focuses on the demographic upheavals associated with industrialization in the nineteenth century, as the major population shifts in Europe during this period presented churches with logistical problems that most were unable to adequately resolve. Some workers, for example, remained very mobile after moving to towns and therefore did not form close relationships with any particular congregation, while others who were more settled gave up practices that had been meaningful in a rural context, but no longer seemed so in an urban environment (McLeod 1996: xxi). The second form of the argument sees cities as by nature pluralistic spaces: because surveillance of practices, attitudes, and beliefs by employers, the Church, or magistrates was not possible in cities, differing subcultures could flourish, which meant that, in nineteenth-century Europe, religion declined as the urban population enjoyed greater freedoms than they could elsewhere (p. xxii). Some sociologists developed this to argue that urban pluralism encourages relativism, which breeds scepticism and challenges both the social support and plausibility of any one religious tradition (p. xxii). The third form of the argument proposes a further psychological relationship between urbanization and secularization, positing that cities develop a rationalizing and mechanistic disposition, and transcendent or supernatural realms lose their credibility. Weber argued that these bureaucratic, rationalizing modes of interaction became an 'iron cage', leading to the 'disenchantment of the world' (2001: 123).

Although not specifically addressing the spatiality of this, Peter Berger's early secularization theory draws on all three forms of this argument, and has been influential on subsequent studies of evangelicalism. He argues that processes of rationalization and the social and the structural differentiation of systems such as the state, institutional education, science, healthcare, markets, and religion led to the privatization of religion. This specialization of semi-discrete spheres of social life removed most 'non-religious' aspects of social life from the control of religious authorities and institutions in a process of macro-level secularization of the social order. This differentiation means that the social order cannot be reduced to any one overarching frame of reference, such as capitalism, technocratic instrumentalism, state bureaucracy, 'or even a neoliberal variation of the three. Modern society is an irreducibly fragmented patchwork of differentiated institutions' (Wilford 2012: 31). Berger argued that this process of differentiation, as part of the rationalization of the social order, also entailed the fragmentation of shared sacred frames of reference and meaning. These had previously legitimated social institutions and imbued the transient and fragile constructions of human activity with a sense of ontological security, order, and permanence (1969: 33, 36).

---

[4] I draw here on Hugh McLeod's summary of these arguments (1996).

The erosion of shared structures of meaning through differentiation leads to the fragmentation and privatization of cultural life in general, but secularization theorists specifically posited this as leading to individuals' loss of religious faith in a process of micro-level secularization (Wilford 2012: 33). Berger argues that the technological, bureaucratic, and pluralizing processes of modernization associated with capitalistic industrialism engender feelings of anxiety and confusion, and lead to a loss of a sense of belonging and an experience of psychological 'homelessness'. Differentiation leads to the pluralization of sources of meaning and identity, while at the same time, bureaucratic and managerialist forces contribute to individualization and a process of 'subjectivization', as individuals experience themselves as their own source of moral authority and meaning. However, because social identities require recognition and support from external sources such as religious traditions and institutions, this process of meaning-making is precarious. Mobile populations during periods of urbanization lacked the support of durable agencies that would reinforce sources of value and identity, and this engendered increasing existential uncertainty in the absence of any overarching 'sacred canopy'.

Berger argues that subjectivization offers two possibilities for religions: they can 'accommodate themselves to the situation, play the pluralistic game of religious free enterprise, and come to terms as best they can . . . by modifying their product in accordance with consumer demands', an approach described as cultural accommodation. *Or* they can 'entrench themselves behind whatever socio-religious structures they can maintain and construct, and continue to profess the old objectivities as much as possible as if nothing had happened', an approach described as resistance to the processes of modernization and subjectivization (1969: 153). Berger has since become a critic of secularization theory, arguing that societal secularization does not necessarily lead to secularization at the level of individual consciousness (1999: 3). Yet, as Wilford argues, he was correct in diagnosing that there is no longer any one shared 'sacred canopy' serving as a unifying framework of meaning and order for society, and that individualization, fragmentation, and compartmentalization—processes intensified in pluralistic urban spaces— 'serve as the social context within which religious organizations in civil society must adapt' (2012: 33).

These secularization approaches shaped dominant approaches to evangelicalism, and the binary construction of rural/urban led to a sense of 'urban religion' as something of an oxymoron, with 'nature' understood as a sacred form, for example, in the work of Mircea Eliade, who described the modern city as an 'end product of a long history of spiritual alienation and decline' (Orsi 1999: 42). Alasdair MacIntyre's depiction of urbanization is also articulated in these terms. He writes that with the migration of the working class from the countryside to industrial cities 'they were finally torn from a form of community in which it could be intelligibly and credibly claimed that the norms which govern social life had universal and cosmic significance, and were God-given. They were planted instead in a form of community in which the officially endorsed norms so clearly are of utility only to certain partial and partisan human interests that it is impossible to clothe them with universal and cosmic significance' (cited in Orsi 1999: 42). Within theology, Harvey Cox's *The Secular City* (1965) also reflected (and indeed celebrated) this understanding of cities as secular spaces.

How have these different views of the relations between cities and religion in modernity shaped understandings of evangelicalism? Given the influence of secularization theories within the history of the sociology of religion, it is not surprising that some of the most influential studies of evangelicalism have focused on the question of how it confronts pluralist modernity, and mostly answered this through theories of cultural accommodation or resistance.[5] Rejecting the thesis that urbanization causes secularization, and opposing the grounds of secularization theory more broadly, Rodney Stark and Roger Finke have argued that urbanization fuels the growth of religions. Like McLeod, they posit that the pluralism accompanying urbanization stimulates a religious 'marketplace', in which different religious groups are forced to compete with each other for 'customers'. This leads to an increasing array of distinctive religious 'brands', with the result that the customer is in this situation *more* likely to find something that caters to her taste (Finke and Stark 2005). In this context, religious groups, including evangelical churches, that utilize entrepreneurial methods to market their products most effectively will be those most likely to thrive. They argue that people want their religions to offer rewards such as miracles, and to impart 'order and sanity' to the human condition. They argue that institutions such as conservative evangelical churches, which offer these, are therefore likely to be the most attractive, even while they also make stringent demands on what the 'customer' must pay to obtain these rewards (p. 282).

Statistics demonstrating declining church attendance and religious affiliation in the English context throughout the twentieth century do not straightforwardly fit with Stark and Finke's theory that pluralization stimulates

---

[5] Hunter offered one of the most influential 'cultural resistance' approaches, arguing (1983) that American evangelicalism has thrived because it has been 'sheltered' from modernity, with evangelicals living disproportionately in rural and small town areas. His approach is mostly rejected, since the demographic location of evangelicals no longer corresponds with his thesis. Kelley (1972) and Iannaccone (1994) offer an alternative approach, 'strictness theory', which posits that churches demanding an absolutism of beliefs and behavioural conformity produce high levels of commitment, which engenders a sense of meaning. Others have argued that the growth of conservative evangelicalism is part of a global rise in religious fundamentalism, which should be explained as a response to economic uncertainty (e.g. Thurow 1996).

religious growth.[6] However, their argument that religions that impart a sense of order thrive does, as I will show, correspond to a certain extent with the appeal of St John's for its members. Steve Bruce also argues that urbanization can give rise to religious revival movements, suggesting this as an explanation for the growth of evangelicalism in the late eighteenth and nineteenth centuries. Through dissenting Nonconformist traditions, 'the formerly deferential middling and lower orders marked their withdrawal from the old system of dependency on parson and squire, asserted their autonomy, and embraced the religious values and practices that endorsed their recently acquired socio-economic and democratic aspirations' (Bruce 2002: 34). At the same time, evangelicalism encouraged self-discipline, hard work, and sobriety, which assisted these orders in their upward mobilization in society (p. 34). However, Bruce sees urbanization as in the longer term undermining community life and thereby contributing to secularization, even if in the short term it causes an increase in religious participation and historically led to the growth of evangelicalism.

Christian Smith's work on US evangelicalism has attempted to move beyond the either/or of the cultural accommodation/resistance explanations. Smith argues that when the old 'sacred canopies' split apart, ripped pieces of fabric fell to the ground and 'many innovative religious actors caught those falling pieces of cloth in the air and, with more than a little ingenuity, remanufactured them into umbrellas' (1998: 104). In the pluralistic modern world, he states, people no longer need 'macro-encompassing sacred cosmoses to maintain their religious beliefs. They need only "sacred umbrellas," small, portable accessible religious worlds—religious reference groups—"under" which their beliefs can make complete sense' (p. 104). Within this framework, Smith developed 'subcultural identity theory', an approach that explains evangelicalism's vitality in terms of both its cultural engagement *and* the symbolic boundaries of distinctiveness it maintains. He argues that American evangelicalism maintains its strength as a religious movement 'precisely because of the pluralism and diversity it confronts ... American evangelicalism ... is strong not because it is shielded against, but because it is—or at least perceives itself to be—embattled with forces that seem to oppose or threaten it' (p. 89). These cultural conflicts and a sense of threat enable evangelicalism to thrive, since without these it would 'lose its identity

---

[6] Peter Brierley's analysis, based on the 2005 English Church Census, shows that greater London is the only county in England to have seen an increase in church attendance in the twenty-first century. London has 11 per cent of the churches, but 20 per cent of the churchgoers, and its churches are on average twice as large as those elsewhere. It is home to 23 per cent of evangelical churchgoers, 53 per cent of Pentecostals, and 57 per cent of churchgoers aged twenty to twenty-nine (2006b: 249–50). This might accord with Stark and Finke's thesis; however, London's singularity in terms of church growth as an urban area suggests that it is not *only* plurality that contributes to this, but a range of other factors to do with London's cultural specificity as a global metropolis.

and purpose and grow languid and aimless ... [T]he evangelical movement's vitality is not a product of its protected isolation from, but of its vigorous engagement with pluralistic modernity' (p. 89). Thus he argues that 'modernity's cultural pluralism can ... benefit religious subcultures by providing a greater variety of other groups and subcultures against which to "rub" and feel distinction' (p. 116). Smith argues that evangelicals' sense of distinction from 'the world' is reinforced through discourses of 'us' and 'them', and can create a sense that they are on the receiving end of hostility from 'the world' (p. 140). This does not mean that they are defensive or wounded, and Smith argues that they also place significant emphasis on the important of contentment and self-assurance, and expressed 'very little doubting' (pp. 29, 145).

Several features of these different approaches fail to resonate with the lifeworlds of members of St John's, and the British context more generally.[7] While raising important questions about the effects of processes of modernization, these debates mainly charted macro-level religious changes through analyses of quantitative surveys and censuses of beliefs and institutional affiliation, which promoted a simplistic notion of evangelical culture and subjectivities as unified. However, the repeated emphasis by members of St John's on their sense of moral struggle and their articulated sense of shame suggests complex forms of simultaneous connection with and separation from 'secular' others outside the church that these standard approaches to evangelicalism have failed to address.

Studies of secularization paid little attention to the experience of inhabiting secular urban spaces and the multiple textures of evangelicals' everyday life afforded by these. As religion was mostly perceived to be disappearing in cities, few were drawn to tracing the religious lives that were being lived there, with ethnographers working in urban sociology by and large little interested in religion, and anthropologists and sociologists of religion not much interested in cities. As Wilford argues, the perception of secularizing processes as themselves 'corrosive of place' further contributed to a lack of sociological interest in space when addressing secularization, reflected in approaches to evangelicalism (2012: 25). Studies of evangelicalism that have explored space have mostly focused on suburban and rural contexts, since as Eileen Luhr comments, evangelicalism has often been seen as helping believers to cope with the 'chopping up' of life through processes of differentiation by

---

[7] This difference is also partly related to the difference in sociocultural location between conservative evangelicalism in London compared with evangelical cultures in the United States. The 2005 English Church Census, for example, showed an estimated 2.5 per cent of the English population attending an evangelical church on an average Sunday (Brierley 2006b: 52). Although 23 per cent of these evangelical churchgoers are located in London (p. 249), this still represents a far smaller constituency of evangelical affiliation than in most parts of the United States (see, for example, Pew Forum 2010).

sacralizing the 'private' spaces of home and family life, and by emphasizing voluntarism, moral freedom, and 'choice' in free market economies, making 'evangelicalism the perfect belief system for suburbia' (2009: 16). While evangelicalism has flourished in suburban and rural environments, in contemporary Britain, urban settings—and specifically London—are of strategic importance for understanding the location and potential futures of evangelicalism. In the twenty-first century, Greater London is the only county to have seen an increase in church attendance (Brierley 2006b), and is home to 23 per cent of evangelical churchgoers, 53 per cent of Pentecostals, and 57 per cent of all churchgoers aged twenty to twenty-nine (Brierley 2006b: 249–50).

If the study of religion has historically been marked by lack of interest in the urban, the past decade has however seen a proliferation of research on urban religious life, of which Robert Orsi's edited *Gods of the City* (1999) can be seen as marking the beginning. This development is not only related to growing interest in 'the urban' in social theory, but is also part of increased focus in the study of religion on 'lived religion'. This was a move against how established sociological methods of inquiry, privileging survey data on beliefs and affiliation to religious institutions, perpetuated a Western construction of religion that effaced the significance of practice and materiality. Lived religion scholars developed approaches to explore the messiness of how religious lifeworlds flow beyond the orderliness of categories of doctrine and institutions. Colleen McDannell's work on the material culture of religion (1995), for example, drew attention to how ideas of 'proper' religion shaped the normative thrust of the study of religion, reflecting wider power relations: it was the religion of educated male elite 'specialists' that was the standard focus of scholarly attention, with forms of religion that fell outside this constructed as 'other' and 'deviant'. The move towards urban religion can be seen as part of this broader move in the study of religion towards focusing on those whose religious lives have been rendered opaque by moralizing constructions of 'real religion', including immigrant and ethnic minority groups. Yet the urban settings of their lives also offered analytic lenses to explore the messiness, materiality, and embodied nature of religious practice. Orsi argues that there are distinctively *urban* forms of religious life, and describes urban religion as 'the site of converging and conflicting visions and voices, practices and orientations, which arise out of the complex desires, needs, and fears of many different people who have come to cities by choice or compulsion (or both), and who find themselves intersecting with unexpected others' (1999: 44).

Growing interest in urban religion stems also from broader factors that have put both 'the urban' and 'religion' back on research agendas in other social science disciplines.[8] An expanding body of work has examined how

---

[8] This can be connected with a 'spatial turn' in research on religion (see Knott 2010).

globalization and migration shape forms of transnational religious connections,[9] and this focus on diasporic groups has shaped understanding of urban religion to the extent that this is now often taken to be what the term describes. Because conservative evangelicalism has historically often been located in suburban areas, there has been little focus on middle-class urban evangelicals. The 'return of religion' to public prominence has also contributed to a growing interest in urban piety movements in diverse global settings. The urban nature of these movements is not necessarily brought sharply into relief in these studies, yet analysis of the strategies through which such groups differentiate themselves from others has raised questions about the politics of religious place-making and the nature of 'othering' practices in urban religious marketplaces (Turner 2011: 285).

An interrelated thread in several of these studies, particularly in the 'media turn' in anthropology of religion, has explored the significance of new technologies in shaping religious mediations and transcendent connections, with a focus on the emotional, embodied dimensions of these (e.g. Hirschkind 2006, Meyer 2008, 2010). Focusing largely on religious lives in cities outside Western urban contexts, these studies have opened up questions about the means by which religious groups can exert power in secular spaces, connecting with wider theoretical debates about the meanings of secularism, secularity, 'post-secularity', and the public sphere (Habermas 2008, Taylor 2007).

These different threads of research demonstrate the strategic importance of cities as spaces where the interrelations of religious practices and desires and broader social changes materialize and can be studied. Yet the field is still rather fragmented, and the distinctive significance of 'the urban' is not always brought into analytic focus. There are few shared resources among scholars in this field—partly a result of the historical lack of interest in urban religion. Therefore to develop an approach that opens up analysis of the lifeworlds of members of St John's and also draws out the urban further in this field, I propose that returning to the work of Simmel on cities, and drawing this together with his work on religion, frames key questions about religious lives being lived in secular spaces. Simmel's work draws us away from straightforward narratives of urbanization as leading necessarily either to secularization or stimulating religious growth, and allows us to consider the extent to which forms of religious life simultaneously provide a creative response to, are shaped by, *and* contribute to conditions of cultural fragmentation. This moves us beyond ideas of individuals as either religious *or* secular and opens up more complex understandings of the complex interrelations between space, faith, subjectivity, secularism, and materiality.

---

[9] See, for example, McCarthy Brown Tweed (2006); Vertovec (2001); Waghorne (1999).

SUBJECTS OF THE CITY: SIMMEL AND
THE METROPOLIS

The idea that the experience of modernity is one of fragmentation and flux, ephemerality and change, has been widely articulated. In *The Painter of Modern Life*, Baudelaire famously described modernity as 'the transient, the fleeting, the contingent; it is the one half of art, the other being the eternal and the immutable' (1995: 13). Marshall Berman evokes the ambivalence of this condition:

> To be modern is to find ourselves in an environment that promises adventure, power, joy, growth, transformation of ourselves and the world—and, at the same time, that threatens to destroy everything we have, everything we know, everything we are. Modern environments and experiences cut across all boundaries of geography and ethnicity, of class and nationality, of religion and ideology; in this sense, modernity can be said to unite all mankind. But it is a paradoxical unity, a unity of disunity; it pours us all into a maelstrom of perpetual disintegration and renewal, of struggle and contradiction, of ambiguity and anguish. To be modern is to be part of a universe in which, as Marx said, 'all that is solid melts into air.'
>
> (1983: 15)

This ambivalent promise of modernity, and in particular the relationship between the individual and the social collectivity it promoted, preoccupied Simmel. Living in Berlin at the end of the nineteenth century when migrants were swelling European cities and leaving Europe for America, industrialized cities were becoming increasingly densely populated, and ever more culturally diverse, Simmel sought to examine the social effects of this rapid urbanization and to address the question, as Richard Sennett articulates, of 'What could arouse mutual understanding among these people, who knew one another not even though they were pressed together?' (Sennett 2012: 37). Other contemporary social theorists lamented these changes, for example Ferdinand Tönnies's nostalgic contrast between the intimacy of social relations in small-scale rural community life and the impersonal individualism characterizing urban life. Yet Simmel was a celebrant of urban difference and, as Sennett notes, thought the presence of strangers can 'deepen social awareness; . . . life with others is bigger, richer' (2012: 38). As discussed earlier, Simmel's contemporaries mostly understood the increased cultural plurality that urbanization wrought as contributing to secularization. Simmel, however, located religion as offering creative responses to these conditions, which he saw as opening up new kinds of freedoms. Before considering his approach to religion, let us examine his approach to urban analysis.

Cities are complex and dense physical entities, yet urban experience is also shaped at the levels of perception, emotion, memory, and desire. For Simmel, the city was the paradigmatic site of modernity and he sought to explore the interrelation of space, time, the senses, embodiment, culture, and subjectivity through studying urban modes of 'sociation'. This idea of sociation was central to Simmel's approach: he wanted to avoid both individualism and sociological holism, in which particular social structures are reified and treated as autonomous. Simmel argued that we can understand neither individual nor society without beginning from social interactions and examining how social structures are formed out of the processes of sociation (Turner 1986: 95). This approach, beginning with the nature of social interactions and opening onto broader questions of social order, is apt for tracing multi-sited and intersecting modes of relationality in increasingly networked societies, particularly in contemporary urban life, connecting with understandings of cities as 'node [s] of social relations in time and space . . . they are essentially *open*; they are the foci of interconnections with a wider world. Cities are *open intensities*' (Massey 1999: 122).

Simmel's influential 1903 essay 'The Metropolis and Mental Life' examines how modes of urban sociation distinctively shaped subjectivities, addressing how individuals' micro-level interactions were affected by and contributed to wider processes of change such as rationalization, individualization, and the commodification of social life. This allowed a means of exploring 'much broader questions regarding the modern social condition and what Simmel sees as its central problematic—the uneasy relation between individuality and collective life, played out more vividly than anywhere else in the lonely and crowded spaces of cities' (Tonkiss 2005: 113). The essay contemplates how individuals respond to the sensory bombardment, fluidity, and range of experiences characterizing modern urban life. His analysis moves between the registers of individual personality, mundane modes of interaction, and the wider nature of collective order to explore the relationship the city promotes between 'individual aspects of life and those which transcend . . . single individuals' through considering how subjectivities are formed in response to wider social forces (Simmel 1971b: 324–5). This connects with Simmel's preoccupation throughout his work with how processes of individualization associated with the Enlightenment project interact with the depersonalizing 'sovereign powers of society', how individuals resist 'being levelled, swallowed up in the social-technological mechanism' (1971b: 324). 'The Metropolis and Mental Life' brings this central question to life with particular vividness and clarity, and as Tonkiss notes, one of the pleasures of this text more than a century later 'is in part the tremor of recognition for anyone who has ridden a subway or enacted the drama of the crowded street' (2005: 115).

Simmel describes the human as a creature who differentiates, who makes sense of things by drawing distinctions and making connections between sensory impressions. In the metropolis, we encounter excesses of stimulation that challenge our capacity to filter perceptions: we are faced by waves of random visual, mental, and other sensory forms so that the basic condition of urban life is overstimulation, and it becomes difficult to process the multitude of cultural forms we see and hear 'daily, everywhere, and in the most mundane ways' (Tonkiss 2005: 116). This intense sensory stimulation is a source of attraction for some but has the potential to overstimulate to distraction. Simmel argues that it most often produces an adjustment of the senses in a disposition of detachment, what he terms a 'blasé' attitude. This works against the process of categorization by flattening impressions and encouraging a stance of detachment, exemplified in avoiding eye contact with the stranger on the street or pressed up close in the tube train. Tonkiss notes the prescience of this observation: Simmel's Berliners had to construct this social distance themselves, whereas in contemporary cityscapes, smartphones 'realize the logic of urban detachment perfectly. Immersed in a private soundscape, engaged in another interactive scene, you can set limits to the city as a shared perceptual or social space' (2005: 117).

Simmel argues that this urban detachment was bound up with the development of the modern money economy. The impersonality of money shapes social interactions, which become increasingly patterned through a dominance of quantitative values over qualitative, and rationalizing, instrumental modes of engagement, with 'all float[ing] with the same gravity in the constantly moving stream of money' (1971b: 330). The world is transformed into 'an arithmetical problem and . . . every one of its part[s] [fixed] in a mathematical formula' (p. 327). As the money economy throws all into circulation, fragmenting stable and constant relations and creating ever more transitory constellations, the city dweller responds to the continuous shift of stimuli through increasingly abstracted processes of rationalization. Prefiguring Walter Benjamin's treatment of the homogeneous, empty time of modernity (1970: 266), Simmel describes this circulation of money as shaping urban orientations towards time, leading to a dominance of 'now' time and a particular sense of temporal suspense. A focus on the present means of exchange becomes predominant, and the ultimate end and significance of transactions is forever deferred, leading to a loss of meaning:

> A feeling of tension, expectation and unresolved insistence runs through modernity . . . as if the main event, the definitive one, the actual meaning and the central point of life and things were yet to come. That is certainly the emotional outcome of that excess of means [associated with the money economy], of the compulsion of our complicated technique of life to build one means on top of another, until the actual end which they were supposed to serve recedes further and further towards the horizon of consciousness and ultimately sinks beneath it.
>
> (1997b: 251)

At the same time, the city dweller's orientation towards time becomes governed by logics of precision, utility, and calculability. 'The technique of metropolitan life in general is not conceivable', he writes, 'without all of its activities and reciprocal relationships being organized and co-ordinated in the most punctual way into a firmly fixed framework of time which transcends all subjective elements' (1971b: 328).

These urban norms of exactness, indifference, and impersonality have the effect of abridging social contact, marking and maintaining psychological barriers of separation between people (Tonkiss 2005: 117). Ideas of separation and solitude as conditions of urban life have been influential, and suggest a melancholy story of urban coldness and rationality. Yet despite the increasing instrumentality in human relations Simmel describes, this indifferent urban attitude is a fundamentally social condition: 'civil inattention' (Goffman 1971) is a form of non-interference that is the only manageable way of being together with so many countless strangers in crowded city spaces. As Tonkiss argues, this dissociation and psychological separation 'is in fact a basic form of urban sociation, one that allows us to coexist with all these largely unknown others. Refusing interaction is not... merely a matter of social withdrawal but is instead a primary condition for urban social life, securing individual calm together with relative social peace' (2005: 11).[10] While there were psychological costs to urban life, Simmel saw the increasingly diverse range of cultural forms as offering the potential for greater freedom and enhancing individuals' horizons, and the presence of strangers as enriching social life.

Simmel argued that urban plurality has further effects, leading to experiences of subjective fragmentation. Cities are always crossed by social and spatial lines of separation, which today are increasingly concretized in global cities by processes of socio-economic polarization (Dorling 2011; Sassen 2001). The city dweller moving between different planes is addressed as a different kind of subject in each. Robert Park famously captured how urban social differentiation entails the construction of distinctive moral spaces: 'processes of segregation establish moral distances which make the city a mosaic of little worlds which touch but do not interpenetrate. This makes it possible for individuals to pass quickly and easily from one moral milieu to another, and encourages the fascinating but dangerous experiment of living at the same time in several different contiguous, but otherwise highly separated worlds' (1925: 608). As only fragments of the personality are involved in most urban interactions, the over-optioned experience of life in the city leads to subjective fragmentation, as the individual cannot assimilate the multitude of cultural forms and sensations that are faced, each with their own associated

---

[10] This is not to suggest that this form of urban indifference necessarily translates into more than the negative freedom of not being interfered with. Valentine notes a 'worrying romanticization of urban encounter' in strands of urban literature which 'reproduce a potentially naïve assumption that contact with "others" necessarily translates into respect for difference' (2008: 325).

moral logics. In 'the buildings and in educational institutions, in the wonders and comforts of space-conquering technique, in the formations of social life and in the concrete institutions of the State', Simmel writes, 'is to be found such a tremendous richness of crystallizing, depersonalized cultural accomplishments that the personality can, so to speak, scarcely maintain itself in the face of it' (1971b: 338). While all social interactions inevitably make a plurality of claims on individuals who simultaneously belong to different groups, and all subjectivities are formed at the intersection of interests and expectations, Simmel saw this process as intensified in cities.

Simmel's attention to the subjective effects of this fragmentation is significant for understanding the formation of evangelical subjectivities. Before considering his approach to religion, let us briefly consider his understanding of the formation of subjectivity. Simmel's conceptualization of subjectivity follows a Hegelian understanding of subjectification/objectification, in which the subject can only be constituted through differentiating subject-object relations, with this process influenced by modes of exchange shaped in the money economy.[11] He sets this approach out in *The Philosophy of Money*, stating that the distinction 'between subject and object is not as radical as the accepted separation of these categories and in the scientific world would have us believe' (2004: 66). He describes mental life as beginning 'with an undifferentiated state in which the Ego and its objects are not yet distinguished; consciousness is filled with impressions and perceptions while the bearer of these contents has still not detached himself from them' (p, 66). The human capacity for differentiation guides the formation of subjectivity, and is inseparable from objectivity: the subject is only able to recognize itself as a subject through the recognition of the existence of other subjects external to the 'I' (p. 66). This takes place not only through the objectification of what is external to the subject, but also through the objectification of the subject, as 'we can observe, know and judge ourselves just like any other "object"' (p. 67). Subjectivity depends on the creation of distance, including the reflective distance that allows the individual to become conscious of herself.

This process of subjectification/objectification does not just produce an intellectual worldview: 'the distinction between the desiring, consuming, valuing subject and the valued object', shapes practical activity, interaction, and understanding (p. 68). However, acts of enjoyment and consumption transcend subject-object relations, as within 'such moments we have an experience that does not include an awareness of an object confronting us or an awareness of the self as distinct from its present condition. Phenomena of the basest and of the highest kind meet here' (p. 68). Simmel describes the enjoyment of an art work in these terms: 'here "we forget ourselves", but at the same time no

---

[11] See Miller (1987: 68–82) for detailed comparison of subjectification/objectification in Simmel with Marx and Hegel's approaches.

longer experience the work of art as something with which we are confronted, because our mind is completely submerged in it, has absorbed it by surrendering to it' (p. 68). Simmel characterizes the distance between subjects and objects in terms of desire, with the space of desire depending on objects' resistance to our desires, which shapes how he understands the nature of humans' relations with God. The value of the object emerges from the contrast between the subject and desired object, and those objects that resist our desires are more valued: 'we call those objects valuable that resist our desire to possess them. Since the desire encounters resistance and frustration, the objects gain a significance that would never have been attributed to them by an unchecked will' (p. 69).

In modernity, new forms of cultural production present the subject with an ever-increasing number of objects, and she finds that other subjects also desire these objects. The values of objects become then further objectified, and this entails increasing abstraction, as things are no longer valued for their intrinsic qualities but rather for what makes them exchangeable (Miller 1987: 71). As these cultural forms become increasingly separated from the content of human interaction, they follow their own logic and become independent of their producers (Simmel 1997c: 76). For Simmel, subjectivity entails not only the externalizing process of objectification but is also a dynamic process of internalizing these cultural objects: 'Individuals must include *these* constructs and constraints within themselves, but they must really include them within the individual *self*, and not simply allow them to continue to exist as objective values' (1997c: 58). The formation of subjectivity therefore requires both the externalizing, differentiating movement of objectification and the internalization of these external cultural forms within the self.

Simmel differs from Marx, as Miller notes, in stressing not only the nature of production in industrialized societies, but also this aspect of consumption and assimilation, seeing the quantitative increase in material culture as constructing new developments in the possibilities of societies. 'Whether the objects are books, furniture, or cars, individuals are seen by Simmel as increasingly coming into relationship with them, not as producers who fail to recognize their products, but as consumers who have to determine their own development in this world of goods' (Miller 1987: 76). However, the increased production of cultural forms in modernity makes the subjective assimilation of all these cultural forms impossible, and this leads to a condition of subjective fragmentation, which is exemplified in urban environments, although it is by no means restricted to these. 'Countless objectifications of the mind: works of art, social forms, institutions, knowledge', Simmel writes, confront us 'like kingdoms administered according to their own laws,... demand[ing] that we should make them the content and norm of our own individual lives, even though we do not really know what to do with them, indeed often feel them to be a burden and an impediment' (1997f: 92).

This Simmelian modern circulation of subjects and objects has 'shifted up several gears in the postmodern era of mass air travel and ubiquitous motorways. If relationships in the era of organized capitalism were already ephemeral, then how much more so they are now. In the postmodern, again only taking to excess what already is to be found in the modern, not just objects but also subjects would be depleted of meaning' (Lash and Urry 1994: 13). The effects of the rationalization of time and the ever-faster circulations of cultural objects made possible by new media technologies have been theorized by social theorists as a process in which time and space 'empty out' (Giddens 1990) or become compressed (Harvey 1989), resulting in people becoming increasingly disembedded from concrete space and time (Lash and Urry 1994: 14). Lash and Urry argue that this emptying out of time and space is necessary for the contemporary circulation of subjects and objects so that markets 'can "stretch" over national and international space' (p. 14) leading to an intensification of the processes Simmel identified over a century earlier: 'We have here a seemingly endless profusion of "space odysseys", of subjects and objects travelling at increasingly greater distances and speeds. Objects are emptied out of both of meaning (and are postmodern) and of material content (and are post-industrial). The subjects in turn are increasingly emptied out, flat, deficient in affect' (p. 15).

As Simmel described cultural forms as assuming independence from their producers, so the increasing agency of mass media forms following their own logics shape contemporary experiences of space and time. While modernist metanarratives of progress can be seen as contributing to the increased rationalization of time Simmel identified in urban spaces, media logics shaped by the development of new technologies have reduced time further 'to a series of disconnected and contingent events... If modernist time is based on a literary paradigm, postmodernist time is based on a sort of video paradigm, where attention spans are short, and events jumbled out of narrative order via re-wind, fast forward and channel hopping' (Lash and Urry: 16). In this context, as Miller describes, the overwhelming quantity of meanings and things that confront us everyday—with this experience not limited to but perhaps felt most intensely in the rush of busy urban spaces—intensifies the problematic Simmel identified of how people respond to this fluidity and fragmentation.

If Simmel's approach to urban sociation raises questions about experiences of time, space, cultural plurality, and the formation of subjectivities in cities, how then does this relate to evangelicalism? Within the study of religion, cultural and subjective fragmentation and processes of rationalization have often been central to secularization narratives. Simmel, however, allows room for both the secularity of urban space—as impersonal principles of utility, rationality, and the sovereignty of money increasingly shape urban interactions—*and* for the religious desire for a transcendent source of coherence and security to be intensified under these conditions. While Weber saw the pluralization of values in modernity as denying the possibility of any ultimate unity or coherence (1948: 356), Simmel posits religion as potentially responding to the subjective dislocations of modernity, offering individuals creative resources to draw together the diverse fragments of their experiences into a sense of coherent order, while simultaneously further contributing to this cultural fragmentation. Let us consider how both this and Sennett's *Flesh and Stone*, which builds on Simmel's concerns, open up questions about how ideas of coherence and fragmentation sedimented within Christian traditions of practice and interrelate with modern urban logics of detachment.

COHERENCE, DESIRE, AND TRANSCENDENCE

As cities are sites of difference confronting individuals with a range of cultural forms, so the urban subject can be seen as fundamentally fragmented, and this, as already noted, has been seen as the condition of modernity. In 'Religion and the Contradictions of Life', Simmel argues that religious practices create an orientation to a transcendent beyond this fragmentation, bringing 'peace to the opposing and incompatible forces at work within the soul, by resolving the contradictions they create' and offering a pattern of coherence and unity (1997e: 36). Simmel sees the subjective effect of encountering and moving between differing cultural forms as creating a desire for a sense of coherence, for a transcendence in which life 'manifest[s] itself beyond all forms in its naked immediacy' (1997c: 90). Simmel emphasizes that this desire for an unmediated transcendent is ultimately unattainable, with this very idea of moving beyond cultural forms itself only mediated through our immanent experience of cultural objects. In Simmel's view, this promise of coherence has to be transcendent: 'The point of our religious endeavor must be placed . . . in a sphere beyond the empirical world, because it would be impossible to reconcile our manifold and diverse spiritual concerns in an empirical context' (1997e: 37). Simmel argues that the personality of God exemplifies this promise of transcendent coherence, experienced as opening up a pure unity in the religious life. He describes the religious orientation towards the transcendent divine as structured in terms of desire: every fulfilment of desire also contains within it a further longing, reaching an 'ultimate climax' in the feeling an individual has for God in terms of simultaneously both having and not having (p. 39).

While this desire for a divine transcendent enables the individual to draw together the fragments of her life in a sense of unity, Simmel also sees religion as contributing to the experience of fragmentation, introducing orientations that sit in tension with those developed through participation in other social structures. The sense of coherence that religion allows in response to conditions of fragmentation is therefore both present and always deferred (p. 43). I will examine Simmel's approach to the personality of God further in Chapter 5, but it is worth underscoring that one of the specific advantages of his work in understanding evangelical intersubjectivity is this attention he gives to the personality of God. His work opens up questions not only of evangelicals' engagement with the multiple forms of difference they encounter in everyday modern life, but also how they experience God as 'other' and the agency this has in forming their subjectivities.

This thematic interrelation of transcendence and cities as spaces of difference is also central to Sennett's *Flesh and Stone* (2002b), which explores the interrelation between dominant images of the body and the experience of urban space in pivotal moments in the history of Western cities. Sennett's focus here on how narratives and images of the body within Christianity shaped Christians' interactions in ancient and medieval cities builds on Simmel's focus on issues of fragmentation and transcendence, opening up questions about how culturally sedimented Christian practices and narratives have agency in forming evangelical cultures today. Sennett argues that the condition of subjective fragmentation is not only characteristic of urban modernity: civilization has *always* worked to confront people with differing forms of experience and contradictions that cannot simply be pushed away, and cities have always been pluralistic spaces where people encounter difference.

Sennett argues that throughout the history of Western cities, people's responses to the others they encounter are shaped by how they relate to their own bodies. He argues that unhappy, stressed experiences of our bodies make us more aware of the world we live in and encourage us to respond to others, whereas a passive relation to bodily pain and pleasure encourages indifference towards others. He outlines how throughout the history of civilization these themes have been recast in master images of the body. Some of these images, he argues, have attempted to convey the unity of the body as a system and emphasized unity, wholeness, and coherence, while others have presented this though 'a more sacred image of the body...a source of suffering and unhappiness', which encourages people to 'acknowledge this dissonance and incoherence in themselves' and to be more aware of the sufferings of others (p. 25). While Stoics cultivated passivity towards their own and others' bodily sensations, he describes their Christian heirs as seeking to combine an indifference to their own bodily pain and pleasure with 'an active engagement in the pains of their brethren' (p. 25). This was bound up with how Christians related to master images of the body offered in descriptions of God in the Bible.

Sennett describes how Yahweh was a wandering God, and Christians learnt to identify themselves likewise as exiles and strangers. Writing about early Christians in Rome, Sennett described how the narrative of exile was spiritualized into an understanding of the people of God as not 'at home' in this world. Learning this orientation towards a heavenly City as 'home' required loosening attachments to the immanent places in the earthly cities where these Christians lived. St Augustine 'expressed this injunction as the Christian's obligation to make a "pilgrimage through time"', which entailed attempting 'to break the emotional bonds of place' through specific embodied practices (Sennett 2002b: 130). The early Christians had to develop this orientation through rituals such as baptism and Eucharistic meals, through which they sought to direct their attention away from their own bodies towards the transcendent Word and Light. Sennett argues that as they learnt to focus on the narrative of the transcendent Word's movement to and from flesh in incarnation and ascent, this roused in them a sense of their individual incompleteness and embodied vulnerabilities. 'Crucified for man's sins,' he writes, Christ's 'gift to men and women is to rouse a sense of the insufficiency of the flesh; the less pleasure His followers take in their own bodies, the more they will love one another' (p. 371).

In contrast with the orientation to the body these Christian rituals created, Sennett argues that the master image of the body in contemporary Western cities is increasingly solitary and passive. This, he writes, was shaped through the technological development of mundane comforts such as armchairs and forms of seating on public transport. 'Leaning back,' for example, 'in a spring-held, tilting office chair is a different experience from leaning back in a wooden rocking chair; to experience comfort, the body moves less; the springs do the work of the feet' (p. 342). As ancient cities had public spaces where strangers came alive to each other in the performance of rituals, by the early twentieth century the modern city lacked these forms of public space. While eighteenth-century coffeehouses had been sites for gathering information and sharing news, in modern cafés, as Simmel identified, the café-goer expected to be left alone rather than talk to others, and 'the café thus provided a space of comfort which joined the passive and the individual' (Sennett 2002b: 347).

At the same time, modern urban architecture further served to detach city dwellers from each other. Sennett describes how central heating, new forms of ventilation, the development of electric lighting, and elevators meant that new urban buildings could be constructed that were entirely sealed from the streets around them, like those surrounding St John's today. He describes the Ritz Tower in New York, which opened in 1925, as an example. Then the tallest building of its kind in the Western world, it was both efficient and dramatic, with the engineering of heat and air meaning that apartment dwellers in the building no longer relied on the window for the circulation of air and light. 'Even today,' he writes, 'when the Ritz Tower is surrounded by other skyscrapers and Park Avenue is a hideous scene of traffic congestion, inside the building one has a great sense of calm, of peace, in the heart of the world's most neurotic city' (p. 349). As these modern designs eased the burdens of work and compensated for tiredness, they lightened the body's sensory weight and suspended it 'in an ever more passive relation to its environment. The trajectory of designed pleasure led the human body to an ever more solitary rest' (p. 375).

Sennett's narrative builds on and deepens Simmel's conceptualization of cities as characterized by increasing psychological detachment and individualization. Seeking to interrupt modern emphases on individualistic self-sufficiency, Sennett argues that a disturbance of the self and an awareness of individual insufficiency, such as was historically formed through Christian rituals marking collective belonging, is necessary to turn people outwards in compassion towards others. Sennett's approach, like Simmel's, does not posit the subjective fragmentation arising with cultural plurality in cities as necessarily engendering meaninglessness, but rather as offering the potential for self-transcendence and for people to turn towards each other in civic responsibility. Taking forward Simmel's celebration of the presence of strangers and urban cultural difference, Sennett invites us to consider the extent to which forms of religious and secular practice—and their interrelations with ideals of coherence, incompleteness, and individual insufficiency—contribute to or inhibit ethical conditions of freedom, tolerance, and civic compassion today.

CONCLUSION

The growing interest in urban religion has rich potential for deepening understanding of how religion is implicated in increasingly complex ways in wider processes of social and cultural change. Since cities are where such changes often materialize and can be constituted as sites of study, exploring evangelicalism in an urban context opens up wider questions about how the formation of religious subjects in secular times and places is affected by these processes. Historical neglect of religion in cities in sociology and anthropology has meant that there are few shared disciplinary resources to orient discussions in this field. I have argued that Simmel's work on cities and his work on religion can be brought together to stimulate conversation about how religious subjectivities are formed through interplays of cultural plurality, fragmentation and social division, orientations towards transcendence, and the forms of intersubjectivity implicated in relations with multiple urban 'others'. Simmel's micro-level approach to everyday sociation has the potential to advance understanding of evangelicalism through opening up how urban norms of individualism, impersonality, rationalization, and tolerance interrelate with desires for evangelism and the ambition to proclaim the gospel to all people everywhere, a logic also shaped by the urban beginnings of the church in the ancient cities of the Mediterranean.

In the following chapters, I consider the extent to which conservative evangelicalism is patterned on this interplay between the image of wholeness that the personality of God offers, and the acknowledgement of fragmentation and incompleteness formed through rituals that encourage people to turn towards each other. I will explore how Christian traditions of practice inter-relate with modern urban comforts and logics of interaction that tend towards privacy, detachment, and self-sufficiency as individuals move through differ-ent city spaces. I will thereby unpick assumptions treating evangelicalism as a unified culture that thrives because of its homology with modern individual-ism and address the questions posed by Simmel's and Sennett's analyses about the interrelation of religion, individuality, plurality, and the wider social order. To what extent do evangelicals' practices entail a normative tilt towards a sense of individual insufficiency? How do their practices affect their connec-tions with and separations from others? To what extent do these encourage them to address discordances within the self, and how does this shape their subjectivities? How is their experience of the personality of God implicated in this, and what does this reveal about the interplay of fragmentation and coherence in their everyday lives? Addressing these questions requires an approach that looks at how subjects move through and engage with a multi-plicity of 'others' across different urban spaces, which the following chapter develops.

2

Dividing the Subject

Embodiment, Interrelationality, and Ethical Subjectivity

> My body is the fabric into which all objects are woven, and it is, at least
> in relation to the perceived world, the general instrument of my
> 'comprehension'...
>
> [M]y body is not only an object among other objects, but an object which
> is *sensitive to* all the rest, which reverberates to all sounds, vibrates to all
> colours, and provides words with their primordial significance through
> the way in which it receives them... [T]he body... is that strange ob-
> ject... through which we can consequently 'be at home in' that world,
> 'understand' it and find significance in it.
>
> (Merleau Ponty 2002: 273, 275)

As I walked towards St John's one late November evening, a young couple
walked ahead of me into the church, the man wearing a warm-looking winter
jacket and jeans, and the woman wearing a short skirt, nude tights, and knee-
high, high-heeled boots. I was by that point used to the fact that women at
St John's do not necessarily dress especially modestly for church, but nevertheless, her outfit struck me as somewhat insubstantial for the late autumn
weather. The theme for that service turned out to be sex, or more specifically,
as Freddie explained at the beginning of the sermon, 'sexual immorality and
sexual temptation'. I sat next to Kate, a lawyer in her late twenties I had got to
know on the Rooted groups' weekend away. After the congregation had sung
the opening songs and recited the confession, a man with blond hair,
probably in his twenties, wearing jeans and a blue checked shirt, came to
lead the prayers. As the congregation sat with bowed heads and eyes closed,
he prayed: 'Lord, we can find it hard to believe that we are forgiven, as we
walk around in blemished, sinful bodies. Help us to believe the promises of
your Word.'

The passage for that evening was 1 Corinthians 6:12–20. When Freddie stood up to preach, he opened by describing the situation facing the church in Corinth and comparing this with London today:

> The Corinthian culture and our culture are . . . very, very similar. Corinth was sexually liberated, they had a Las Vegas, or an Amsterdam sort of reputation; the red light district was official, and many of the prostitutes worked for the temples. But a church in that culture is always gonna have to battle to live God's way, isn't it? And it's the same with our culture, and the danger is, it'd be the same with our church. We live in the middle of a city that is a lot like Corinth, where for the most part, young people care very much about sex, are very interested in it. Very easy to have the same attitudes and therefore the same behaviour. And faced with that sort of battle in Corinth, some of the men had begun visiting those temple prostitutes.

Freddie said that while you would have expected Paul to 'come up with some practical solution' for the Corinthians, 'cold showers, sex addiction groups, that kind of thing . . . In fact, he goes after their thinking. He wants them to change their minds utterly on sex and about their bodies in particular. He expects that that sort of change of thinking would transform their lives and their behaviour.' Freddie said that wider culture today treats sexual desire like hunger, as an appetite needing satisfaction, and warned:

> If you try and live as a Christian but think about your body the way the rest of the culture does, then sexual immorality will destroy you, like as not . . . Sex is not all you are, and sex is not all your body is for. Your body was certainly not meant for sexual immorality, your body has a much more important purpose, do you see it? Your body is meant for the Lord . . . So our culture says, 'be free, satisfy your natural appetites, your body is your own,' and *this* is the piece of Bible thinking you need in your brain: My body is *not* my own, it is the Lord's . . . He [Paul] begins with a question, verse 15, 'Do you not know that your bodies are members of Christ?' That is basic to what happens when you become a Christian. We, as a church, we are Jesus's body, so each of our bodies is a tiny part of His body, we are united to Him, and the point here is wherever you go, Jesus goes because you're united to Him. So if you take your body to the prostitute, Jesus goes to the prostitute . . .
>
> Start the day with verses like this, wake up in the morning, remind yourself that the body you admire in the mirror is for Jesus and is His body. So instead of whatever you think your body looks like . . . it's actually a small section of Jesus's toenail or whatever you're looking at, and whatever you do today with that body, you do with Jesus's body. And what I do with His body matters to Him . . . Read this verse just before regular times of temptation . . . Maybe read this before the Sunday night, watching the film on the sofa, or whatever it is for you. Read this verse: her body is part of Jesus's body, my body is part of Jesus's body, so . . . flee sexual immorality.

Freddie emphasized that 'the Bible isn't . . . down on sex', but challenged the congregation to think about 'how much sex figures in our thinking about our friendships here, and in our thinking about our behaviour here, and our time here and what we speak about here...How many times leaving the house having got ready to come here do you look at the mirror on the way out and think, "mm, sexy"?'

As I chatted with Kate after the service, she said she tended to think of sex in terms of rules, and saw the sermon as challenging that. She added she did tend to think a lot—'too much, perhaps', she said—about what she looked like when going to church, 'as it's here I'm most likely to meet someone'. As she spoke, I took note properly of her appearance: smart-looking beige jumper, pearl necklace, skinny jeans, knee-high brown boots, shiny auburn hair in a stylish bob, subtle mascara, rosy cheeks, and freckles. She would not have looked out of place in a magazine story about the Cotswolds.

Sex and sexual morality figure prominently not only in the thinking of members of St John's but also in many people's perceptions of evangelicalism. This is part of a history of Christian ambivalence towards the body and construal of this in terms of moral and immoral behaviours. The contested significance of the body in Christianity derives in part from the centrality of the doctrines of the Incarnation and Resurrection: the transcendent God becoming flesh and redeeming humanity through a suffering and dying body, in a sequence of descent/ascent that marks a pattern for Christians to follow in their spiritual journey. Much writing on Christian practice has focused on the asceticism this paradoxical narrative introduces into the social order, on how the invisible soul has been elevated above the visible body. Yet, as Fenella Cannell notes, 'Christian doctrine in fact always also has this other aspect, in which the flesh is an essential part of redemption...[T]his ambivalence exists not just in theory, but as part of the lived practice and experience of Christians' (2006: 7).

This ambivalence towards the body was evident in multiple ways in this evening service at St John's: through what Freddie preached about sex, and the idea of changing the body through changing *thinking* about the body—learning to imagine one's own body as part of Jesus's body—and this way of thinking being achieved through the embodied practice of repeating biblical verses. This idea of the moral importance of thinking about the body differently was practically mediated through Freddie's preaching a sermon, and the church members learnt the significance of this as the means by which God addresses His people through the habituation of their listening. This incident also suggests individuals' self-consciousness about how their presentation of their bodies in clothing and interactions with each other make the church not only a space for the worship of a transcendent God, but also a sexualized space that can lead to 'sexual immorality and sexual temptation'. Caroline Walker Bynum's assessment of Thomas Aquinas's conceptualization of the body seems still to reverberate here: 'The concept of the body implicit here is not entirely coherent or consistent...Aquinas is ambivalent about body itself. Body is the expression, the completion, and the retardation of soul' (Walker Bynum 2013: 266).

Ambivalence about the flesh is not, however, the unique preserve of Christianity. Philip Mellor and Chris Shilling describe modernity as 'Janus-faced' in its divergent cultures of embodiment, characterized by both Enlightenment ideals of rationality and Cartesian dualism and 'another modernity: that of Schopenhauer's "senseless will", Nietzsche's "will to power", Baudelaire's *flâneur*, and the reassertion of sensuality in baroque culture' (1997: 131). Modern cultures of embodiment are shaped by the uneasy interrelation of these phenomena, and Simmel's writing captures how the metropolis intensified this uneasy cohabitation, as the multitude of sensual experiences cities afford combines with the abstraction and rationalization of everyday life.

Ambivalence about the body has also shaped the construction of 'religion' as an object of study. In this chapter, I argue that focusing on evangelicals' embodied practices and how these form their subjectivities helps us to understand their everyday experiences, ethical orientations, and concerns. I begin by locating my focus on speaking and listening practices in relation to the increasing interest in materiality in the study of religion. Focusing specifically on word-based practices, I describe how the work of Webb Keane and Simon Coleman has opened up attention to the interrelation of Protestant linguistic practices and the formation of modern subjectivities, helping frame my focus on how evangelicals' speaking and listening practices intersect with urban logics of interaction. In the second half of the chapter, I outline how the concepts of body pedagogics, interrelationality, and ethical subjectivity are helpful for developing an account of conservative evangelicals' everyday experiences. I begin by outlining the concept of 'body pedagogics' in the work of Shilling and Mellor, and suggest this can be brought together with Foucault's work on technologies of the self, and consider how these approaches have been applied to the study of Christianities. However, as conservative evangelicals' desire to listen and speak is inseparable from their sense of relationship with God, understanding their experiences requires an approach that is sensitive to their forms of connection with (and distance from) the divine. I suggest that Bruno Latour's irreductionist empiricism offers this, and outline how this approach leads us to be more attentive to modes of relationality between self and other. In the final section of the chapter, I consider why focusing on *ethical* subjectivity, drawing on the philosophy of Emmanuel Levinas, enlarges our perception of evangelicals' everyday social lives and opens up new approaches to religious intersubjectivity.

STUDYING EVANGELICAL EMBODIMENT

'What difference does Christianity make? What difference does it make to how people at different times and in different places understand themselves and the world? And what difference does it make to the kinds of questions we are able to ask about social process?' (Cannell 2006: 1). Within the history of anthropology, these are relatively recent questions. They were central to classical sociology, with Weber demonstrating the agency of Protestant culture in forming Western capitalist modernity. Yet despite the centrality of religion in the work of the founders of sociology, religion throughout much of the twentieth century was a neglected area of the discipline, particularly in the decades following the 1960s, as declining participation in institutional religion in the West was accompanied by theories of the secularization of society. Writing in 1983, Bryan Turner argued that sociology of religion 'has not played a role in or constituted a part of any major theoretical debate in modern sociology' (1983: 3), and Gordon Lynch comments that 'it is an unfortunate irony that at the same time as questions about the social signifi-cance of religion have become pressing for academics, policy-makers and wider publics, we are reaping the fruits of the relative lack of engagement with these questions by social theorists and researchers over the past forty years' (2012: 73). Mellor and Shilling argue that the methodological default position of many sociologists throughout the twentieth century has been to treat religion as always the dependent variable relative to other economic, political, and cultural phenomena deemed more significant, thereby effacing the analytical significance of religion (2010: 27). It is possible to see some of these tendencies as underlying some of the dominant sociological approaches to evangelicalism, which explained its strength as a response to the uncertain-ties of modernity.

Turner argues that one of the reasons for the marginal contribution of sociology of religion to broader debates in social theory for much of the twentieth century was an inward-looking preoccupation with the question 'what is religion?' The difficulty of providing a satisfactory answer to that question dominated debates about secularization, with 'the effect of inducing a certain theoretical sterility and repetitiveness within the discipline. The endless pursuit of that issue has produced an analytical cul-de-sac' (Turner 1983: 3). Moving beyond this theoretical impasse, Turner argues that bringing 'the corporality of the individual and the corporation of society' into view allows examination of the significance of religion 'in the interchange between nature and culture in the formation of societies and the creation of human attributes' (pp. 12, 13). He highlights that the word 'religion' is derived 'from *religio* – the bond of social relations between individuals' and that 'sociology' comes from '*socius*, the bond of companionship that constitutes societies' (p. 8). He describes sociology generally and sociology of religion in particular as 'concerned with the processes which unite and disunite, bind and unbind social relationships in space and time' (p. 8), and argues for the central importance of embodiment in analysing these processes. These were also Simmel's central sociological concerns, as his work explored the nature of

individuality and collective life, and the new freedoms and constraints afforded by modernity. Following this approach, I will not focus primarily on
addressing what 'religion', 'secularity', or 'Christianity' are per se, but will
explore how conservative evangelicalism shapes and is shaped by processes
that 'bind and unbind' particular kinds of relationships in the times and
spaces of the metropolis.

Since Turner argued for the importance of focusing on embodiment in
1983, there has been a marked increase in interest in the body and materiality
in the study of religion. This can be seen, as Manuel Vasquez notes, as 'but an
instalment of age-old epistemological debates in Western thought' (2011: 21).
Within the history of sociology, the body has been a somewhat *absent
presence*' (Shilling 1993: 11). Although the sociology of the body and of the
emotions are now established subfields, classical sociology rarely focused on
embodiment as a specific area of inquiry. This did not mean that the body was
absent, as society's workings are inseparable from embodiment, but the body
was not a central focus of interest (Shilling 1993: 9).[1] In the sociology of
religion, the body has also been an absent presence, as the discipline has
focused on beliefs, values, and attitudes, neglecting practice and embodiment
as areas of inquiry. This neglect of the body has not marked anthropology in
the same way, and the recent turn towards embodiment in the study of
religion has been influenced by work on materiality and practice within
anthropology (e.g. Asad 1993; Latour 1993, 2005; Miller 1987), as well as by
broader social theory focused on practice (Bourdieu 1984, 1990), discursive
constructions of embodiment (Foucault 1979; Judith Butler 1990), and the
lived body (Merleau Ponty 2002).

While interest in embodiment is part of a broader recent materialist impulse
in the social sciences, in the study of religion it is also specifically bound up
with a reflexive concern about academic constructions of 'religion', articulated
by scholars working in the 'lived religion' approach. As noted in the previous
chapter, this is a move against several features of established sociological
approaches to the study of religion. In *Lived Religion*, Meredith McGuire
argues that scholars of religion, especially sociologists, need 'to rethink fundamental conceptualizations of what we study and how we study it' (2008: 4).
Her dissatisfaction with quantitative sociological research methods is bound
up with how these frame 'religion' primarily in relation to established religious
institutions and statements of belief, failing to engage with the complexities
and nuances of lifeworlds that cannot be 'stuffed into . . . [a] questionnaire's
categories' (2002: 196).

Lived religion scholars argued that dominant sociological methodologies
perpetuated a Western construction of religion that effaced the importance of

---

[1] There were of course exceptions to this, for example Elias (1994), Mauss (2006).

bodies and objects in the practice of faith. Moving beyond this, lived religion scholars have called for approaches that explore the messiness of how religious lifeworlds flow beyond the orderliness of these categories and the coherence of doctrine. Orsi, McDannell, and others have described how the study of religion has been shaped by Western political and educational landscapes, as scholars formed in liberal Christian traditions formulated 'a vision of "religion" that developed out of liberal and modernist Christianity [which] acquired a normative status in the work of nineteenth- and twentieth-century scholars of comparative religion' (Orsi 2005: 189). Orsi describes how this construction of 'true' religion—rational, respectful, 'unmediated and agreeable to democracy . . . emotionally controlled, a reality of mind and spirit not body and matter . . . concerned with ideal essences'—shaped scholarly lack of interest in embodiment, materiality, and practice (p. 188). These established approaches normalized forms of religion that conformed with elite, liberal norms as 'healthy', and exoticized those that did not as 'other', thereby fortifying the liberal, rational self (p. 198). To move beyond this moralizing construction requires, as Orsi argues, attending to how it is through the practices of an experiencing body that the sacred can become real. Lived religion scholars have therefore worked to refocus the study of religion through a lens that is attentive to embodiment, emotion, materiality, and—as discussed in the last chapter—place.

Reacting against the academic construction of religion as rational and emotionally controlled, lived religion scholars have focused on forms of religious embodiment that involve the body in heightened emotional states. McGuire, for example, argues: 'Collective embodied experiences, such as singing or dancing together, can produce an experiential sense of community and connectedness . . . Without the full involvement of the material body, religion is likely to be relegated to the realm of cognition (i.e. beliefs, opinions, theological ideas)' (2008: 115). This implication that there could be forms of religion—those that focus on beliefs, opinions—that do *not* fully involve the material body has the potential to reinforce the mind/body dualism she sees as operative in standard sociological approaches, since all forms of religious practice—including those privileging belief—involve the body. There seems an ironic suggestion that the messiness of religious practices outside the boundaries of institutions is somehow more 'real' religion than its social construction in the West, rather than acknowledging that academic practices are also a form of realizing religion in ways that do not necessarily stand outside the social lifeworlds we study. Focusing on conservative evangelicals' speaking and listening practices therefore provides a window into how the kind of construction of religion that lived religion scholars are reacting against (self-consciously rational, focused on cognitive beliefs, in many senses privatized) *has* been internalized in some contexts.

Anthropology has had a longer focus on embodiment. Anthropologists of Christianity working on evangelicalism have largely focused on charismatic and Pentecostal cultures,[2] and words and language have become a specific focus of inquiry. This is unsurprising given that Protestants place significance on the centrality of words. Susan Harding's research on Christian fundamentalists in the United States (2000) emphasized the central importance of rhetoric and narrative techniques over ritual in conversion, although, as Coleman argues (2006: 168), her approach is limited through its divorcing of language from sensual forms. Coleman's work on Swedish Pentecostalism and the Word of Life movement and Keane's study of the encounter between Calvinist missionaries, their converts, and those who resisted conversion in the colonial Dutch East Indies and post-independence Indonesia have pioneered reflection on how the centrality accorded to words in Protestant cultures is achieved through specific embodied performances. Both address how Protestant language ideologies shape particular kinds of subjectivities. My focus on conservative evangelicals' speaking and listening practices draws on these approaches to examine the interplay between urban logics of interaction, experiences of fragmentation, and forms of evangelical intersubjectivity. How then do their approaches situate the relation between words, subjectivities, and modernity?

Keane's broader project highlights the inevitability of material forms and processes of objectification in communication and language, arguing that religious doctrines 'only become real to the extent that there exist concrete semiotic practices by which they can be embodied, experienced, and transmitted... [T]hose practices will be subject to such factors as logistics, aesthetics, economics or prior history... Their push and pull must be understood within what could be called an economy of language practices and ideologies' (2004: 443–4). In *Christian Moderns*, Keane traces the relations between language practices, personhood, and 'the moral narrative of modernity'. His account demonstrates how particular Protestant practices shaped modern subjectivities as individualized and autonomous, as 'moderns' understood language and moral agency as beginning in the self. An example is the semiotic form of the creed, which locates agency in the self through objectifying belief as an internal state. He points out that the Apostles' Creed states an objective claim (that Jesus Christ was conceived of the Holy Spirit, born of the Virgin Mary, etc.): 'As such it appears to be merely a proposition. But it begins with

---

[2] See, for example, Austin-Broos 1997; Bialecki 2008, 2011; Coleman 1996, 2000; Luhrmann 2004; Meyer 2008, 2010; O'Neill 2010a, 2010b; Poewe 1994; Robbins 2004; Coleman outlines the reasons why these Christian cultures have had particular significance within anthropology, allowing renegotiation of notions of the local and traditional, and examination of how such missions are 'a sign of and response to modernity' (2010: 799). Crapanzano (2000), Harding (2000), Elisha (2008, 2011), and Bielo (2009) have focused on non-charismatic Protestant lifeworlds, but this literature is small compared with that on charismatics and Pentecostals.

the explicit first-person assertion, "I believe". It asserts the speaker's alignment with the claims...Moreover, it publicly reports that alignment' (2007: 71). The repetition of the creedal form 'entails a normative tilt toward taking responsibility for those words, making them one's own' (p. 71). Keane here shows Protestant language practices as having, as Jon Bialecki puts it, a 'centripetal' force in the kinds of subjectivity they create, which created the conditions for the emergence of the secular, individualized, autonomous subject of modernity (2011: 682). At the same time, Keane aims to trouble this notion of individualized subjectivity, showing how the borders between self and other are porous, as 'our' language always comes from another.

Bialecki contrasts Keane's account with Coleman's, which posits a 'centrifugal' conception of subjectivity. Coleman's analysis draws on anthropological theories of exchange to argue that sacred words can be understood as 'things'. As these words circulate, they show the porosity of the subject formed through the objectification of particular forms of language. Whereas for Keane's moderns, the normative tilt towards sincerity requires that speaking originates in the self, Coleman describes how the Pentecostals he studied internalize external words from the Bible through practices such as memorizing particular verses. In this way 'the mind and body of the believer are to be colonised by the transcendent world of the Spirit, with sacred language as the mediating vehicle between the two' (Coleman 2000: 127). The individual externalizes what they have received in performances through which words 'are turned into physical signs of the presence of divine power' (p. 131).

Coleman's approach draws on Daniel Miller's Hegelian (and Simmelian) understanding of objectification as a process of becoming: the subject is created and developed through an ongoing process of externalization and sublation (Coleman 1996: 109). In this sense, there is *both* a centrifugal force to the externalization of words *and* a centripetal force as the subject reabsorbs these external forms and thereby reconstitutes the self. This process of objectification implies, Coleman argues, 'a Foucauldian technology of the self...whereby inner and outer states are objectified and monitored in order to maintain a socially derived ideal' (p. 115). The self that is created through these processes is understood as a kind of 'living icon', colonized by the Spirit and sacred language, thereby representing 'principles of collective faith and truth' (p. 115). In the global Word of Life movement, this collectivity is not tied to the local spatial community, but rather through the circulation of words in portable forms such as cassettes encourages a 'translocal religious consciousness not tied to any particular institution or national culture' (p. 124). Here '[b]elieving does not appear to depend on belonging' in the sense of connections to a bounded religious community (p. 124).

The work of Keane and Coleman demonstrates how focusing on word-based practices opens up theoretical questions about the nature and boundaries of the self in modernity. My focus on listening and speaking arises from conservative evangelicals' understanding of these practices both as the means by which they form a relationship with God and as symbolic boundaries of separation, marking them as different from others around them. Focusing on these practices therefore illuminates the interplay of modes of urban sociality and opens up how individuals can struggle to perform the moral ideals promoted by their religious culture as they move across different spaces, troubling the simplistic stereotypes of evangelicals that arise through focusing on particular leaders' public statements rather than the exigencies and ordinary tensions and textures of their everyday lives. While anthropological focus on the formation of Christian subjectivities has often been confined to the specific setting of a religious culture and its ritual life, understanding conservative evangelicalism within a complex, pluralist city requires examination of the interrelation of urban norms of practice and those encouraged through church participation. The work of Mellor and Shilling on 'body pedagogics', brought together with Foucault's conception of 'technologies of the self', offers an approach sensitive to these complex interrelations.

BODY PEDAGOGICS

In *Social Theory and Religion*, James Beckford argues that much sociological theorizing about religion is problematic because it lacks theoretical resources to account for how religion (and its frontiers with non-religion) is interrelated in increasingly complex and subtle ways with other social, cultural and political phenomena (2003: 9–10). Taking up his call for scholars of religion to be more attentive to developments in wider social theory and to advance understanding of the increasing public prominence of religion, Mellor and Shilling argue that new sociological approaches can draw on established disciplinary resources. In 'Body Pedagogics and the Religious Habitus', they draw on Durkheim, Weber, and Luhmann to develop an approach attentive to the contemporary complexities of religion. Their approach follows Durkheim's understanding of embodiment as 'actively implicated in the internalization and reproduction of religious social facts' (Mellor and Shilling 2010: 28). They argue that his engagement with embodiment has been overlooked by interpreters who have either prioritized emotions or cognitive factors 'without acknowledging that *both* are important aspects of human embodiment for Durkheim' (p. 29). The specificity of 'religion' in their account draws on Berger and Luhmann, who 'remind us that being "religious" is to do with the adoption of specific modes of (transcendent) orientation to (immanent) social realities' (p. 30). The body pedagogics approach examines how transcendent experiences that shape orientations to the immanent social world are formed through 'distinctive techniques, rituals and cultural systems' (p. 30).

Mellor and Shilling use the phrase 'body pedagogics' to denote the centrality of embodiment as the experiential mediator of religious social facts and the basis on which 'a creative religious habitus' might be the outcome of these processes (p. 28). They propose that the study of body pedagogics involves 'an investigation of the central institutional *means* through which a religious culture seeks to transmit its main embodied techniques, dispositions and beliefs, the *experiences* typically associated with acquiring these attributes, and the embodied *outcomes* resulting from these processes' (p. 30). They suggest that this helps us examine how religious practices, techniques and experiences have significant consequences for forming '*embodied orientations* to the self and world, characterised by a *transcendent* configuration of *immanent* social realities' (p. 30), and enables us, following Weber, to analyse the directional logic towards the world formed through these means. This extends approaches to studying religious practices by exploring how embodied techniques are affected by broader social and cultural factors that may inhibit as well as enhance the reproduction of particular religious cultural forms.

The body pedagogics approach is similar to Marcel Mauss's focus on 'techniques of the body' and Michel Foucault's conception of 'technologies of the self'. In 'Techniques of the Body' (2006), Mauss focuses on specific embodied techniques through which a particular habitus is formed.[3] The body pedagogics approach builds on this by focusing not only on the cultural specificities of body techniques but also addressing the experiences these allow and the means by which these are carried between persons, space, and time. Foucault's focus on 'technologies of the self' in his later work can be drawn together with the body pedagogics framework to explore how evangelicals' embodied practices create particular orientations towards self and other as they seek to form themselves as particular kinds of subjects. Although theorists of embodiment sometimes accuse Foucault of lack of interest in embodiment and tending towards discursive reductionism, in his later works Foucault draws back from these tendencies. In 'Technologies of the Self', he states, 'Perhaps I've insisted too much on the technology of domination and power. I am more and more interested in the interaction between oneself and others and in the technologies of individual domination, the history of how an individual acts upon himself, in the technology of self' (1988: 19).

Within this later work, Foucault describes practices constituted in Greco-Roman philosophy in the first two centuries AD as forms of 'care of the self' and examines practices of the self in early Christian spirituality and monasticism. Through this he develops an approach to understanding the hermeneutics of

---

[3] Mellor and Shilling differentiate their account of *habitus* as 'the contingent *outcome* of religious practices and beliefs' from Bourdieu's, in which habitus is both *medium* and *outcome* of the embodied transmission of cultural phenomena (Mellor and Shilling 2010: 30n2). My use of the term follows its use by Mauss and Mellor and Shilling.

the self. Foucault defines 'technologies of the self' as 'permit[ting] individuals to effect by their own means or with the help of others a certain number of operations on their own bodies and souls, thoughts, conduct, and way of being, so as to transform themselves in order to attain a certain state of happiness, purity, wisdom, perfection, or immortality . . . [This] implies certain modes of training and modification of individuals, not only in the obvious sense of acquiring certain skills but also in the sense of acquiring certain attitudes' (p. 18). This is helpful for considering how conservative evangelicals train themselves to think differently about their bodies through such practices as reading the Bible and listening to sermons, learning to discipline their thoughts and sexual desires through internalizing an understanding of the self as part of Jesus's body, a technology they would themselves describe as a form of 'discipleship'. Foucault's terminology is often criticized as aestheticized, with morality becoming 'a matter of style, pleasure and intuition . . . turning oneself into an artifact', and this being 'a subject-centred morality with a vengeance' (Eagleton 1990: 368, 394). Yet Foucault is clear that the engagement with the self is a thoroughly social process. He describes technologies of the self as 'patterns that he finds in his culture and which are proposed, suggested and imposed on him by his culture, his society and his social group' (cited in Campbell 2010: 27).

For Foucault, practices of 'care of the self' are inseparable from morality and ethics. He defines 'morality' as 'the set of values and rules of action that are recommended to individuals through the intermediary of various prescriptive agencies such as the family (in one of its roles), educational institutions, churches, and so forth' (1985: 25).[4] These may sometimes be formulated as a coherent doctrine, but may more often be 'transmitted in a diffuse matter, so that, far from constituting a systematic ensemble, they form a complex interplay of elements that counterbalance and correct one another' (p. 25) Morality also refers to individuals' 'real behaviour . . . in relation to the rules and manners that are recommended to them', designating 'the manner in which they comply more or less fully with a standard of conduct, the manner in which they obey or resist an interdiction or a prescription; the manner in which they respect or disregard a set of values' (p. 25). He suggests that studying morality in this sense means determining 'how and with what margins of variation or transgression individuals or groups conduct themselves in reference to a prescriptive system that is explicitly or implicitly operative in their culture, and of which they are more or less aware' (pp. 24–5). Considering the 'morality of behaviours' implied in evangelicals'

---

[4] Throughout, although I tend to use 'morality' with this sense of rules of action and 'ethics' for implicit logics of interaction in socially situated forms of practice, I follow Keane in treating a strict separation of these terms as difficult to maintain, a difficulty that, as he argues, 'may ultimately reflect the dialectical relations between [these] modalities' (2010: 65).

modes of speaking and listening therefore invites attention to the values that evangelical culture seeks to reproduce, and how these interact with other ethical norms.

Subject formation involves more than just learning to follow rules of behaviour: it is also to do with how individuals establish their relations to these rules and how they recognize themselves as obliged to put these rules into practice (p. 27). As an example, Foucault considers differing reasons an individual might recognize for practising a norm of conjugal fidelity. Moving away from the determinism of his earlier work, his focus on practices of 'care of the self' sees individuals as performing ethical work on themselves, 'not only to bring one's conduct into compliance with a given rule, but to attempt to transform oneself into the ethical subject of one's behavior' (p. 27). This self-formation is 'a process in which the individual delimits that part of himself that will form the object of his moral practice, defines his position relative to the precept he will follow, and decides on a certain mode of being that will serve as his moral goal' (p. 28). This process requires that the individual acts on himself, 'to monitor, test, improve, and transform himself' (p. 28). Foucault's interest in techniques of the self is part of his broader thesis that modern societies are shaped through the integration of two distinctive forms of power relation: 'the mode of the *polis*, structured according to principles of universality, law, citizenship and the public life and the mode of what Foucault calls "pastoral power", which instead accords an absolute priority to the exhaustive and individualized guidance of singular existences' (Gordon 1987: 297). The modern state is for Foucault *both* individualizing and totalizing, and his focus on 'technologies of the self' is part of his analysis of the individualizing aspects of governmental rationality (p. 297).

Examining religious technologies of the self in complex, pluralist modern spaces opens up questions about knowledge and power, and how it is that individuals come to perceive their ethical self-formation as having significance within particular understandings of reality. We will see how evangelicals' desire to form themselves as subjects acting in obedience to God is bound up with their coming to understand God as the really real, whose commands have greater authority than those they experience as normative in the secular city. As the behavioural codes of conservative evangelicalism summon the individual to recognize herself as a subject who will discipline her thoughts and body according to the values of her faith, so deepening our understanding of evangelical experience requires attention to the practical means through which this takes place and how this is affected by secular norms of interactions. Foucault's 'technologies of the self' and the body pedagogics approach together enable us to explore how practices encouraged in a Christian culture shape orientations to the social order and form individuals as subjects in particular ways. Let us briefly consider how these approaches have been applied to Christianity.

Mellor and Shilling argue that within Christianity, in the process of individuals being incorporated into a church, social identities and bonds are transcended simultaneously as the seeds of individualism are sown: in emphasizing conformity to the will of God, Christianity also foregrounds the centrality of individual consent to this (2010: 31). As the individual body receives redemption through believing in the Word of God or receiving Christ's Body in the Eucharist, it 'becomes itself a source of redemption, in the sense that ultimate religious meaning becomes incorporated within the individual' (p. 32). This carrying of a transcendent meaning within the self then 'facilitates a cutting across "immanent" ethnic, economic or cultural loyalties, creating an inter-corporeal and reflexive space for Christians to experience and reflect upon them in a critical manner' (p. 32).

Mellor and Shilling argue that Christianity's 'directional logic' towards the world is as much to do with how it generates an embodiment of an orientation towards social realities as with its cognitive plausibility. They note the centrality of the New Testament teaching 'that Christians are *called out* of the world (John 15:19), and . . . that this involves *changing their bodies* so that they walk, talk, desire, think and feel in a way that is entirely at odds with their previous existence' (p. 33). As mentioned in the previous chapter, Sennett describes how the ritualized practices of early Christians provided the means by which they attempted to sever their emotional attachments to the present city and to orient their attention towards the City of God (2002b: 148). While the means of the transformation have varied across space and time, anthropological literature on Pentecostalism has conceptualized this in terms of 'ruptures', shaped by particular practices, with the effect of locating 'immanence / transcendence tensions primarily in the individual body' (Mellor and Shilling 2010: 33). This understanding of faith in terms of rupture does not translate to British conservative evangelicalism, however, in which the broader culture has been shaped by the historical influence of Christianity. Yet the body pedagogic formation of an immanence/transcendence tension is useful for reflecting on the struggles evangelicals experience as they seek to live as individuals called out of this world, and we will see how this leads them to knot themselves into relationships of accountability that encourage them to keep going in their faith.

Foucault sees techniques of confession and moral self-reflection as central to the formation of the Christian subject. He acknowledges that Christianity requires 'a duty to accept a set of obligations, to hold certain books as permanent truth . . . not only to believe certain things but to show that one believes' (1988: 40), but he characterizes it as 'not only a salvation religion, it's a confessional religion':

Each person has the duty to know who he is, that is, to try to know what is happening inside him, to acknowledge faults, to recognise temptations, to locate desires, and everyone is obliged to disclose these things either to God or to others in the community and hence to bear public or private witness against oneself. The truth obligations of faith and the self are linked together . . . It's not the same in the Catholic as in the Reform tradition. But the main features of both are an ensemble of truth obligations dealing with faith, books, dogma, and one dealing with truth, heart and soul.

(p. 40)

There is perhaps, as Jeremy Carrette notes, an overdependence on the verbalization of truth in Foucault's account, underplaying the importance of silence. While Foucault locates the importance of silence in relation to operations of power that silence subjects in regimes of oppression, Carrette emphasizes that there are a range of registers of silence (2000: 30). We might therefore consider how within conservative evangelicalism, individuals seek to discipl(in)e themselves and each other through different kinds of silence. This includes the silences of women who are excluded from practices of preaching, as well as the silence required to listen to one another and to God, together with practices of confession and self-reflection, as the means by which Christ's redemption is located in their individual and collective body as a church.

The term 'practice' is central to conceptualizations of both body pedagogics and technologies of the self. Drawing on Bourdieu, Courtney Bender highlights how this turn to 'practice' emphasizes elements of hybridity, making do, habituation, instability, and the potential for change (2012: 274). Bender argues for an analytical shift away from 'practices' as 'things' which might appear to be 'self-evidently "religious"' to the verbal form of 'practising', which redirects attention towards the processes that make things 'religious'. Such an approach allows attention to how religion is always entwined in the practice of other cultural forms, such as law, politics, family life, and education (p. 275), moving us away from a view 'that it is religious people or individuals (or groups) that are keepers or containers of religion who then mobilize or play out "religious practice" in an unmarked social landscape' (p. 280). Focusing on practising religion opens up how 'the self and the social world are constitutively interlinked, made for and by the other' (p. 280). Studies of evangelicals often operate with a concept of individual agents who mobilize religion in response to cognitive factors, rather than attending to how evangelical praxis is interwoven in a dense fabric of cultural norms shaping subjects who make and re-make their social worlds with and for each other.

To develop an account that opens up this interrelationality of evangelical praxis and moral self-formation further, we need to explore their modes of sociation with others, and indeed how senses of 'otherness' are created, and how body pedagogic techniques of speaking and listening come to be experienced and understood in terms of a responsibility to a divine Other. Let us consider how the work of Latour, together with Simmel, opens up further these modes of evangelicals' relationality with others (human and non-human) who address them with multiple demands for response.

IRREDUCTIVE INTERRELATIONALITY

Moving away from mechanistic metaphors that conceptualize social life in terms of structures, in recent years, social theorists have increasingly turned to metaphors of relations, liquid flows, assemblages, processes, networks, and mobilities to evoke the dynamic and changing constellations of the contemporary social world.[5] Within this move, Latour's work (e.g. 1993, 2005) has been influential in drawing into question what we mean by 'the social', extending sociology as the study of 'associations'—the processes by which particular forms of connection are formed in space and time—to include forms of relationality with non-human actors. Simmel likewise saw sociology as the study of 'sociation', and was attentive to the agency of objects and media in shaping subjectivities and the social world. In his approach to religion, Simmel considers the nature of human desire for God, extending understanding of religious sociation to include forms of relationality with the non-material. As discussed in the previous chapter, he did not only consider *human* attachments to God, but also the agency of the personality of God in creating an orientation towards a transcendent source of coherence, which introduces a specific form of fragmentation into the social order. Within sociology, study of the nature of interrelationality with God and other sacred figures has mostly been avoided because of concerns that this raises metaphysical questions beyond the empirical limits of the subject. Chapman, Naguib, and Woodhead also argue that social scientists have written little about God because '"God" has become the great taboo of the post-war period' (2012: 173). Within anthropology, relations with sacred figures have often been constructed as fetishistic in colonial encounters. Yet, relations with supernatural beings are amenable to social scientific study, since they 'are mediated by words, symbols, actions and other things which we can investigate, whether or not their referents are "real"' (p. 173).

Orsi's work on mid-twentieth-century Catholic cultures in the United States has explored how sacred figures became real presences in the lives of individuals, and within the anthropology of Christianity, there is also a growing literature addressing modes of interrelationality with the divine or the

---

[5] See, for example Bauman 2000; Deleuze and Guattari 2004; Massumi 2002; Thrift 2008; Urry 2007. See Olli Pyythinen's illuminating discussion of this turn in social theory (2010: 3).

transcendental (Luhrmann 2004, 2012; Meyer 2008, 2010). As standard socio-logical theorizing has tended to bracket out questions opening onto the ontological contours of sacred figures, such accounts, as Orsi argues, fall short of engaging with lived experiences of social reality, for example, the ways in which for a Pentecostal woman, 'Jesus has an existence that is greater than the sum of her intentions, desires, needs, hopes, and fears, and ... cannot be completely accounted for with reference to her social circumstances. He has a life of his own in her life' (2012: 85). If we are to develop a *realist, empirical* account of conservative evangelicalism, we therefore need an account that engages with the complex textures of individuals' experiences of Jesus and God as real in their everyday lives. Latour's object-oriented ontology has been influential in helping refocus the study of religion on what its 'modern' constitution has effaced: the material practices and mediations by which religious lifeworlds are formed. Latour's more recent work on modes of existence (2011, 2013) also invites attention to the agency of *non*-material actors, including sacred figures, and the 'thingly' properties of words and concepts, offering conceptual tools to attend to forms of sociation between humans and non-human actors, including, in my analysis, God, in ways that avoid the kinds of metaphysical speculation that worry social scientists.

Latour's approach to 'modes of existence' is bound up with his aim to show the instability of the binary that is posited between 'facts' and 'socially constructed knowledge'. His specific emphasis on 'irreduction' draws atten-tion to the resistance of all 'objects' to either the explanations of a 'realist' scientific approach—the 'fact' position—or the explanations of a social con-structionist 'fairy' position:

> Once you realize that scientific objects cannot be socially explained, then you realize too that the so-called weak objects, those that appear to be candidates for the accusation of antifetishism, were never mere projections on an empty screen either. They too act, they too do things, they too *make you do* things. It is not only the objects of science that resist, but all the others as well, those that were supposed to have been ground to dust by the powerful teeth of automated reflex-action deconstructors ... Is it not time for some progress? To the fact position, to the fairy position, why not add a third position, a *fair* position?
>
> (2004: 242–3)

The influence of Feuerbach on Marx, and the secular roots of sociology as a discipline differentiated from theology, have influenced sociological ap-proaches that have either treated sacred figures as projections of human needs or as epiphenoma of broader social and economic processes, that is, as 'weak objects', or bracketed out questions concerning transcendental orien-tations altogether.

By questioning the binary that has constructed sacred figures as 'weak objects', Latour's approach asks us, when considering evangelicalism, to take seriously the ways in which God, Jesus, and other non-material actors have particular kinds of agency in individuals' lives. This is not to say that thinkers such as Marx failed to see the social agency of people's relationships with sacred figures: it was precisely *because* he recognized the social power of religious faith that he sought to expose it as an illusion. However, to really understand the experience of faith in contemporary religious lives means engaging with the mundane textures of people's forms of sociality with sacred figures and how these shape their everyday social interactions and orientations. Taking seriously the social agency of sacred figures in this way does not mean entering into theological speculation. It rather entails recognizing that as evangelicals experience God as real, any empirical account of their lives needs to pay heed to how these relationships affect and are affected by their relations with other social actors, and to explore the material and embodied means by which these relationships are formed and experienced.

Orsi argues that greater attention should be given to the experience of 'the holy' in the study of religion, arguing that in studying experience, we should avoid the use of the phrases 'believe in' and 'have faith in': 'because the holy is met as the really real . . . this renders otiose such terms that in their modern meanings connote subjective experience on a stark subjective/objective grid' (2012: 104). Latour also encourages social scientists to move beyond the binaries of the subjective/objective grid and realist scientist/social constructionist. To do this, he proposes that to understand social realities empirically we need to acknowledge their 'gathering'. Drawing on Heidegger's articulation of the 'thingness of the thing', this approach does not examine the conditions of possibility of a fact, but is rather 'a multifarious inquiry launched with the tools of anthropology, philosophy, metaphysics, history, sociology to detect *how many participants* are gathered in a *thing* to make it exist and to maintain its existence' (Latour 2004: 246). Latour notes that the closer we draw to things, the more we see how they always resist both 'fact' and 'fairy' explanations. The examples he gives are suggestive of how the things closest to us— 'the God to whom I pray, the works of art I cherish, the colon cancer I have been fighting, the piece of law I am studying, the desire I feel, indeed the very book I am writing'—always resist being fully accounted for by either type of explanation (p. 243).

Latour's approach—attending not just to people, but to things, facts, gods, and other non-human entities—allows us to explore how forms of interrelationality between different actors shape practices, values, and orientations towards these. Bryant, Srnicek, and Harman label Latour's realism as 'irreductionism'. In this, 'all entities are equally real though not equally strong insofar as they act on other entities. While non-human actors such as germs, weather patterns, atoms, and mountains obviously relate to the world around them, the same is true of Harry Potter, the Virgin Mary, democracies, and hallucinations. The incorporeal and corporeal realms are equally capable of having effects on the world' (Bryant, Srnicek, and Harman 2011: 5). This 'irreductionism' has potential for advancing understanding of religious life-worlds: extending the body pedagogics and techniques of the self approaches, it invites us to consider how incorporeal entities, such as concepts, doctrines, and sacred others, are mediated and experienced as real through specific body pedagogic means and how these act within the process of ethical subject formation. Latour states that work is 'rare in ethnography, no less than in theology... that respects the exact ontological contours of religious beings' (2011: 329). Part of the challenge of the turn towards practice, embodiment, and materiality in the study of religion is to consider the experience of these ontological contours of God and other non-material actors in everyday religious lives, a challenge that, as Orsi notes, unsettles established modern binaries of knowing, such as the real and imagined, past and present, self and other, here and there (2012: 14).

Attempting in his recent work to get away from the language of 'construction' with its 'metaphorical baggage of constructivism' and unsettle the subjective/objective grid that effaced the agency of what were posited as constructed, 'unreal', weak objects, Latour suggests that Étienne Souriau's term 'instauration' is more useful. The term 'construction', he states, draws attention to the *subject* who constructs, whereas 'saying of a work of art that it results from an instauration, is to get oneself ready to see the potter as the one who welcomes, gathers, prepares, explores, and invents the form of the work, just as one discovers or "invents" a treasure' (Latour 2011: 311). Instauration allows for the agency of the 'thing' as well as the human in the gathering, and 'allows exchanges... with rather different types of being, in science and religion as well as in art' (p. 311).

Developing this realism, Latour argues that we should conceptualize experience in terms of prepositions. Following William James, Latour states that it is undignified 'to call oneself an empiricist yet to deprive experience of what it makes most directly available: relations' (p. 306). He argues for a radical empiricism that puts experience 'at the centre of philosophy by posing a question that is both very ancient and very new: if relations (prepositions in particular) are given to us in experience, *where then* are they leading us?' (p. 306). He suggests that conceptualizing modes of existence as prepositions enables us to go beyond the bifurcation of nature that insists on 'the strict separation of objectivity and subjectivity, science and politics, the real world and its representations' and see how these bifurcations are the effects of a particular history (p. 305). He questions whether the deployment of this understanding of modes of existence as given through different forms of relations (prepositions) might 'allow... a total rephrasing of the question of knowledge? Can the bifurcation of nature be brought to an end?' (p. 306). He cites a passage from Souriau that shows how it is in attending to prepositions that we can draw closer to understandings things' different modes of existence:

> The modulations of existence *for*, existence *before*, existence *with*, are just so many types of the general mode of the synaptic. And by this route one can easily cure oneself of the over-importance given in certain philosophies to the famous man-in-the-world; because the man before the world, or even the man against the world . . . are also real. And inversely, there is also the world in the man, the world before the man, the world against the man. The crucial thing is to get the sense that existence in all these modulations is invested neither in the man nor the world, not even in them together, but in this for, in this against where the fact of a genre of being resides, and from which, from this point of view, are suspended the man as much as the world.
>
> (cited in Latour 2011: 331)

The turn towards materiality in the study of religion has drawn attention to how the academic construction of religion is part of a history that has often rendered the agency of objects and bodies invisible. Latour here brings into yet clearer focus the challenges of finding ways to describe the relational nature of *all* forms of existence, including relations with God, Jesus, and other non-material actors, and others 'before' and 'after' in time, and to explore the affectivity implied in these modes of relationality.

Drawing on Latour, Thomas Tweed argues for an understanding of religions that emphasizes their interrelational formation, specifically the means by which they enable movement 'across' and 'with', and the means by which they are a form of 'dwelling': 'Religions designate where we are *from*, identify whom we are *with*, and describe how we move *across*' (2006: 79). This emphasis on religion as a means of 'dwelling' resonates with Merleau-Ponty's description of how it is through our bodies that we can be 'at home' in the world. Yet, as discussed in the previous chapter, Christianity is patterned on a logic of learning to understand 'home' as the transcendent Kingdom of God, an orientation that exerts pressure on the everyday times and spaces and spaces of the immanent city. While we will see that there is a sense in which conservative evangelicals' modes of interrelationality are a means of dwelling 'at home' in the world, we will see how their body pedagogics also entail learning to inhabit the 'in between' space of being an 'alien' and 'stranger' in the city.

Latour's irreductionist approach to relationality invites us to develop prepositional modes of description to describe how conservative evangelicals dwell with, but are also simultaneously oriented *towards* and sometimes *against* the world, as they experience God *in* them, the disciples *before* them, act *for* each other, and so on, and the flows and stymies of these connections and separations moving in different directions. In the following chapters, I explore the extent to which the continued reverberation of this Christian narrative of exile is both a way of dwelling in and finding meaning in the world, responding to conditions of fragmentation and impersonality, and how this is also a way of becoming *not* at home, as individuals seek to discipline their thoughts and bodies according to the address of a transcendent ideal that calls them out of the world. To explore the intersection of the differing modes of interrelationality formed through conservative evangelicals' simultaneous urban dwelling and their seeking to direct orientation away from the city towards a transcendent Other requires addressing the means by which these identifications of self and other are formed. The final concept I draw on to develop this is 'ethical subjectivity'. Standard sociological approaches to evangelicalism have failed to acknowledge how evangelicals' subjectivities are formed through the interconnection of differing and sometimes contradictory currents and the extent to which they are often conscious of these tensions through particular reflexive modes of practice. To develop more nuanced understandings of evangelicalism, we need a concept of subjectivity as the space where these cross-cutting currents of practice intersect and are shot through with dreams, desires, memories, and perceptions. And as subjectivity entails the experience and negotiation of differing logics of practice in how we respond to and feel we ought to respond to others, this is inseparable from the realm of the ethical.

ETHICAL SUBJECTIVITY

Several scholars have criticized the concepts 'subjectivity' and 'intersubjectivity' as limiting in the study of religion. Turner, for example, argues that sociological focus on the subjectivity of the social actor, 'manifested in the analysis of religious beliefs, world-views, definitions of alternative realities, commitments to the sacred cosmos and so forth,' resulted in the neglect of rituals and practice (1983: 3–4). Jean and John Comaroff have also argued against 'intersubjectivity' as privileging modern Western understandings of society, culture, and economy as 'aggregate product[s] of individual action and intention' (cited in Orsi 2005: 170). They argue that the agency and creativity of the individual human over the social order is exaggerated in intersubjective ethnographic accounts and that these lead to limited understandings of the social and cultural, through a decontextualized focus on dialogical encounters between anthropologist and informant. The Comaroffs argue that to construe others' gestures, 'we have to situate them within the systems of signs and relations, of power and meaning, that animate them' (cited in Orsi 2005: 170).

The main objections that scholars have to subjectivity and intersubjectivity is the overemphasis on the intentionality of the human actor and decontextualized individualism they take the terms to imply. Some work in the lived religion approach does overemphasize intentionality on the part of the individual actor, who seems to play out their religious practices with a considerable degree of agency and choice. However, subjectivity and inter-subjectivity do not necessarily entail the neglect of practice or broader social contexts, nor do these terms necessarily imply inattentiveness to operations of control and constraint. Indeed, these issues seem to be implied within the concept subjectivity, which invites attention to how the subjection of subjects takes place through practices in which forms of power inhere, leading to certain kinds of relationality, shaped by the conditions of human embodiment. Focusing on subjectivity does not then imply the givenness, as theologian Graham Ward posits, of atomized, 'modern, secularized individuals' (2009: 189), but rather draws into question how the formation of subjectivities takes place through modes of responding to, identification with, and separation from particular others, formed by practices that delimit future possibilities. But what then does *ethical* subjectivity specifically add to this?

In recent years there has been a proliferation of interest in 'the moral' and 'the ethical' in anthropology and sociology. Although questions about 'the good' and how people engage with ideas about how we ought to live might seem basic to any study of social and cultural life, specific attention to 'the ethical' has historically been something of a blind spot within social scientific theorizing. This absence might seem surprising, given that the early canonical texts of both anthropology and sociology were preoccupied with 'moral facts' and cultural values. James Laidlaw, an influential advocate for developing an anthropology of ethics, suggested that it was in part precisely the Durkheimian origins of anthropology and Durkheim's identification of the moral law with the social collective that inhibited anthropological examination of ethics (Laidlaw 2002: 312). Jarrett Zigon argues similarly that, 'in replacing Kant's moral law with society, Durkheim . . . negated morality as a particular topic of study . . . For when morality is equated with society (or culture), it is quite difficult, if not impossible, to analytically separate a moral realm for study' (2007: 132). The same could also be said of sociology: the idea of an anthro-pology or sociology of ethics seems at first glance somehow odd, since most anthropologists and sociologists might have felt that in studying social and cultural practices they were studying morality all along. Robbins (2012) suggests that the rapidly growing recent interest in 'the ethical' is precisely because it is such a ubiquitous element of society and culture that once questions about the interrelations of ethics and social interaction have been brought to the fore, most anthropologists are able to relate this to their own intellectual projects.

This increasing interest in ethics among anthropologists and sociologists opens up new avenues for approaching fundamental existential questions about what it is to live a good life, offering the potential to 'shift or deepen our understanding of social life more generally' (Lambek 2010: 7). Much of this growing body of work has been influenced by Foucault's later work on ethics.

Yet although Foucault's work invites attention to technologies of the self, his approach to ethics does not focus on 'the exigencies of actual practice . . . which always entails articulation with other persons, nor, perhaps, is he attending sufficiently to those dimensions of virtues like responsibility or cohabitation that respond in the first instance to the call of the other' (2010: 25). While Latour's irreductionism opens up affective modalities of social relationality, the concept of ethical subjectivity adds to this, helping us construe both the differentiating movement of subjectification/objectification, entailing a separation between self and other, and also the effects of the interrelations of *different* modes of relationality as subjects simultaneously inhabit and move across different social spaces. This concept is therefore pertinent for thinking through how people negotiate differing logics of practice associated with pluralist urban spaces, and we will see that particular evangelical practices intersect with—and are sometimes caught in tension with—other logics of practice, and subjectivity is where these tensions are felt. In contrast with methodologically individualist sociological approaches, in Simmel's approach, the individual is, as Olli Pyythinen notes, 'an intersection, a crossroads . . . where "social threads tie themselves". The individual is not an absolute, final element, but . . . traversed and given to us by a specific set of relations' (2010: 39), which are the starting point for understanding the constitution of both social order and individuals. Yet subjectivity is not reducible to a bundle of subject positions, as if these were independent of each other. While formed through the experience of differing social norms of practice and discourse, subjectivity is also the space of the interconnection of these modes of relationality, providing 'the ground for subjects to think through their circumstances and to feel through their contradictions' (Biehl, Good, and Kleinman, cited in Prasad 2012: 363).

Simmel's approach opens up questions about how modern subjectivities are formed through responding to the different cultural forms that confront the individual, and his distinctive conceptualization of subjectivity raises fundamental social questions about how forms of difference and connection are created and maintained. Within the conditions of industrialist capitalist modernity with its myriad cultural forms and sensations, his approach specifically invites us to think through both how religious subjectivities are shaped in responding to the cultural practices, things, and others (including non-material others) that address them, and how the subject learns to say 'I' through processes of objectification and internalization as she responds to these. Yet to appreciate more fully the ways in which the 'I' is formed in responding to the claims of multiple others, the philosophical work of Emmanuel Levinas can deepen our understanding of *ethical* subjectivity in ways that move beyond the voluntarism and overemphasis of individual intentionality that has marked some other approaches to subjectivity. In the final section of this chapter, I will briefly address this.

Simmel's analytical approach starts with neither the individual nor society but the process of sociation. Levinas's philosophical approach likewise begins not with the primacy of the self or society, but with the condition of being addressed and called into question by another, the constitution of both self and society emerging in responding to that call. Levinas describes subjectivity as beginning not with the intentionality of the subject who *chooses* to respond, but rather with the statement 'Here I am' in response to the address that another makes to me, an address that individuates me as I am asked *how* I will respond (Levinas 1987: 170). I will not here provide an extensive discussion of Levinas's theoretical aims, since I have already addressed these at length elsewhere (Strhan 2012), but Levinas's decentring of the human subject and his aim to draw to attention the ways in which all social life, knowledge, and language are founded on the *ethical* conditions of subjectivity was fundamental to his philosophical project. This has significance in three areas for deepening our understanding of evangelical life.

Firstly, Levinas's account of ethical subjectivity centrally conceptualizes subjectivity as beginning with responsibility as responsivity, through describing how forms of difference confront the subject and invite her response. Although Levinas often writes about this in terms of an Other who addresses the subject, so that this is sometimes perceived as a dyadic relation, the ways we are always addressed by *myriad* others—both near and distant, past and present—who look for our responses is a fundamental aspect of this notion of subjectivity. Levinas's philosophy is concerned with how we respond to these others and with the nature of civility and compassion in our responding to difference. He saw these questions as bound up with both the practical and political nature of our responsibilities towards others, and with how our thinking about others within the traditions of Western philosophy are also implicated in our responses to others. Levinas was critical of Hegel's philosophy (and much of the history of Western philosophy more broadly) as totalizing, aiming to reduce all others to *my* knowledge in the pursuit of individual autonomy. His own approach to subjectivity begins not with the Hegelian moment of the subject externalizing itself, but with the moment of being addressed *by* the other. There are therefore fundamental differences between Simmel's Hegelian approach to subjectivity and Levinas's conceptualization—for example, Levinas rejects the assimilation of the other in the Hegelian dialectic as a form of violence. Yet the specific attention Levinas gives to how subjectivity emerges through our responses to myriad others, and the affective qualities of being addressed, shifts the analytical focus of subjectivity away from the process of externalization, and this is consonant with Simmel's attention to how multiple and contradictory modes of cultural address shape the conditions of modern subjectivities. This shift in analytical emphasis allows us, in line with Latour's empiricism, to engage more deeply with how evangelicals experience themselves as being addressed by others in the secular spaces they inhabit, by others in the church, and by God, and how they seek to listen and speak in response, in acts that form them as disciples.

Levinas's concept of ethical subjectivity therefore adds to Simmel's and Foucault's approaches through drawing attention to the experiential qualities of how people respond to and are formed as subjects by the multiple demands addressed to them by many different others, which are the basic civic problems, pleasures, and intensities of living in a pluralist, metropolitan context. Levinas's work sought to expose the ideas of the individual self-sufficiency and rational autonomy of the Western Enlightenment modern actor as a myth (since our knowledge, language, and social life always depend on our responsivity and responsibility to others). He encourages us to be attentive to how subjects are formed in responding to the claims that multiple others make, while also inviting us to consider how humans' primary conditions of impressionability and vulnerability are always interrelated with cultural forms of power and norms of recognition (Butler 2005: 45). This offers a richer conceptualization of subjectivity through which to explore the nature and lived experience of social relationality than many standard sociological approaches to the human actor.

Secondly, Levinas pays particular attention to both the significance of language in the formation of subjectivities and to the conditions of embodiment for the emergence of meaning. He emphasizes that our having language, being able to speak and to respond, must always depend on the fact of 'our' language having come from another, through the embodied conditions of address and response. Keane argues that despite the individualizing tendencies of modernity that arose with particular Protestant language ideologies, our words are always already someone else's. Levinas likewise theorizes subjectivity as only possible through our having received language from another, so that the other is always in me, and I in the other. We will see how conservative evangelical listening and speaking practices imply this porous sense of a subjectivity that is always also a self-transcendence.

This fundamental dividualism—indeed multiplicity—of individuals' subjectivities raises particular questions about the interrelations between words, monotheism, and the formation of ethical subjectivities. In the previous chapter, I outlined how Simmel's approach to monotheism sees the pure unity and coherence of God in monotheism as encouraging an orientation towards transcendence that ultimately fragments the subject, as it introduces into her orientations that are at odds with those she encounters in everyday life around her, and as God becomes the object of faith, He represents an absolute object of a desire that can never be satisfied within immanent social conditions. Levinas also sees the subject as fundamentally divided, as the subject's having language depends on her experiencing within herself the (ethical) demands that come to her from outside as she is addressed by multiple others who make claims on her as they ask for her response. Levinas's conceptualization of this process is not meant as a straightforward developmental description. Yet his approach encourages us to be attentive to how evangelicals' subjectivities are divided through the specific ways they come to experience the personality of God within themselves and inviting their response. Thinking through how monotheistic orientations towards transcendence divide the subject invites us to consider the significance of the unity, coherence, and moral perfection of God that evangelicals experience within this specific system of religious intersubjectivity, encouraging them to (continually) work on themselves in obedience to the demands they come to understand God as making of them. I will consider how this intersubjective Christian imaginary is shaped through particular body pedagogic modes, such as listening to sermons that encourage individuals to experience themselves as simultaneously both a 'sinful' inhabitant of the present age and as belonging to the transcendent City of God.

Thirdly, Levinas directs our attention towards the everyday aspects of moral life. He describes the ethical moment as found not only in moral acts of confronting local and global injustices, inequalities, and forms of political violence, but also in the most mundane act of saying 'after you' to another. Ethical theory often focuses on particularly contentious issues—such as abortion, euthanasia, capital punishment—that are matters for public debate. It would be fair to say that much of what is known about evangelicals by those outside the movement stems from focusing on their stated—often countercultural—positions on such controversial issues. It would be too simplistic to say that by focusing on individuals' 'everyday' ethical practices we are refocusing on their 'private' moral concerns, since these public discussions also play a role in shaping evangelicals' intimate self-understandings and mundane social interactions. Yet by considering the ways in which the ethical is implicated in evangelicals' ordinary interactions helps develop more nuanced understandings of how they seek to respond to all the different others that confront them in everyday social situations. This enables us to open up the effects of their moving between different moral terrains and deepens understanding of the complex location of 'religion' in the modern world. Levinas has a particular normative impulse underlying his work—aiming to *show* us the ways in which moments of ethical possibility are already there in everyday social interactions, and how these are related to the possibilities of more just and more humane societies as people respond to the claims of others (Strhan 2012). In drawing on his approach to consider evangelicals' ethical practices, I am not seeking to advocate for their positions, but rather to explore the significance of particular moral (religious and non-religious) logics in their everyday lives. What are the norms of responsibility that they experience as binding, and to what extent do they struggle with these in practice? Yet in seeking to tell this story, *I* am responding to the claims of many others, including both my informants and my academic interlocutors, who have addressed me in multiple ways as I have assembled this text, inviting a response that will be responsible.

CONCLUSION

These concepts of body pedagogics, interrelationality, and subjectivity allow an account of conservative evangelicalism sensitive to how 'self and the social world are constitutively interlinked, made for and by the other' (Bender 2012: 280), opening up what is invested in these processes of identification and separation between 'self' and 'other'. The body pedagogics approach allows investigation of the increasingly complex ways in which religion is interrelated with a variety of other social and cultural phenomena in the contemporary world. In the setting of London, it focuses attention on how embodied practices shaped through participation at St John's intersect with broader urban norms of interaction. Mellor and Shilling outline how the teachings of Christianity call Christians to be strangers in this world, entailing a demand to change modes of behaviour, and Foucault's attention to 'techniques of the self' provides resources to think through how conservative evangelicals seek to form themselves, through specific practices, as ethical subjects according to the norms of their faith, which they locate as out of step with those dominant in the city around them.

As conservative evangelicals seek to form themselves as ethical subjects according to the logics of their faith, understanding their lived experiences requires explicating how their ethic of obedience arises not only through their connections with each other but also out of an experience of desire for a God who is understood as moral purity and unity. My narrative will consider how His personality has agency in shaping their subjectivities as they form a sense of relationship with Him through particular listening and speaking practices. Developing this approach requires the notion of 'interrelationality' to draw into focus the affective qualities of their being addressed as subjects across different spaces and how this divine personality is a social actor, shaping their interactions with others in the city, and how they think of and experience themselves.

This sense of relationship with God and desire to be subject to His demands is something conservative evangelicals experience as countercultural in London, as is the orientation to morality they develop. The concept 'ethical subjectivity' provides a means of exploring the effects of negotiating incommensurable logics of practices in the city and how these senses of separation between self and other, subject and object, are the result of particular practices and histories. This, together with interrelationality, also invites us to consider the affective and ethical qualities implied in the often-excluded middle of relationality, between self and other. What is *in* the address, where the self is put into question, and is being made and re-made through the responses that are given to, with, and for others?

My analysis in the following chapters describes forms of practice that will help advance understanding of the directional logics of conservative evangelicals' orientations to self, other, and world. I begin by exploring conservative evangelical speaking (*with, to, for*, etc.) and listening (*to, with, in*, etc.), and how these practices are implicated in the formation of particular kinds of subject. Speaking and listening are fundamentally relational practices—whether one speaks for, with, to, or against another—in which the boundaries between self and other are called into question, as the self is both individuated and transcended in speaking and listening. This focus on word-based practices draws into question the norms of how people learn to speak with and listen to others who are different from them. Under what conditions do people speak or not speak to others of their faith in workplaces, schools, on the streets, and elsewhere as a practice of civility? What shapes what they both do and do not want to say and hear, and how is this bound up with broader ideals about how we live together in city spaces? What forms of connection, separation, freedom, individuality, and community do their everyday modes of practice enable? And what does this mean for how we understand the norms shaping ideas of public, private, and intimate spaces?

Let us turn to examine the modes of speaking (and not speaking) to, listening with, longing for, difference from, through which evangelical subjectivities are formed, and the orientations towards self, other, and the social order these allow as they respond to the multiple demands addressed to them by many others. Despite the ambivalence towards the body noted at the start of the chapter, we will see that it is through specific forms of embodied practice that individuals learn to be both 'at home' in the world, and experience themselves as 'called out of that world' and separate from those around them, leading them to desire God and experience their own bodies as the site of tensions between immanence and transcendence. We will begin with practices of speaking, exploring how evangelicals' desire to speak of their faith to others is formed through participation in their church, but experienced as constrained in secular spaces of the city, leading to a consciousness of subjective fragmentation.

3

Speaking Subjects

Difference, Indifference, and Moral Fragmentation

[A]s the modern public expands, it shatters into a multitude of fragments, speaking incommensurable private languages.

(Berman 1983: 17)

I had arranged to meet James, an investment analyst in a large, multinational corporation in the City, in a café he suggested round the corner from his office. When I arrived at the café, which at 5.30 p.m. was still busy, James was already there, finishing a meeting with a client. As I waited for him, I surveyed the large selection of teas available, and sat at one of the rustic wooden tables with a pot of Earl Grey. James's schedule was tight, and I was grateful he had made time to talk to me. Aged thirty-six, tall and blond, wearing jeans and a red fleece, James first started going to St John's after graduating from Durham and beginning work in the City. As we talked, he told me about his experience of evangelism during his time working in the City, describing how he had set up his firm's Christian prayer group, which had organized his company's carol services. He said that he was aware, however, that while around 200 people had regularly been along to the carol services, there were 1,500 people in his office, and he was 'wracking my brains for a way, if I couldn't get my colleagues to the gospel, how could I get the gospel to all my colleagues?'

A few years before that, he told me, he had written 'a little sort of tract', which took the six principles Warren Buffett uses before making any investment decision, and 'applied them to the claims of Jesus Christ, to see whether He was a good investment'. Some of his friends encouraged him to get this written up and published professionally, and he decided, in order to 'get the gospel to' his colleagues, to hand a copy of the published booklet and an invitation to a follow-up talk with a guest speaker to every single person at his firm. About half his Christian group were supportive and helped him with this; 'the other half didn't want anything to do with it'. To prevent any accusation they were doing this in company time, they distributed these before

7.30 a.m. one morning. By 7.45 a.m., James had been summoned to the company's head of human resources, who, James told me, had said to him, '"What you have done [James]"—these were his exact words—"is no different from giving people an invitation to join a Nazi rally, or an invitation to join a jihad". He was absolutely furious, so I apologized for any sort of offence caused—it wasn't meant to cause offence.' The head of human resources told James to go round to all 1,500 of his colleagues, take the pamphlet back, and apologize in case it had caused anyone offence. James said, 'it took me about thirteen minutes to realize that this was just the best possible thing that could have happened, because it took me three and a half hours to go round the whole firm, and this was a work-sponsored opportunity to have one-on-one follow-up time with every single individual in the firm'.

James's practice of evangelism in this corporate environment—meeting up with other Christians in office meeting rooms to pray about how to 'reach' the rest of the firm, planning Christmas carol services, and walking round to put copies of a Christian pamphlet he had written on colleagues' desks—helped shape his experience of the City as peopled by 'the lost' who are in need of redemption and as a space that is hostile to Christians. When I asked why he thought the head of human resources had been so angry, James said, 'I don't know whether he felt threatened. What I do know is that Jesus promises that Christians will be opposed, and Christians will be persecuted and will be hated, so the response wasn't a surprise.' But James does not see his 'witness' to his colleagues only through distributing his tract and organizing carol services: he described working hard and doing a good job for his firm as a means through which he could be seen as 'blameless' and therefore also as a form of evangelism at work.

It is possible to discern differing moral logics—appearing to pull in contradictory directions—running through James's evangelism: as a good evangelical, he has internalized the sense that he should tell his colleagues about his faith and be a 'witness' for Christ in the workplace, but this is simultaneously bound up with a norm of reserve, which means he also feels he ought not to impose his views about his faith on others and therefore would not strike up conversations about his faith unprompted, and so is grateful for the 'persecution' that allowed him to have conversations with colleagues about his faith. As James's desire to share his faith with his colleagues led to his actions being labelled 'offensive', having breached workplace norms of interaction, examining how members of St John's practise evangelism illuminates the means by which these practices effect barriers of separation from particular others, and shapes their sense of a bounded moral community of 'the saved'. This reveals the complex ways in which they learn to imagine and experience the city as a culturally fractured space and opens up their everyday manoeuvres through different moral milieu, and how these lead to a desire for coherence that transcends these forms of fragmentation.

I begin by outlining how ideals for evangelistic speaking are promoted at St John's. I then show how the leadership of St John's aim to encourage a specific habitus through which members of the church feel both compassion for and a sense of distinction from what David described as 'this desperately lost city of London' and develop the desire to speak 'publicly' about their faith in workplace and other social spaces. I then describe how individuals often struggle with this, revealing how their subjectivities are formed through the complex interaction of behavioural norms associated with different spaces they inhabit. As they become conscious of tensions in their logics of practice shaped through their simultaneous inhabiting of differentiated social spaces suffused with differing moral norms, they narrate their subjective fragmentation according to biblical narratives of guilt and sin. This enables them to draw these fragments together into an overall pattern of meaning that shapes their sense of self.

SPATIAL AMBITIONS: '*PUBLIC AND UNPOPULAR*'

The centrality of the idea of conversion throughout the history of evangelicalism has made the duty to preach the gospel to others a privileged duty of the believer. This is bound up with the conviction that an individual is justified and redeemed through faith in God. Following a theological trajectory from Martin Luther, justification by faith became one of the distinguishing doctrinal elements of evangelicalism in the eighteenth century: acceptance by God came through faith, not works, and this required individuals to have heard the gospel, so that they could respond in faith. The quest for souls in evangelistic and missionary movements drove British evangelicals in the nineteenth and twentieth centuries out to distant mission fields and encouraged them to take their faith out to the people through house-to-house visitations and other forms of missionary work in the inner-city areas increasingly populated by the non-churchgoing masses (Bebbington 1989: 6, 118). This orientation towards conversion-shaped styles of preaching in church services with the aim of drawing in outsiders, as the language of sermons was 'adapted to the supreme task of implanting the gospel in the hearers' from different social backgrounds (p. 118). This desire to express the gospel in terms clear and relevant to non-Christians underpinned James's use of investment culture language in his evangelistic pamphlet, and has shaped the style of contemporary evangelistic endeavours across different evangelical traditions, such as The Alpha Course, developed by the charismatic Anglican church, Holy Trinity, Brompton.

The nature of mission has, however, become an area of disagreement in contemporary evangelicalism. Within the evangelical movement, forms of missionary engagement with non-Christians have often extended beyond preaching the gospel to modes of philanthropy, humanitarianism, and social justice activism, from Wilberforce's anti-slavery campaigns to the more recent involvement of organizations such as Tearfund in the 'Jubilee 2000' and 'Make Poverty History' campaigns. Many evangelicals also understand their personal social relationships with non-Christians as a form of 'mission', through which they can 'witness' the moral values of their faith in their everyday social interactions. Although some British conservative evangelicals are involved in social justice movements and humanitarian work, and many would see their relationships with non-Christians as constituting a 'field' for their evangelism, there is a strong emphasis coming from dominant voices within contemporary British conservative evangelicalism on an understanding of mission in terms of 'preaching the gospel' and *verbal* evangelism, articulated in relation to the doctrine of justification by faith. This stands in self-conscious contrast with charismatic evangelicals' emphasis on both the 're-evangelisation of the nations and the transformation of society'.[1]

A key body pedagogic means through which the conservative evangelical subject internalizes this sense of their privileged duty to speak to non-Christians as a mode of evangelism is their listening to sermons that articulate this understanding. This emphasis was expressed in many sermons at St John's. In a sermon focusing on a chapter from Luke's Gospel, David stated that 'Christian mission is only Christian mission if it has to it *verbal* content, declaring the possibility of reconciliation with God. The disciples are sent to announce, and to offer the possibility of being reconciled with God: that is a *verbal* thing.' He differentiated this from approaches other Christian churches might take, stating 'it's a wonderful godly thing to care for your neighbour, to love others. But it is not *Christian* mission unless the gospel is being proclaimed *verbally*. We hear of medical missions, of aid missions, of peace missions, but it's actually only as the gospel is proclaimed that such activities become genuine *Christian* mission.'

David's words indicate how the sermon form plays a role in creating the boundaries of 'genuine *Christian*' orthopraxis as separated not only from non-Christians, but also from other Christian (including evangelical) groups who do not emphasize verbal proclamation. Members of the church internalized this sense of *their* obligation to proclaim the gospel verbally, and could be critical of Christians who did not share this view. Joy, a middle-aged teacher, for example, described how this sense of difference had led to some painful exchanges with a more liberal Christian teacher, Jane. She said that she had

---

[1] From the website of Holy Trinity, Brompton, <http://www.htb.org.uk/about-htb> (accessed 8 June 2012). This is not to say members of St John's do not talk about the need for a transformation in society, but their understanding of how this will be effected centres primarily on the need for individuals' redemption, with this privileged in churches' teaching, over the need for activism based on a principle of transforming society as an end in itself.

suggested to Jane that they might together invite some of their 'nominal Christian' colleagues to evangelistic events at St John's, and that Jane hadn't been especially keen. This had led to a conversation in which Jane had said that you didn't necessarily need to be a follower of Jesus to be saved, and that pleasing God meant 'doing God's will in terms of feeding the hungry, clothing the poor'. Joy said that she felt that Jane's position was 'really shocking' and was 'an issue of evangelism, about how people are saved', and that Jane is 'a false messenger if she gives the impression that Christianity's about being a lovely person'. She said that Jane 'genuinely loves God, and so is a Christian, and does fabulous work for the community, but I can't square her belief that you don't need Jesus with her love of Jesus'. Joy said she found their disagreement on this point 'the more painful because we're both Christians; it would be easier to discuss this with a non-Christian than a Christian', and said she now avoids this topic in conversation with Jane.

However, despite this positioning of evangelistic speaking as symbolic of orthopraxy, in practice this is not felt as an easy task in Britain in which, in many public arenas, the open expression of religion has become, as Woodhead argues, 'highly contentious. "God" becomes the great taboo – far more than sex or violence' (2012: 25). In this context, members of St John's are encouraged to interpret their struggles to speak as a battle, part of a cosmic spiritual warfare in which, David stated, the world is divided between Good and Evil. David described the 'verbal proclamation of the finished work of Jesus Christ on the cross' as 'warfare, in which we announce verbally the victory of Jesus as we declare the defeat of Satan . . . No wonder it's so hard'. He said to the congregation: 'We are authorized by Him to go out into battle, proclaiming the truth of the gospel, announcing the victory of Christ', and added, 'You will find opposition, and indeed the more we . . . plan to proclaim the gospel, my expectation is the more we will see the opposition rise up . . . I think Oscar Cullmann . . . got it right . . . when he suggested it's a bit like the Allied Forces following D-Day. Once the D-Day landings had happened, victory was essentially secure. Hitler was defeated. But there was still battle raging all through Europe.' David then asked the congregation: 'What is *your* personal plan of action where God has placed *you*? Maybe you're in your office or your school: you're there as a warrior, as a member of God's army, and the war God wants us to be involved in . . . is the proclamation making the truth of Jesus known.' He concluded by inviting members of the congregation to chat over supper after the service about what their 'own personal plan of campaign is . . . Not all of us will be proclaiming from the pulpit . . . What is *your* particular role in the campaign?'

In another sermon, George, one of the curates, articulated this understanding of evangelistic speaking as the means through which God works: 'those words we have, the apostles' words here in the New Testament, through those words, the Spirit convicts the world, shows people that they utterly need Him'.

George said that for most of the week, members of the church would be surrounded by non-Christians—'maybe you'll get on the bus, driven by someone who's not a Christian, maybe the bus will take you up to your hall of residence, and you're going past the porter, who's not a Christian, up the lift to your floor, populated by people who mostly aren't Christians'. He said that these people '*need* the words of Jesus . . . These are the words that will convict the security guard, the bus driver, the tube passenger, your next door neighbour, your parents that they have a desperate need of Jesus.' He concluded with a prayer, as the congregation bowed their heads: 'We pray, Father, for us as your people with your words in our hands, that we would speak these words to those who aren't at the [guest event] dinner tomorrow . . . maybe neighbours, security guards, bus drivers, people on our course, people in our office, family, we pray that we would speak these words to them, that the Holy Spirit would be at work, that they would be convicted, that they would come to Jesus.'[2]

In these sermons, we see the individual summoned to recognize herself as a subject whose duty it is to proclaim the gospel to others in spaces outside the church, playing her own part in this 'army' as she speaks of her faith. The objectification of most people she interacts with in everyday life as 'other', in need of Jesus's words, is bound up with the subjectification of the evangelical as one whose task is to speak the words of Jesus to others in the unique situation in which she is located, differentiating her from other Christians who do not share this understanding of mission. She is thereby encouraged to experience her mundane movements through London as affording multiple opportunities to engage in these acts of speaking, and to interpret difficulties she may encounter in this task through a narrative of warfare.

This privileging of *verbal* mission is bound up with a stress on the importance of 'public' speaking about faith, as part of a narrative emphasizing the de-Christianization of Britain. This emphasis, also evident in the campaigns of organizations such as Christian Concern, can to a certain extent be interpreted according to Casanova's thesis of the de-privatization of religion. As discussed earlier, Casanova (1994) argues that a response to processes of universalization may be that groups whose lifestyles are disrupted by these processes seek to mobilize and re-enter the public sphere. In the UK, these universalizing processes are evident, for example, in the Equality Acts of 2006 and 2010, the extension of marriage rights to gay couples, and debates about women bishops in the Church of England. As conservative evangelical teachings on gender, sexuality, and other faiths rubbing up against universalizing modern norms come to represent particular cultural flashpoints of tension, conservative

---

[2] St John's holds regular 'guest events'—dinners and other events with a short evangelistic talk from one of the clergy, followed by a question and answer session with questions for the speakers.

evangelical leaders' public responses to these issues locate their movement as increasingly countercultural, with religious freedom described as increasingly under threat, while members of their churches come to understand those outside the Church objectifying them as increasingly 'intolerant' and 'out of date', as, in David's words, 'this country careers away from its Christian heritage'.

This sense of a periodization of time, moving from a Christian past to a secular, liberal modernity increasingly inhospitable to evangelical standpoints in tension with norms of equality, was clearly articulated in a question and answer session following a sermon at a Sunday evening service. In this, David said that the 'social and political tectonic plates of Britain are shifting radically, as we move from once-Christian—at least nominally—through to post-Christian Britain'. He then asked the congregation: 'given that the tectonic plates are beginning to shift, well, are you not finding that to speak openly of your faith, to make mention publicly of your views of sexuality, or gender, or other faiths, the absolute supremacy of Christ and the impossibility of salvation through any other religion . . . are you not finding that as you say these kind of things, you're facing increasing hostility?' David mentioned individuals who had been challenged by their human resources departments as examples of individuals who were engaged in the kind of 'public and unpopular' speaking he described, and encouraged members of the church to speak publicly about their faith in their workplaces and universities, likening this to the situation of Christians in China: 'The worst they can do is kill you. I think that's unlikely in our culture, but the worst they can do is sack you. Actually, you will find that if they sack you that the law is on your side, because they are threatening your human rights . . . Jesus says in Luke's Gospel that anyone who is ashamed of Him in this generation, He will be ashamed of them, when He comes in His glory. Now which would you rather: face the rejection of your peers, or face the disapproval of God Almighty?'

In these sermons, we see a naming of the evangelical subject as one who not only speaks of her faith to non-Christians, but who chooses to speak publicly of her faith in what is perceived as an oppressively secularist setting. David labelled the contemporary British context 'totalitarian', stating that what masquerades under the title 'multicultural, liberal diversity' is in fact 'illiberal, intolerant, secularist fundamentalism. This is not multiculturalism or liberal diversity. It is totalitarian.' George said in another sermon that if Christians 'stick with the words of the Bible' they will be 'hated'. He gave examples of his own practice modelling this, all demonstrating a sense of tension with norms of equality, for example, describing how in his Church of England ordination selection conference, other candidates had said they'd be happy for their churches to be used as multi-faith spaces, whereas he had said he would not, and discussing how there'd been a dispute about a local church performing a blessing of a civil partnership, and in their local diocesan meeting, he had taken a stand against that. He said, 'you could feel the hatred in the room from many of those there'. He stated that the apostles 'stuck with the words of Jesus' and were hated as a result, and likens that to the situation Christians experience today. He said, 'if you insist on sticking with the Bible, the kinds of words that people might use about you are things like 'dogmatic', 'black and white', 'judgemental', 'narrow-minded', and closed the sermon by reiterating: 'the only kind of Christian that is authentic' is one who is 'hated' for speaking the words of Jesus.

Coleman has explored the significance particular language practices have within charismatic evangelicalism for constructing the speaking subject. He describes the practices of members of the Word of Life movement such as speaking in tongues or exchanging personal testimonies as developing a sense of the self 'reaching out' to affect the world and learning to deploy biblical language in ways that put it 'into a kind of verbal circulation', these sacred words taken as showing the power of God at work in the individual (2006: 173). This idea of the evangelical subject as extended outwards is also deeply embedded at St John's, with the individual oriented towards the world as they seek to speak the words of Jesus they have learnt to internalize and thereby convert others while simultaneously learning to interpret hostility to their speaking as indicating a wider spiritual 'warfare'. But other than sermons articulating this emphasis on the centrality of speaking to non-Christians, by what other means does the church seek to create this habitus in which the evangelical subject's body is the medium through which Jesus's words reach others in the city? And how does this affect the interactions of members of the church in their everyday lives?

Members of St John's learn to experience London as peopled by non-Christians on whom they should show compassion and speak to them of their faith through various means. One method is encouraging identification with the emotional responses of Jesus and His disciples in biblical narratives. Ross, another curate, described to the congregation one evening how Jesus, in the feeding of the five thousand, 'looked out over the crowd of people, and had compassion on them, because they were lost, like sheep without a shepherd'. He said, 'That's how I feel when I look at London, at the crowds of people here', and asked: 'Do you feel like that when you think about London?' The physical, built structures of the city are also described in ways that connect it with individuals' past experiences of evangelism. As many members of St John's identify their student years as the period when they became Christians, the university occupies a privileged place in evangelical imaginations as a field for evangelism, and the city is described through the spatial image of a collegiate university. Matthew, a former lawyer, now in charge of city ministry at St John's, said he told members of the church working in city ministry that 'the way to reach the city is like reaching a collegiate university. You have your Christians dotted around in colleges, well here, it's just glass and chrome buildings, steel walls . . . Our role then is to facilitate and encourage them in their ministry there.'

The leaders of St John's also use the figure of the skyscraper to position the relation between church and city in the imaginations of the congregation. In perhaps his most famous and reproduced piece of writing, Michel de Certeau likens viewing the city of New York from the top of one of the towers of the World Trade Center to being lifted out of the city's grasp: 'When one goes up there, he leaves behind the mass that carries off and mixes up in itself any identity of authors and spectators. An Icarus flying above these waters, he can ignore the devices of Daedalus in mobile and endless labyrinths far below. His elevation transfigures him into a voyeur . . . It transforms the bewitching world by which one was "possessed" into a text that lies before one's eyes. It allows one to read it, to be a solar Eye, looking down like a god' (de Certeau 1984: 92). While skyscrapers are not the same dominating feature of the London skyline that they are in some other global metropolises, the ways skyscrapers are used in the church's visual media illustrates how members of the church are encouraged to 'read' London.

A promotional video for its ministry with city workers opens with a frame of what de Certeau would describe as the 'ordinary practitioners of the city', walking across London Bridge, their bodies following 'the thicks and thins of an urban text they "write" without being able to read it' (p. 93). The video then cuts to viewing these workers from above, their walking speeded up to show them rushing from place to place. The video closes with Matthew speaking as a voice-over while the screen cuts from the shot of people walking across London Bridge to him in a room high up a skyscraper, asking the viewer, in his softly spoken voice, 'Do we share the compassion that the Lord God has, that Jesus has for those around us? Are we that passionately concerned for people's eternal destiny? We're not in it alone. Jesus says, "And I am with you always, even to the end of the age."' Following de Certeau, this view from above can be interpreted as constructing a position that allows Matthew speaking and the viewer of the video—addressed as a Christian—to read the city as peopled by the 'lost', for whom they are encouraged to feel compassion and invite them to one of the midweek talks at St John's.

As well as these methods of re-imagining the city to encourage a response of compassion towards non-Christians, the leaders at St John's also use logics of expansion, production, and growth from the corporate world to describe the key aims of the church as to reach as many non-Christians as possible, to build them up in their faith, and then to send them out to 'reach' other non-Christians. At the church's Annual Parochial Meeting in 2010, David described his vision for St John's to the couple of hundred members of the church present using a visual image of a flow chart with numerous arrows branching off the various small groups and congregations of the church to show the ambition to 'grow' the church and reach more and more non-Christians. As the cosmopolitan sensibilities of St Paul shaped the amplitude of his desire to proclaim the gospel throughout the ancient cities of the Mediterranean, so there is a distinctively transnational dimension to how the words spoken at St John's extend this 'reach' globally, both through short-term overseas missions that members of the church participate in and through their financial support of and prayers for 'mission partners'—members of the church based as missionaries in diverse global contexts. These global connections are enacted when mission partners return to St John's and talk about their missionary work to the congregation, modelling for the congregation what it means to be involved in the kinds of 'verbal mission' David described, and detailing what they would like the congregation to pray about for them. While away, fridge magnets that church members have at home—each with a photo of the 'mission partner' and a map showing their global location—remind the congregation of their presence overseas.

The church leadership repeatedly emphasizes that it is the task of *all* members—not just the ministry team or overseas missionaries—to engage in this evangelistic work, 'partnering' with the church in the gospel. In a Sunday morning sermon, David described this ideal of 'partnership' as coming 'from the business world', and said: 'we should think of partnership or fellowship... in terms of the Olympic stadium, or Twickenham... Tolkien got it right with "the fellowship of the ring" – this is nothing cocoa-ish about Frodo, Sam, and, I can't remember the name of the other one'. David defended this use of self-consciously masculine language to describe ideals of verbal mission as a corrective against the 'feminization of society', suggesting a sense of space as divided between a public, masculine, sphere of speaking and the feminine sphere as private. He said, 'over the last forty years or so, our society has been feminized. Some of that has been a good thing... However, with our rejection of a godless model of what it is to be a man, we have lost the idea of what it is to be a godly man.' He said that secular society promotes either 'lad culture' or a 'metrosexual' idea of manliness, 'like Chandler from *Friends*. Men are left asking what do we do with our testosterone? Here is our answer: we are godly men engaged in Christian warfare.' Paradigmatic of this idea of godly masculinity as publicly engaging in verbal mission, ordained ministry—an option that conservative evangelicals hold as only open to men—is held in high esteem. Members of St John's were frequently asked in sermons whether this was something to which they were called. Inviting the whole congregation to consider whether they had 'the right gifts' for such ministry, David said, 'Can you imagine anything more wonderful than having that part in the warfare? Anything *more* important?'

While the leaders of St John's address the congregation to encourage them to feel compassion for those outside the church, configuring London as peopled by the lost and themselves as fighting in a spiritual battle as they speak to non-Christians of their faith, the leaders are nevertheless aware that the majority find this hard. They therefore offer a course that aims to train individuals in techniques for speaking about their faith with colleagues and friends. This runs over ten weeks, held at the church once a week, beginning with supper, and followed by a half-hour talk and small group discussion designed to help members of the congregation feel confident in speaking about their faith. The aim is to equip members with a 'framework' with which to explain the gospel, encouraging the use of particular strategies, such as asking questions to encourage their interlocutor to interrogate their own values and beliefs, and there are group-work activities and role-plays to practise the kinds of conversation they might have with non-Christians in which they could bring up their faith. These techniques function as a body pedagogic means for forming the evangelical as a speaking subject.

Throughout these sessions, the minister giving the talks, Pete, emphasized that it's the usual Christian experience to find it difficult and awkward to speak about faith with non-Christians. One explanation he gave for why many put off speaking about their faith with non-Christians is because the other person's 'eternal destiny' might depend on the outcome of that discussion. Several members of the group I observed talked about how they often felt embarrassed or awkward trying to talk about their faith with non-Christian friends, family, and colleagues, and prayed for forgiveness for these feelings of shame. This, together with the fact that the leadership of St John's felt it necessary to devise a course specifically teaching people how to speak about their faith seems to demonstrate that despite the desire of the leadership to encourage members of the church to speak about their faith in public contexts outside the church, many members have internalized the sense that faith is a private matter. Nevertheless the dominant idiom individuals used to describe the kind of interaction they *hoped* to have with friends and colleagues—'conversation'—demonstrated their desire to speak, and their relational understanding of this enactment of difference.

These then are some of the ways in which the church leaders aim to encourage a habitus oriented towards evangelistic speaking, bound up with a sense of the city as divided between 'genuine' Christians and others (including non-Christians and inauthentic Christians). But to what extent can we see the desire for the public speaking of faith highlighted by the church leadership as the marker of faith played out in the everyday practices of members of St John's? *Is* London named in their actions and speaking as peopled by those for whom they must have compassion, and if so, how does this shape their subjectivities and interactions? *Do* their practices make Christianity 'public and unpopular' through articulating traditionalist moral positions in tension with the secular modern spaces they inhabit outside the church?

To sketch differing ways in which individuals respond to the demand to speak about their faith, I will outline the practices of two individuals: Clara and Simon, one a lawyer, the other an accountant, both working in large multinational firms, both in their late twenties, both white, middle-class graduates of Oxford and Cambridge. Because of the long working hours and high demands of competence required by both their professions, the conflict between the ideal expectations of the church that they spend time evangelizing, studying the Bible, and 'serving' others and the expectations of their workplace bring into clear relief the different ways in which evangelicals experience urban cultural fragmentation. Both are typical of a certain type of English evangelical who appear ostensibly similar in terms of their socio-economic status and patterns of church involvement, with, like James, intense participation at university that has been maintained since starting work in high-earning professions in London. By looking closely at how these two individuals engage with ideals for evangelistic practice in the city, and considering how these compare with other church members' experiences, we can identify different forms of and responses to social and subjective fragmentation, and consider how this contributes to the desire for coherence Simmel describes religion as offering.

CLARA: 'REACHING THE UNREACHED'

Smiley and petite, her dark hair cut into a bob, Clara always looks stylish, both when I met up with her a couple of times at her workplace, and at church. In many ways, she seems to embody the ideal of the evangelical subject promoted at St John's. She organizes a Christian group at her firm, leads a weekly Bible study group at church, writes film and book reviews for a Christian magazine, is on the committee for both a local church plant from St John's and a Christian lawyers' association, and is involved in an evangelism project on local council estates. She generally goes to two of the Sunday services each week at St John's, in addition to mid-week lunchtime services at the church plant. In contrast with James, she experiences her firm as supportive of her faith. When I met her for lunch at her office canteen, she told me that her work Christian group is allowed to hold fortnightly meetings in one of the client rooms, put posters up around the office, advertise in the firm newsletter, and every six months to hold evangelistic events with outside speakers, often from St John's, for which the firm provides lunch. At the most popular of these—on Richard Dawkins and atheism—about fifty of her colleagues came. In addition to organizing the Christian group at work, she also helps lead an 'Introduction to Christianity' course, aimed at non-Christians, and meets up with a woman who has recently become a Christian to read the Bible together in the canteen in her lunch hour.

Clara seems in many ways to be modelling the 'public' Christian practice David encourages, and she told me she is mostly 'pretty open' about her faith with colleagues. She added, however, that while she would tell the woman she shares an office with that she is off to a Bible study in her lunch hour, she would not tell the partners on her team. She mentioned that members of the team she works with are all aware that she's a Christian, but after six years working there, she has 'not had the opportunity to share the gospel with them'. Clara's busyness and hard work in terms of time spent preparing to lead Bible studies and organizing events at her workplace might be seen as reflective of broader cultural ideals of productivity, showing how her Christian practices interact with rationalized urban impulses, intensified through working in corporate law with its emphasis that employees account for their time so that their hours of work can be charged to their clients. Although she has not, as she puts it, 'shared the gospel' with her close colleagues, in many other respects, the performance of her faith in this corporate environment seems to be straightforwardly 'public' in the way David advocates, through activities such as organizing prayer meetings and evangelistic events.

Clara is also part of a team from St John's involved in attempting to evangelize to local council estates near the church. If we compare this form of practice with her workplace evangelism, we begin to see more clearly that her evangelistic practices at work are more reserved than they first appear, suggesting that processes of the privatization and de-privatization of religion can take place unevenly within an individual's subjectivity, formed through the intersection of differing practices associated with particular segregated urban spaces. The project evangelizing to council estates was set up out of a concern about the exclusively middle-class culture of conservative evangelical Christianity in the UK, and is part of a broader national network called Reaching the Unreached, aiming to take the gospel to areas of urban deprivation. The website of this network, quoting American conservative evangelical minister and author Tim Keller, states:

> Most evangelical churches are middle-class in their corporate culture. People value privacy, safety, homogeneity, sentimentality, space, order, and control. In contrast, the city is filled with ironic, edgy, diversity-loving people who have a much higher tolerance for ambiguity and disorder. If a church's ministers cannot function in an urban culture, but instead create a kind of non-urban 'missionary compound' within it, they will discover they cannot reach out, convert, or incorporate many people in their neighbourhoods.
>
> (cited in Chester 2010b)

What this translates to in the experience of members of St John's who are involved in the project is an emphasis on hoping to convert the local urban poor through speaking to them about their faith and reading the Bible with them. The main way Clara and other church members are involved is spending Sunday afternoons walking around local council estates in pairs 'cold calling'—knocking on doors—and asking anyone who answers to do a questionnaire about their values, and then offering to read the Bible with them. This walking around the estates and knocking on doors provides an example of one way in which London—and here, the specific area local to the church—comes to be felt in the experience of members of St John's as 'lost', inhabited by individuals for whom the church shows 'compassion' through trying to convert them. Members of the estates team meet together weekly for Bible study and eat lunch together every Sunday after the morning service before heading out to knock on doors, and have developed close friendships with each other. Some members of the team have also developed friendships with people on the estates they have got to know over the extended period of time they have spent on one particular estate.[3]

The UN Report on global cities describes how urban areas are increasingly divided into distinct areas parallel with particular forms of work, each of which can be seen as a 'subcity'. The report identifies five subcities: '(1) the luxury city of those who make decisions about capital and development; (2) the gentrified city of professionals, managers, technicians, and college professors; (3) the suburban city of families of workers and managers in new manufacturing centers; (4) the tenement city of lower-paid workers and unskilled providers of service; and (5) the abandoned city of the very poor' (cited in Gunnemann 2005: 106). The urban professionals at St John's, such as Clara, James, and Simon, belong to the second and first subcities, while those with whom they are trying to engage through their work on the estates belong largely to the fourth and fifth subcities. Sassen (2001) has argued that the 'glamour' of global cities such as London is increasingly supported by large populations of blue-collar immigrant workers, leading to a widening polarization between the lives of high-income workers of the first and second groups, and low-wage, menial workers inhabiting a different subcity. As world finance is dominated by London and New York, this has led to particularly excessive inequalities between those on the highest and lowest incomes in these cities, affecting not only living standards, opportunities, and aspirations, but also life expectancy. Danny Dorling notes that in the borough of Westminster a woman who has reached the age of sixty-five living on the Church Street estate can expect on average to live another twelve years, whereas a woman of the same age living in the wealthy Little Venice enclave in the same borough can expect to live another twenty-six years (2011: 287). Dorling argues that geographical divides and boundaries come in different degrees of contortion, but 'it is hard to find social statistics as extreme and environments

---

[3] Their practices can be contrasted with the short-term urban missions of the suburban evangelicals Omri Elisha studied. Elisha (2011) describes how such missions among urban black neighbourhoods fortify the white middle-class evangelical self. At St John's, evangelistic practices likewise construct boundaries between Christian and non-Christian; however, the leaders of this project at St John's live in a flat in one of the estates in these neighbourhoods, demonstrating their longer-term commitment to the local area.

as different but so close together as are found within the hearts of London and New York. The intertwining of rich and poor neighbourhoods is far greater in the centres of these two cities than anywhere else in the rich world' (p. 288).

The self-consciousness that the Reaching the Unreached project shows of the classed character of conservative evangelicalism demonstrates the desire of those involved in the project to disrupt the ways in which urban space is divided by lines of socio-economic inequality as reflected in the make-up of largely affluent middle-class urban conservative evangelical congregations. When several of the team involved in this project spoke to the congregation one Sunday evening, the minister leading the team stated, 'It's sad but true that in the UK, evangelical Christianity is primarily a middle-class phenomenon,' and said that 'if we could look with X-ray spectacles beyond the walls of the church, we would very quickly come to these estates, and see the proximity of these unchurched people who are facing God's wrath'. He said the gospel 'must mean breaking down socio-economic barriers between people'.

Yet it is a minority of members of St John's who are practically involved in this project, and the ways some members of the church narrate these evangelistic practices has the effect of objectifying those living on the council estates as 'other', demonstrating how deeply rooted these socio-economic separations are within urban subjectivities. At one of the weekly Bible study groups I observed, the church invited a former member of the church now involved with Reaching the Unreached in a church in a white working-class area of Essex to talk about his work. When asked what he would like prayer for, he asked for prayer that 'God would raise up more indigenous pastors... For me, this ministry is cross-cultural, I'm a middle-class toff.' At another prayer meeting in which one focus was the estates work, the members of the small group I was with—not themselves involved in visits to the estates—discussed 'how scary it must be to go round the local estates', and how 'unpleasant they must be'. Straight after praying that anyone who came to a service at St John's from the council estates 'would be able to fit in', the two men I was sitting next to—highly paid professionals, both wearing pinstriped suits and pink shirts—started chatting about their recent skiing holidays and fine dining in Verbier, and Lucy, with pointed wit, commented to them on the irony of this. The fact that people from the estates who do want to engage in Bible reading are not necessarily encouraged to start attending St John's—the estates team suggests other 'Bible-teaching' churches nearby—demonstrates the extent to which the estates team are also conscious of these cultural divides shaping urban meanings and experience.

The evangelistic speaking practices members of St John's use on local council estates stand in contrast with the evangelistic techniques they employ with middle-class non-Christians. These are typified by either the workplace methods of organizing events, such as carol services used by Clara and James, or more commonly by inviting friends to church 'guest events'. Clara lives

near the council estates she evangelizes, in a modern apartment block with a
security man on the door, but neither she nor other members of the church
practise door-to-door evangelism in these middle-class spaces. While this is in
many ways because they see door-to-door evangelism as the *only* way to reach
the urban poor, so separate are their existences that they would not have the
opportunity otherwise to engage with them, at the same time, the contrast in
how they speak about their faith across these contexts illuminates the everyday
dynamics of different forms of urban fragmentation.

Their attitude of *comparative* reserve in speaking about their faith with non-
Christian friends and colleagues, evidenced by feelings of anxiety and embarrassment, suggests that in spaces associated with middle-class privilege it is
harder for evangelicals to go public with their faith. In practice, one of the
main ways members of St John's 'speak' about their faith is not through
verbally articulating the gospel themselves, but through inviting a friend or
colleague to a 'guest event' at which a minister, as a religious specialist,
explains the gospel in a setting that is constructed for this purpose. Even
this act of invitation can create feelings of anxiety. When the church leaders
encouraged members to invite friends to a forthcoming evangelistic guest
event by giving out cards asking what one question they would like to ask of
God, they asked people who had given out these cards to talk about how that
went to the rest of the church. Several of these—while encouraging use of the
cards—said that they had felt embarrassed or awkward about giving them out.
Before a different event, Stevie, one of the young curates, said to the congregation that it can feel 'very nerve-wracking' inviting people to guest events,
and described a time he had 'broken out in a sweat' in front of his computer as
he emailed a friend an invitation.

Such incidences of embarrassment demonstrate a moral fragmentation
arising from the conflict between an internalized sense of reserve and propri-
ety demanding that Godtalk be avoided in the workplace and amongst friends,
and the countercultural demand addressed to members of the church to
practise their faith in a way that is 'public and unpopular'. Jonathan, another
graduate in his late twenties, said he found it difficult in his open-plan office
'to talk about Christian things, because people can just come in halfway
through a conversation, and then it would probably sound quite strange
what we were talking about . . . It's hard to have a chat about personal, spiritual
things . . . I find it quite difficult, but I love it whenever I get the chance to.'
This indicates his internalization of a secular cultural norm that faith is
'personal' and 'private', running in tension with the ideal of 'public' speaking
encouraged by ministers at St John's and in wider conservative evangelical
discourse.

In contrast with the sense of awkwardness associated with speaking to
middle-class colleagues and friends, no-one involved in the work on the
estates spoke of this work as causing them embarrassment or anxiety, despite

other members' prayers describing this work as 'scary'. A teaching assistant in her twenties described how in 'coming out as a Christian, it's easy to lose face', which she said makes it harder to be 'out' as a Christian among colleagues and others with whom one is in regular contact. In contrast, other than giving up time on a Sunday, those involved in the work on the estates do not risk this loss of face through going public with their faith in door-to-door calling. The estates work, therefore, demonstrates the extent to which urban space is divided across lines of social stratification, and that the anonymity this creates for middle-class evangelicals in deprived areas means their evangelistic practice in these spaces is not marked by the awkwardness with which their evangelism directed towards middle-class acquaintances is imbued. While those involved in the estates work seek to challenge the urban separations caused by wealth and cultural inequalities, in practice, they find these difficult to undo.

Thus the desire to locate Christianity in public city spaces is both appropriated *and* contested within Clara herself, in her busy organization of evangelistic events and door-to-door evangelism bound up with her *comparative* reserve about speaking to the colleagues with whom she works most closely about her faith in everyday conversation. Given Clara's commitment to the different forms of evangelistic practice she is engaged with, it is perhaps unsurprising that she says she is considering leaving the world of corporate law to devote herself to full-time paid Christian ministry. This is indicative of how the idealization of the speaking subject privileges full-time paid Christian ministry as the highest aspiration for the individual who has 'the right gifts'. Despite this aspiration, Clara said, however, that she was unsure whether she would be able to pursue this ambition, since options for women in full-time ministry within conservative evangelicalism, with ordained Christian ministry ruled out, are significantly more limited than for men.

SIMON: 'LONDON TO ME IS NOT WHAT IT IS TO MANY PEOPLE'

Simon has, like Clara, been attending St John's since starting work in the city, yet his attitude towards workplace evangelism is less confident than hers, and in many ways more representative of the experience of the majority of individuals I spoke with. He was wearing shirtsleeves when I met up with him at a café about a minute's walk from his office early one February evening, and after we finished chatting, he returned to his office, as he regularly works until 10 p.m. Simon is a quietly spoken young man, and he told me he doesn't find it easy to talk to either colleagues or family about his faith, saying it would feel 'unnatural' to talk about it, although he added he *should* try to think of his workplace more as a 'mission field'. He said he would find it very difficult to talk to non-Christians about evangelical teachings on gender or sexuality and added that he would also be embarrassed to talk about the church's opposition to the ordination of women with any of his Christian friends from outside St John's.

While the leaders of St John's aim to encourage members to feel more confident in speaking publicly about conservative evangelical teachings on gender, sexuality, and other faiths, even if that will lead to hostility, most members of the church I spoke with said, like Simon, that they would prefer to avoid conversations on these issues. Another accountant said that she lived with a gay housemate with whom she was good friends, and had never mentioned her beliefs about sexuality to him, preferring, as she put it, to talk about 'more positive aspects' of her faith. This framing of evangelical sexual morality as implicitly 'negative' and not something individuals want to address with non-Christians was bound up with an articulated sense that the moral teachings articulated in the church were only applicable to Christians. Gemma said that it would be wrong for her to be judgemental of her colleagues for behaving in ways that went against Christian teaching: 'If they're not Christians, there's no reason for them to be living otherwise; the internal consistency of their own lifestyle makes perfect sense.' In a Rooted group, discussing unmarried cohabitation, Lucy said she wouldn't want to address this issue with non-Christians: 'I wouldn't feel comfortable, if they're not Christians, saying they ought to change what they're doing.'

Within this narrative, the most important thing to speak about 'publicly' with non-Christians was the 'positive' aspect of the possibility of relationship with God. A trader I interviewed articulated this reluctance to discuss his views on sexuality with non-Christians: 'It's the wrong way round to start a discussion ... I don't expect somebody to accept a biblical morality if they haven't accepted God is God ... Why should they? I don't think it works to preach a morality. The first thing to do is for them to recognize who God is, and *if* they do that, *then* what is said [in the Bible regarding sexuality] has to be reckoned with.' Several socially conservative Christian campaign groups argue that Christians should play a role in the public sphere in promoting their views on areas such as sexuality morality and family life, stating that these moral teachings are for the good of the nation.[4] However, the unwillingness of many members of St John's to share their views on these issues with those outside the church in everyday life suggests that running in tension with this 'prophetic' ideal in which these moral norms are understood as universally applicable, their subjectivities are also formed through a principle of toleration, in which expressing their views on such issues would impinge on another's right to live

---

[4] See, for example, the mission statements of Christian Action Research and Education (2010) and Christian Concern (not dated b).

according to their own moral norms and disrupt the calm that urban indifference affords. Describing non-Christians' morality as essentially none of their business and emphasizing the pragmatic impetus to focus on 'more positive' aspects of their faith enables them to craft a coherent narrative that makes sense of this reluctance to speak publicly about issues where their moral viewpoints are in tension with universalizing modern norms.

However, this sense of a strategic decision not to speak was somewhat troubled when colleagues directly asked about their views on these issues. Two women in their early twenties, Jo and Rhiannon, described times when they had been asked about their views on homosexuality and had difficulty expressing these. Rhiannon, who worked in the theatre, said a gay colleague had said to her, 'rather aggressively, "oh, do you think that I'm going to hell?"' Describing her response, she said, 'I was really shocked and really upset... I don't think I said anything at that point, partly because I think I was almost crying. But then, afterwards, I went back and said, "look, I don't think you're going to hell because you're gay... actually, if you've been told that, then that's a wrong perception of Christianity".' She said that she thought negative perceptions of evangelical Christianity in the theatre were because it was seen as judgemental: 'the theatre is very postmodern, and it's a faux pas to say that you disagree with someone's belief or lifestyle choice'. Jo, a physiotherapist, described a time when one of her colleagues had asked her in front of several other colleagues what she thought about the Bulls, the bed and breakfast owners who were taken to court by a couple in a civil partnership, Steven Preddy and Martyn Hall, for refusing to allow them a double room, a case widely reported in the British press.[5] She said she had replied 'people can have a personal view, but we should abide by the law', and when asked directly what her views on homosexuality were, she had said, 'I have views', without revealing what those were, adding, 'I was a bit chicken about it.'

The effect of the prominence of the narrative that Christians will be 'hated' and face hostility for speaking about such issues, combined with the media prominence of cases like the Bulls, seems to be the opposite of what evangelical leaders intend, with most members of the church feeling increasingly anxious in speaking about issues where the church is felt as rubbing up against broader norms of equality. It is worth noting, however, that although a small number of church members expressed disagreement with the church's teaching on these issues, this was a small minority within the congregation. Although individuals' reluctance to speak about such issues (in contrast with their leaders' willingness to preach about them) indicates differences in their and their leaders' symbolic investment in these particular moral issues, it was taken as a given in small group discussions that members of the church agreed, for

---

[5] See Preddy and Hall v. Bull and Bull 2011.

example, with the church's stated positions on male church leadership, wives' submission to their husbands, and so on. This is in part related to the urban context of the church, with many other churches in relative proximity, so that if individuals disagreed with the church's position on these issues, they moved on to a church that was more liberal on these issues. When I asked one of the curates about this, he said that St John's 'set the bar high in terms of our requirements about belief', and that people who left the church were not necessarily moving away from Christianity, but onto churches that were 'less demanding'.

It was not only speaking about these moral issues outside the church that made members of St John's feel uncomfortable. Many, like Simon, felt awkward talking about their faith at all, and some described themselves as 'coming out' as Christians the first time they mentioned to colleagues that they go to church. Feeding into this anxiety is not only media representations but also specific examples of individuals at St John's who got into trouble at work for their evangelistic practices. One student, Steph, for example, was formally reprimanded by her course director for setting up a Bible study group, and Freddie mentioned her in a sermon as a paradigm of heroic evangelistic practice. As such stories circulate around the church, this makes others more anxious about speaking about their faith in their workplaces. Jane, a teacher, said, 'when you hear of cases like Steph's, you think that's not what you're meant to do, to tell the gospel to people', though she qualified that, saying, 'I wonder if it's hard [to speak about faith] not because of the society we live in, it's just that . . . we make it hard for ourselves, 'cos we're rubbish, and lack the confidence.'

When I asked Simon about whether he thought his colleagues knew he was a Christian, he said he thought that a number of them did know, but added that he thought their impression of his faith was that it was compartmentalized, 'a hobby . . . a thing bolted onto my life . . . it's just on Sundays'. Because Simon finds it hard to engage in the kinds of verbal evangelistic practices Clara is involved in, he finds other non-verbal means of 'witnessing' and thereby negotiating alternative boundaries of distinctiveness from non-Christians. One area in which he, like other members of St John's, draws boundaries of moral distinctiveness from others in the city is in the area of drinking culture. Most, including Simon, balance this not by withdrawing from going out for a drink with colleagues, but by limiting themselves to two drinks, although Jenny, an insurance worker, mentioned this didn't necessarily always work: 'the trouble is that if you haven't had something to eat, or you've got the timing wrong, you end up losing your sense of proportion'. Simon said he doesn't think colleagues look down on him for this. However, Matthew said other members of St John's had been made to feel uncomfortable by their bosses not only for making a couple of beers last an entire deal-closing-celebration drinking session, but also for refusing to take clients out to lap-dancing clubs.

He said that for all Christians working in the city, 'you've got to have your own red line', and know where those moral boundaries are drawn.

Performing this distinctiveness from the drinking culture of the city is one way for evangelicals to position themselves as distinctive, even if they feel awkward engaging in the more public 'verbal' performances of faith Clara and James are engaged in. As cities have figured in biblical and other religious narratives as vice-riddled, so in sermons at St John's, London is frequently compared to the Corinth that St Paul was addressing, a hedonistic 'sin city' in which 'money and sex are the twin idols'. David described the church's location in London as 'within the precincts of the temple of Western idolatry: materialism'. Therefore, by giving a significant percentage of their income to the church and by withdrawing from behaviours such as getting drunk or having sex before marriage, members of St John's are able to position themselves as 'aliens' within this reading of London as 'lost', and they narrate these practices as the ways in which they offer a 'witness' in their workplace contexts, when they find it hard to speak of their faith.

Learning to read the city as peopled by 'the lost' for whom they are a witness, both verbally and through performing other boundaries of distinctiveness, entails significant emotional demands, as every interaction becomes loaded with possible ramifications for eternity, every moment including the passing of lost chances and missed encounters. In his sermon on verbal mission, David described London both as a space of battle and as a 'lost city' that affords strategic potential for expansion, and talked about how on a recent visit to Bloomsbury he had been aware of how it was full of students from around the world. He said that St John's has 'incredible opportunities for the spread of the gospel all around the world: God has placed us here, at the centre of this global city', and he prayed for 'this desperately lost city of London, that they would turn, and put their trust in you'. Following Simmel, this mode of concern for the 'lost city' combined with a desire to expand the circulation of the words of the gospel to all, globally, is in tension with the impersonal and instrumental norms of interaction that dominate everyday modes of metropolitan practice. This therefore creates a specific form of fragmentation between the type of emotional response evangelicals learn to feel for non-Christians through the church, and the more instrumentalized ethics of interaction formed in their workplace settings where, as Jonathan described, talking about 'personal, spiritual things' is felt as strange.

This tension of feeling that they ought to speak about their faith and that they cannot, or 'lack the confidence' to do so, is not only because of stories circulating about individuals who get into trouble with their human resources department. It is also related to their habituated modes of speaking practices formed through participation in the church. In *Together*, Sennett describes how when he first moved to London after music school in New York, 'discussions were couched in terms of "possibly", "perhaps", and "I would have thought" ... whether in a local pub or patron-grandee's drawing room, the Brits proved themselves skilled masters in the use of the subjunctive mood' (2012: 22). Sennett argues that this is not just a matter of conversational politeness, but is a tentativeness that issues 'an invitation to others to join in' (p. 22). This mood of conversation was very characteristic of interactions at St John's, especially in the Bible study groups. These followed a repetitive rhythm of practice, each beginning with supper, followed by an academically demanding Bible study run by church members trained in leading small groups. The conversations in the two groups I spent most time with were characterized by this subjunctive mood of 'I would have thought' and 'perhaps', as established members of the groups sought to open up space for quieter and newer members to join in.

Sennett argues that the subjunctive mood is an antidote to paralysed positions and counters 'the fetish of assertiveness by opening up an indeterminate mutual space ... The social engine is oiled when people do not behave too emphatically' (p. 23). Small groups are one of the main body pedagogic means through which members of St John's learn, as Freddie described, to 'preach the gospel to each other' as they 'speak the words of Jesus' in discussing the set passage. Small groups are seen as important to being part of the church community, and the craft of sociality and dialogical conversation is privileged as part of the making of this community. Although the speaking in small groups was not completely indeterminate—there were things that could not be said— the space of these groups, crafted around the interpretation of particular texts, involved a give and take in conversation that refrained from assertiveness and offered social pleasure in the forms of conversation it enabled.

While ministers address the congregation with an assertive message in sermons and encourage them to 'speak Jesus's words' and 'contend publicly for the truth of the gospel', thereby engendering conflict, the ways members of the church actually practise speaking about their faith is mostly with each other, in this more subjunctive mood.[6] This encourages a habitus of sociality that values indirection and avoids confrontation, and this also underlies their reluctance to speak about issues where the moral standpoints of their faith are in tension with those of the secular spaces they inhabit outside the church. This ethic of interaction militates against more definitive public statements of, as David described, 'the objective truth of the gospel', and the tension between these two differing ethics of speaking can be theorized as a specific modality of subjective division.

---

[6] Members of the congregation involved in church politics, for example, in synod meetings, in that context seemed more confident expressing the church's opposition to gay clergy and women bishops. However, it was a minority of lay members of the congregation involved in these forms of interaction, with clergy being more frequently involved in articulating the church's position on these issues, often arousing tension with liberal Anglicans.

Despite—or because of—these tensions, the church becomes a space that offers a sense of coherence and unity through both a sense of relationship with God, as we will see in Chapter 5, and the experience of intimate friendships formed there. Both Clara and Simon said that their closest friendships are with Christians, and when I asked what difference their faith makes to their experience of living in London, both spoke of the importance of the experiences of friendship afforded by the church. Simon said he felt that the city has '*shrunk* in many ways', that London is not to him 'what it is to many people, a large impersonal city', but is where his church is based and where he therefore has a large number of friends and feels welcome, and Jonathan said that since moving to London, 'the only way, other than work, I've found of meeting people is through the church'. This sense of London being changed through the experience of friendships at church was reiterated by almost everyone I spoke to. Jenny said that St John's made life in London 'bearable', both through the friendships it enabled and the teaching she received there in sermons and small groups as 'inspiring' her and supporting her faith.

The friendships formed through the church are related to its physical location: because it is in a central part of London mostly given to commercial buildings where few live (other than those on the council estates they are evangelizing), most of the congregation live about half an hour's journey away. Thus very regular—in many cases twice-weekly—meals together at church in small study groups and after Sunday services form an important means of creating a sense of community, and the practice of sharing prayer requests at the Bible study groups means people are quickly drawn into each others' lives. The time that church members make for this might be seen as bound up with urban impulses towards productivity, as the church seeks strategically to 'build' these individuals in their faith so that they can 'reach' more 'unreached'. Yet the details of these practices—eating together and engaging in rigorous textual exegesis, going to listen attentively for half an hour in the middle of a busy working day to an academically demanding sermon—might also be seen, however, as a means of finding a space outside this and, as we will explore in Chapter 6, these groups provide an important means in enabling individuals to keep going in their orientation to a transcendent source of meaning.

Simon seems, unlike Clara, to have more straightforwardly internalized the cultural expectation that faith is a private matter, not to be spoken of publicly at work, and was critical of some aspects of practice that St John's leaders encourage, for example, criticizing the privileging of 'verbal mission', stating that he felt there's a tendency at St John's 'to downplay social ramifications of the gospel'. While Clara's reading of her office as a mission field and expressed desire to devote herself full-time to Christian ministry shows one response to the problem of urban fragmentation, Simon deals with this differently, finding spaces for reflection within his weekly routines in which he can orientate his attention towards the transcendent and find a sense of coherence beyond experiences of fragmentation. In addition to his participation in Bible study groups, church services, and private devotional reading, he attends choral evensong in another Anglican church, sings in a gospel choir, and at weekends escapes the sensory battering of urban life with a Christian walking group. All of these may be seen as a way of providing a more coherent pattern to urban life, while simultaneously introducing a further fragmentation specific to evangelical faith between these forms of practice that seek to develop an orientation towards transcendence and more instrumental modes of inter-action characterizing everyday urban encounters.

CONCLUSION: '*A UNITY OF DISUNITY*'

In an online article, one of the church staff described how at university, she'd been the 'compartmentalising queen. I had a box for study, a box for CU, for church, a box for my social life, and the most important...a box for sleep...And very oh so very rarely did any of them meet.' An image of stacked cardboard boxes accompanied the piece, and the writer suggested that rather than compartmentalizing, Christians should see the ultimate 'aim of our lives being to see God's name spread, wherever we are or whoever we are with, or whatever area of our carefully boxed out life it intrudes upon, and whatever it cost us. Our aim being to focus on how immense Jesus is...and how little we deserve his love and forgiveness.' The writer concluded by suggesting that instead of experiencing life as a pile of boxed and divided areas it is 'instead one huge box, where the cardboard is Jesus'. This article articulates the tendency in complex, differentiated societies—with London exemplifying this—to cope with the fragmentation of cultural spaces by compartmentalizing and separating religion out as discrete from other areas of life. Modern life is secularized in this sense of functional differentiation, with life separated into public and private spheres. In workplaces, instrumental norms of interaction are shaped, as Simon described, by the 'busyness of work, therefore the conversations also revolve around work'. In such secular contexts, it feels 'unnatural' to talk about faith, as something felt to belong to a separate 'personal' sphere of life.

The impersonality and seeming indifference that characterize everyday interactions allow certain freedoms. While, as Tonkiss describes, 'relations of indifference may be fragile, grudging, uneven...they also can be seen as *ethical* in inscribing an attitude, however minimal, of the self in respect of others' (2005: 9–10). Members of St John's are conscious of the freedom this affords them in relation to their faith: despite the language of persecution and hostility that often reverberates, they *also* frequently express gratitude to God that they are free to practise their faith in contrast with Christians in other global contexts for whom they pray. Formed as modern subjects who value the freedom that privacy allows, they feel uncomfortable expressing moral viewpoints that appear to transgress 'public' impersonal, instrumental norms by expressing beliefs that imply that others' 'private' morality is wrong, and this is most intensely felt in relation to issues where the teachings of their church rub up against broader norms of equality.[7] Yet the teachings of their faith *also* ask them to feel compassion for those around them in 'this desperately lost city in London', and to witness to those in need of Jesus's words through speaking to them of their faith and contending 'publicly' for the gospel.

Members of St John's are conscious of these tensions. Their reflection on the extent to which their own speaking practices fall short of their understanding of what God wants of them encourages them to work on themselves as ethical subjects, as they seek to discipline not only their practices but also their attitudes towards the different codes of behaviour they experience in different spaces. We saw in the last chapter how Levinas and others have conceptualized ethical subjectivity as beginning in the division of the subject, and Foucault also describes the process of subjectification as taking place through 'dividing practices': 'the subject is either divided in himself or divided from others' (1982: 208). At St John's, the naming of the ideal evangelical subject, who speaks publicly about her faith and expresses beliefs about gender, sexuality, and other faiths that go against universalizing norms, functions as a boundary that divides evangelicals from others. It *also* divides the subject within herself, introducing a demand into her that she is conscious she does not meet, and therefore feeling, as Jane described, 'rubbish', and there being an inevitability in this. The experience of a tension between an ideal of practice—here, the public proclamation of faith—and the sense of having fallen short of that is not new within evangelicalism. Practices of reading the Bible, listening to sermons, small group discussion, and the praising of 'heroic' individuals such as Steph and James, name ideals of performance, while practices of confession divide the subject, making her conscious of her falling short of these ideals, and desiring to come closer to them in future.

The tension between the desire to speak publicly and the consciousness of failing to do so is narrativized as an internal battle, through idioms of guilt, sin, and idolatry, and biblical narratives enable individuals to make coherent sense of this tension and shape their orientations towards their own practice. A speech therapist said, 'Jesus talks about "whoever will be ashamed of me and my words, I will be ashamed of him"', and stated that this showed that

---

[7] In contrast to the narrative often presented of evangelicals viewing diversity policies with hostility, several members of St John's spoke positively of these policies in relation to preventing discrimination against gay colleagues (Strhan 2014). Research conducted by Anderson et al. with evangelicals in New York also found that LGBT rights were taken seriously by conservative evangelicals (2011: 627).

feelings of shame are the inevitable experience of all Christians. The leadership of the church are also sensitive to these tensions and articulate a sense that while God desires wholehearted service, He also offers the promise of coherence beyond the fragmentation of the city, providing release for the soul riven by 'internal battles', as I will explore in subsequent chapters.

While Bruce describes the compartmentalization of religion that occurs with structural differentiation as a holding process en route to secularization (2002: 29), examining the different evangelistic practices of members of St John's complicates this narrative. While on the one hand the difficulties they experience in speaking about faith does suggest a secularization of urban space in which speaking of faith is a taboo, on the other hand members of the church are conscious of this fragmentation and learn to desire a sense of overall coherence, for Jesus 'to be the cardboard', showing that the secular city is at the same time the space of religious dwelling.

The cultural and subjective fragmentation Simmel describes is brought into relief in the evangelistic practices of church members. On local council estates in which distance is created through socio-economic inequalities, members of St John's confidently engage in verbal evangelism and experience little discomfort about doing so. Yet in middle-class spaces in contrast, their felt experiences of awkwardness signify a tension between the missionary norms encouraged through their church and a secularization of space that locates the religious within the realm of the personal. Seemingly contradictory ethics of interaction bound up with the different spaces inhabited by members of St John's are thus spun in uneven patterns within their bodies, shaping their engagement with and formation by the city in complex ways, as their desire to speak is inhibited and they find alternative means of 'witnessing'. Through these practices, they draw lines of distinctiveness that separate them from both non-Christians and other Christian groups and connect them more closely with each other.

London is therefore named and experienced in different ways as individuals learn to read the city according to diverse and often contradictory stories: as a 'desperately lost city' and site for busy evangelism, as a space where Christianity is marginalized, as a space of everyday friendship and community, as a space of socio-economic divides, as a site for workplace productivity, as a space resounding with other voices that distract them from attending to the voice of God, and as a site of missed encounters and opportunities for speaking. The desire to *speak* the words of the Bible as a distinctive mark of 'genuine Christian mission' is bound up with the formation of the evangelical subject as one who 'listens' amid the clamour of the city and thereby forms a sense of relationship with God. In the following chapter, we will explore the distinctive forms of this listening, and how this points towards an ideal of subjectivity that is orientated towards a unification of the fragmented and transient cultural forms of the metropolis.

4

The Listening 'I'

> Words strain,
> Crack and sometimes break, under the burden,
> Under the tension, slip, slide, perish,
> Decay with imprecision, will not stay in place,
> Will not stay still.
>
> (T. S. Eliot 1974: 194)

Services at St John's are planned by the church leaders to focus on a particular theme from the chosen Bible passage, with hymns and prayers reflecting the theme. On a cold January morning in 2011, Pete was leading the service. He began by referring to the shootings in Tucson, Arizona, that had taken place the day before, saying it was appropriate to be focusing on the theme that morning of 'looking forward to God's future glorious kingdom'. He said, 'Hear what the apostle John says in Revelation: "I heard a loud voice from the throne saying, 'Behold the dwelling place of God is with man. He will dwell with them, and they will be His people, and God Himself will be with them as their God. He will wipe away every tear from their eyes, and death shall be no more, neither shall there be mourning, nor crying, nor pain any more, for the former things have passed away.'"' This theme of the future kingdom of God reverberated in the words of the traditional organ-accompanied opening and closing hymns and the more contemporary songs accompanied by a band.[1]

Hugo, one of the older ministers at St John's, was preaching that morning. He began by praying, 'Open our eyes, Lord, we pray, that we might see wonderful things in your Word. Open our vision to the future, that it may become increasingly real to us. Strengthen our faith that we may live in the light of these things that you have revealed to us.' He said, 'the book of Isaiah has often been called a tale of two cities . . . Here, in Chapter 1 . . . the faithful city has become a whore . . . and afterwards you shall be called . . . the city of righteousness, the faithful city.' He explained that the faithful city is 'of course

---

[1] See, for example, the song 'Higher Throne', from <https://www.gettymusic.com/hymns.aspx> (accessed 22 September 2014).

Jerusalem . . . with Zion . . . [as] the symbol of the presence of the only true and living God amongst His people . . . He dwells among His people, and He does that in order to make them holy as He is holy, so that Israel can be a light to all the nations of the ancient world.' He said that the question Isaiah is 'grappling with' is: 'how is the faithless city to become the faithful city? . . . How can He produce a people who are characterized by holiness when we know just be looking inside our own hearts that the raw material of human nature is riddled with sin and rebellion? . . . How can you and I, as sinful, rebellious people, ever be in relationship with a God of holiness and righteousness and justice?'

He described the situation Isaiah outlined as a 'picture of a city in a spiral of decline, disintegration and corruption', which God will 'purify' as 'He moves in judgment against His people . . . It will be a sanctifying, restorative work that God does . . . and afterwards, the faithless city will become the faithful city'. He said that Isaiah's aim in describing the 'glorious, faithful city' was to 'motivate Isaiah's hearers to repentance . . . to a changed life, to a holiness of living in the present . . . [which] will make a radical difference to their everyday life and to ours'. He said that this vision of a future city should motivate 'God's people in our own generation' today: 'we're looking forward to an eternal and glorious city . . . in which nobody else really in our cultural context actually believes. It's a great challenge to live by that, to live by repentance and faith, in the light of the future certain reality of God's eternal kingdom.' Isaiah's vision of the faithful city then offers, Hugo said, 'detail about God's eternal purposes, which can focus our present, frankly often wobbly, discipleship and motivate us to holiness of character and life'. Hugo then asked the congregation to focus on a phrase in the first verse of chapter 2: 'The word that Isaiah the son of Amoz *saw*':

> Isn't that interesting? What Isaiah sees is a *word*. Because Old Testament reve-
> lation is always verbal rather than visual. It may use illustrations and pictures and
> visions . . . but they're always expressed verbally. The God of the Bible, you see, is
> a speaking God. Which is why the Word of God is central to everything that we
> do on Sunday mornings. We're not called here to come to see pictures. We're
> called to come to listen to God's Word, to respond to His Word, the Word of God
> Himself in scripture, the Word of total wisdom and total authority. And this is a
> Word of future prediction from the God who makes His promises and who
> fulfils them.

Hugo described how in the passage, people will go up to Zion, and said that the 'source of this magnetic attraction' is the 'revelation of the knowledge of God, which will lead us to living a life that reflects the character of God. And that's what we're all concerned about as Christian people: we want to be effective disciples of the Lord Jesus.' Hugo said this vision of God's future glorious city is something that is future, but has 'a present application: . . . Let us be the people who receive the revelation that He's given and who responding to His teaching walk in the light as He is the light . . . Our responsibility now is to listen to His teaching and to walk in His light.'

Hugo warned that what keeps people from this response is 'idolatry . . . something has become more important than God to us, usually ourselves in some form or another . . . We want what *we* want, rather than what God wants', and said 'this is why we don't long for the heavenly city . . . [This] makes it seem remote and distant to us because much more pressing and immediately in our everyday circumstances are the idols which take over from God at the heart of our lives.' He said that in the passage, Jerusalem, as 'the faithless city in Isaiah's day . . . had the same desires as the pagan nations around them . . . They were indistinguishable in their quest for money and armaments', and he said that the 'root of that' was that 'their land is filled with idols'. He said idolatry allows these idols—'often ourselves'—'to dictate to you what is most important in your life', and contrasted 'merely human' idols with God: 'man has no continuity; his breath is totally dependent on God, he has no dependability apart from God'. He said that 'the mistake fallen human beings like us [make] is to try to make ourselves secure independently of God . . . All the way through our lives the struggle that every Christian faces is that there are little cities that are our endeavours to make ourselves secure, so that we don't really have to bother God, much less depend on Him, and hopefully He won't bother us. That's the story of human history.'

He concluded the sermon by praying, as the congregation bowed their heads:

> We're going to sing in a moment, 'Saviour, since of Zion's city, I through grace a member am. Let the world deride or pity, I will glory in your name'. Lord, we don't just want those words to be sung to a great tune. We want them to be the expression of our hearts and lives today and through the coming days of this week. We pray that in the midst of the world that doesn't really believe anything of what we've been talking about, you will help us not just to withdraw from it into some sort of pietistic ghetto, but to live in it as agents of change. We pray that wherever we are this time tomorrow, at work, in our communities, in our serving, wherever we are . . . that we may be the people who are so aware of the grace that has made us members of this eternal city, that we will glory in your name, and that glory may destroy the idols and focus our eyes on the king.

After the final hymn, as the congregation were still standing, with heads bowed, Pete read some verses from the book of Revelation re-echoing the theme of the service: 'The Spirit and the Bride say, "Come." And let the one who hears say, "Come." And let the one who is thirsty come; let the one who desires take the water of life without price . . . He who testifies to these things says, "Surely I am coming soon." Amen. Come, Lord Jesus!'

In this service, we see how looking forward to the future, faithful city of God is understood at St John's as interrelated with the practice of listening to God and forming a disposition of obedience to His teaching in His Word, and that this disposition is experienced as in tension with the 'idolatry' of a cultural norm of self-determination. This critique of autonomy reverberated in many contexts at St John's, through, for example, sermons that described Jesus as 'a perfect model of dependence on God'. In one of the Rooted discussions, Hannah asked the group what kinds of things they would avoid mentioning as possible 'costs' of Christianity to people who were considering becoming Christians; Emily answered, 'obedience and rules'. Alistair said, 'I think it really is very countercultural. We live in a society that really stresses autonomy, our being our own bosses and doing things *our* own way, so the idea of living in obedience to God just really goes against everything that our culture tells us. I don't think it was that way fifty years ago.' Emily said that faith means 'living in a way that is not about living for me, but about living for Jesus, doing what *He* wants. If I think of most of my colleagues, they're pretty egotistical, to be honest, and living with Jesus as Lord would seem quite different from their ideas of freedom.'

Hugo's words articulate an understanding of God as speaking and a sense that relating to Him in a right moral order involves listening to and submitting to the authority of His Word. People are called to respond to His address in obedience and develop a sense of dependence on Him and trust in His promises of a future city of God, which is partially realized in the actions of His people on earth as they seek not to withdraw from the world 'but to live in it as agents of change'. But we also see an acknowledgement that this is a struggle, that they need help to focus their 'present frankly often wobbly discipleship'. In the following chapter, I explore how the personality of God—described by Hugo as holy and bringing about a relationship of intimacy with His people—has agency in shaping the subjectivities of members of St John's, and in Chapter 6, I consider the difficulty of maintaining an orientation to His promises for the future. Before turning to these themes, this chapter will address the formation of evangelical subjects as listeners, concentrating on the processes through which they develop an orientation towards God and learn to focus on His character. This focus offers a response to urban fragmentation *and* introduces a specific moral fragmentation as individuals learn to understand themselves as divided through their seeking to become oriented to the future City of God while at the same time 'sinful, rebellious people'.

I begin by considering what it means to listen in modernity, drawing on Michel de Certeau's argument that the loss of the ability to hear God speak is associated with a fracturing of meaning as individuals understand themselves as authors of their own meanings and identities. I then describe the techniques through which members of the church seek to form themselves as listening subjects, and discuss the significance of 'rationality' in this. I then consider how members of the church also learn to listen in 'private' and 'personal' spaces and how these different modes of listening imply norms of agency that contribute to their self-identification as 'aliens and strangers' in the city. Yet while these listening practices enable particular forms of connection and an orientation towards coherence, they also lead members of the church to be conscious of the many other 'voices' that distract them from hearing God in the city's soundscapes. I conclude by arguing that their listening serves as an interruption to everyday rhythms of the city, encouraging members of the church to seek to *know* God as a source of coherence and meaning and to discipline their minds and bodies in attentiveness to the demand to listen to Him.

LISTENING, MEANING, AND MODERNITY

In *The Practice of Everyday Life*, Michel de Certeau describes modernity as characterized by a loss of the ability to hear God's Word: the 'disenchantment' of the world was 'fundamentally a predicament of hearing, a fracturing of words and revealer, a loss of God's living voice' (Schmidt 2000: 29). De Certeau outlines a shift from what he terms a 'listening' to a 'scriptural economy', arguing that prior to the modern period, the Bible speaks: 'The sacred text is a voice, it teaches (the original sense of *documentum*), it is the advent of a "meaning" (*un "vouloir-dire"*) on the part of a God who expects the reader (in reality, the listener) to have a "desire to hear and understand" (*un "vouloir-entendre"*) on which access to truth depends' (1984: 137). The 'modern age', he argues, is 'formed by discovering little by little that this Spoken Word is no longer heard, that it has been altered by textual corruptions and the avatars of history. One can no longer hear it. "Truth" no longer depends on the attention of a receiver who assimilates himself to the great identifying message' (p. 137). Within the listening economy, the identity of the Speaker had been certain, and 'attention was directed toward the deciphering of his statements' (p. 138). But the authority of the institutions that guaranteed the credibility of that voice were progressively weakened in Western societies, so that 'the voice that today we consider altered or extinguished is above all that great cosmological Spoken Word that we notice no longer reaches us: it does not cross the centuries separating us from it' (p. 137).

De Certeau argues that when people heard the Spoken Word, their identities had been established in relation to the social institutions that projected the divine voice. With that voice's disappearance, there was 'a loss of the identities that people believed they received from a spoken word. A work of mourning. Henceforth, identity depends on production, on the endless moving on (or detachment and cutting loose) that this loss makes necessary. Being is measured by doing' (p. 137). New substitutes for the unique speaker had to be found, and modern societies worked to redefine themselves without that voice, for example, in revolutions and new nationalist identities (p. 137). The task of 'writing' in this 'scriptural' economy symbolizes a change in relationship with language and meaning. As people no longer believed their identities were received with reference to the Spoken Word, the nature of human subjectivity and society were redefined without that voice: humans sought to understand *themselves* as the authors of meaning. As language in the modern age had to be '*made* and not just *heard* and understood', there emerged a 'vast sea of progressively disseminated language, in a world without closure or anchorage' (p. 138). The individual's place in society could no longer be formally assigned as a 'vocation and a placement in the order of the world', but became a 'void, which drives the subject to make himself the master of a space and to set himself up as a producer of writing' (p. 138). This 'new writing' is formed through 'a moving on (*une marche*) that always depends on something else to provide available space for its advance, to the degree that the voice proper to Christian culture becomes its other and that the presence given in the signifier (the very definition of voice) is transformed into a past' (p. 137).

This depiction of a shift from a 'listening' to a 'scriptural' economy with the advent of modernity is, de Certeau admits, an artefact, constructed to depict a shift from divine to human agency, and a fracturing and deferral of meaning accompanying this. Taking 'writing' as symbolic of the activity of different modes of cultural production, de Certeau's account is consonant with theories positing modern and postmodern culture as characterized by the circulation of products and information taking place at ever greater speed, threatening the possibility of coherence. With the ever-faster production and circulation of the stuff of consumer capitalism, this multiplicity of products and objects produces, as in Simmel's thesis, 'many more cultural artefacts or signs ("signifiers") than people can cope with. People are bombarded with signifiers and increasingly become incapable of attaching "signifieds" or meanings to them' (Lash and Urry 1994: 3). Schmidt cites the composer R. Murray Schafer expressing anguish over the 'polluted "soundscape"' of modernity by invoking Meister Eckhart: 'Still the noise in the mind: that is the first task – then everything else will follow in time' (Schmidt 2000: 29).

This story of the loss of the ability to 'listen' in modernity is, as Schmidt writes, mostly, 'finally, a story of religious absence' (p. 29). While de Certeau tells this through depicting a move from a listening to a writing economy, narratives detailing a move from 'hearing' to 'vision', as the prominent means of knowing the world,[2] likewise suggest that modernity has been marked by a move away from valuing receptiveness towards an Other.[3] Although historians

---

[2] See, for example, Buck-Morss's *The Dialectics of Seeing* (1991) and David Levin's edited *Modernity and the Hegemony of Vision* (1993), including contributions arguing both for and against this position.

[3] In articulating a distinction between orality/aurality and writing, de Certeau does not intend to set up an antinomic opposition between the two: the listening he describes implies listening to the words of a written text. His distinguishing these two modes of relating to language is more

are wary of accounts tracing a generalized shift from cultures privileging hearing to occularcentrism, it is now, as Charles Hirschkind notes, 'widely recognized that the politics, ethics, and epistemologies that defined the Enlightenment project were deeply entwined with a set of assumptions regarding the relative value of the senses' (2006: 13). While vision is predicated on distance between the eye and the object of perception, listening bridges the gap between visible and invisible, interior and exterior worlds, involving the self's 'immersion within a sound from without, an engulfment that threatens the independence and integrity grounds the masculine spectatorial consciousness' (p. 13). The very phenomenology of listening and the receptivity and passivity it implies came to be regarded as a danger to the autonomy of the Enlightenment subject.

Walter Benjamin also explored this theme in *The Storyteller* (1969) which, as Hirschkind outlines (2006: 26), describes storytelling as one of the principal means of transmitting wisdom from one generation to the next in pre-modern Europe, a process depending on dispositions formed through slow rhythms of artisanal labour. This required a 'naïve relationship to the storyteller' (Benjamin 1969: 91) and a form of passivity that would allow the story to sink into the listener's perception. Benjamin, like de Certeau, depicts a loss of the ability to listen as related to changes in the conditions of knowledge associated with a rise of 'information', a form of knowledge that is understandable in itself rather than grounded in the authority of tradition or a speaker. 'Information', in Benjamin's depiction, is a way of knowing that is rootless, which 'has the effect of undermining the forms of knowledge and practice that depended on processes of gradual sedimentation and embodiment' (Hirschkind 2006: 26–7).

Has the time of listening then passed? The contemporary appeal of evangelicalism is often explained in terms of a longing for an authoritative revelatory voice that speaks outside of time and establishes a referential unity that 'stems [the] semiotic drift' arising with the fragmentation of modernity (Comaroff 2010: 29). We will see that members of St John's do come to understand God as a secure originary source of meaning and identity—there is still a longing for a 'holy listening' in their lives and 'narratives about rupture, silence, and devocalization remain narrow and inadequate stories' (Schmidt 2000: 31).

---

meant to suggest that modernity has been marked by a move away from valuing attentive receptiveness towards an Other whose address gives the self her identity and meaning. He emphasizes that his aim is not to create the kind of metaphysical binary of writing/orality that Derrida criticized as having as an 'ultimate reference . . . the presence of a value or of a meaning (sens) that is supposed to be anterior to difference' and functions as a foundation that establishes a 'founding archaeology' for language (cited in de Certeau 1984: 133). De Certeau, like Derrida, assumes that 'plurality is originary; that difference is constitutive of its terms; and that language must continually conceal the structuring work of division beneath a symbolic order' (p. 133>).

Hirschkind's (2006) ethnography of cassette listening in the Islamic Revival in Cairo demonstrates how focusing on forms of religious aurality draws into question conventional binaries such as public/private and reason/affect. Hirschkind addresses liberal modernist suspicions about Muslim listening practices and the ear's vulnerability to being affected by non-rational means, citing an American researcher's discomfort as not uncommon: '"It's scary walking past a mosque on Friday when the preacher is raging away, filling the minds of those people with wild fears about the tortures of hell, or the perversity of sex-obsessed Westerners. All of these bearded men crying and shouting 'Allah' – I'm always half-expecting them to jump up and come running after me"' (p. 18). Hirschkind argues that such visceral discomfort indicates that 'reasonableness' is not something decided abstractly at the level of 'content', as implied in normative political conceptions of rationality, but has its own habitus: 'reason has a feel to it, a tone and volume, a social and structural architecture of reception, and particular modes of response' (p. 18).

Hirschkind describes sermon listening as a technique of shaping and disciplining the self according to pious Muslim virtues, achieved through habituated modes of receptivity, in which the individual learns to feel emotions appropriate to particular verses of the Quran. One of his informants, a taxi driver, stated that through listening, 'one is reminded what Islam really entails... See, I am not very Islamic [pointing to his cigarette], I smoke, but when I hear those things on tape, I am encouraged, steered towards correct practice' (p. 71). Hirschkind argues that listening constructs a 'counter-public' with 'a conceptual architecture that cuts across the modern distinctions between state and society and between public and private that are central to the public sphere as a normative institution of modern democratic politics' (p. 107). Sermons render 'public' issues that the liberal state locates within the sphere of 'private' choice—the danger of gossip, gestures in prayer, or modesty of dress—and therefore 'constitutes an obstacle to the state's attempt to secure a social domain where national citizens are free to make modern choices, as it repoliticizes those choices, subjects them to public scrutiny' (p. 112). Moreover the interpretive norms shaping individuals' responses to these sermons are not based solely in logics of deliberative rationality, as in some liberal understandings of a public sphere, but also in the affective, poetic, and sensory power of language to move people to particular modes of being and acting (p. 113).

Hirschkind's work offers a point of departure for considering other forms of listening, technologies of the self, and the understandings of public, political, and ethical life these imply. Conservative evangelical cultures of listening do seem to imply a liberal, secular separation between 'public' and 'private' and a privileging of discursive rationality over emotions, while at the same time expressing a desire for coherence across all spheres of life that transcends such binaries. Examining the means by which members of St John's listen provides insight into the embodiment of 'rational' sensibilities and public/private distinctions. Yet I also show that this practice of listening—a technology of the self that works to form a sense of obedience to God that will infuse *all* everyday interactions—is also felt as hard work in the modern metropolis, and this divine voice can be lost at times. I also show that norms of receptivity to another symbolized in listening and of 'modern' autonomy (symbolized in visuality and the 'scriptural' economy) are inextricably bound together in the lived experience of the evangelical listener.

What, then, are the means through which members of St John's are formed as 'listeners'? What does this reveal about their modes of relation with God, each other, and the multiple others they encounter in the city? To what extent is their listening shaped by a shift in orientation to language away from receptivity towards humans as producers of their own, forever unstable meanings? And how is this formation affected by the proliferation of cultural forms that confront the individual in everyday urban life?

LEARNING TO LISTEN

For members of St John's, God's voice still speaks in the Bible. The periodization of time implied in the adverb 'still' is pertinent, alluding to the shift de Certeau describes away from a listening economy and to the narrative of British society 'careering away' from its Christian past resonating in St John's and wider public discourses. This privileging of listening,[4] underlined in the image above which accompanied the sermon series in which Hugo's sermon featured, is not surprising for a church that locates its institutional identity squarely within the Reformed tradition. The theological rationale for this focus lies in a Christology positing Jesus as the sole mediator between sinful humanity and a holy, transcendent God through His death and resurrection, offering those who believe in Him the possibility of relationship with God. The Bible is understood as the means by which the person of Jesus and the purposes of God are revealed and therefore as *the* way of entering into relationship with God. Being in relationship with God means having heard Jesus, believing in Him, and choosing to internalize His words and do what He says. As George said in one sermon, the means by which an individual 'becomes clean . . . is through hearing His [Jesus's] Word and believing it'.

---

[4] The language of 'hearing' and 'listening to God' are used interchangeably by members of St John's to denote the ideal of the subject formed, as de Certeau described, in receptivity to God's address. Yet it is the idea of *listening*, denoting the intentionality of the one who hears, that is more central to evoke conservative evangelicals' self-formation as listeners.

David Morgan describes how within Protestantism, the sacred is regarded as 'information, as content-laden delivery of proper knowledge. God is in the information, the knowledge of salvation and divine intention for one's life' (2012: 177). Within the history of Protestantism, there was an emphasis on forming subjects who located their agency to believe and interpret the Word in themselves rather than in the authority of a mediating priest, creating the conditions for the emergence of the autonomous subject of the Enlightenment (Keane 2007: 219). This orientation to words and cognitive belief meant that information given through sensations and emotions was understood as 'knowledge' only after processes of categorization and filtering through the mind (Mellor and Shilling 1997: 23–4). Belief—in terms of an internal assent to propositions, mediated through *hearing*, accepting, and then *knowing* Jesus as saviour—became separated from and privileged over experiences of the sacred gained through 'carnal knowing' (p. 23).

This understanding of a relationship with God shaped by words and knowledge is still central within conservative evangelicalism. As Freddie stated in one sermon, 'The life of faith is the life of the Word. "Abide in me," says Jesus, "abide in my words."' Listening is described as the most important practice of the Christian life, the means of cultivating a relationship with God. David preached in one sermon on the story of Martha and Mary in Luke's Gospel:

> There is only one priority that counts: listening to Jesus. There is only one thing that really matters: listening to Jesus. There is one item that trumps all others on the list of things that you need to do today, tomorrow, this week, next week, next month, the month after, until the day we die. Put *this* in place as *the* priority above all others and everything else will fall into place: listening to Jesus comes ahead of my work. Listening to Jesus comes ahead of my acts of service. Listening to Jesus comes ahead of my family responsibilities. Listening to Jesus comes ahead of my own physical needs, before my pleasures and playthings. Listening to Jesus comes ahead of our church responsibilities. Listening to Jesus comes ahead of our church plans, our church activities. Listening to Jesus comes ahead of our care programme, our mums and toddlers group, our outreach plans, our building projects. There is one thing that matters: listening to Jesus. Martha was distracted; Mary chose the good portion that will not be taken away.

He went on to say that his prayer for the church is that they would be 'people who give ourselves to listen to Him', and described listening to the Word and its explanation as how to have 'a genuine experience of the living God'. David said this listening must be 'personal and public', explaining 'personal' as meaning a programme of daily Bible reading, study and listening to audio-recordings of sermons, and 'public' as meaning listening in church services and Bible study groups. What, then, were the body pedagogics of this 'public' listening?

While modes of practice were broadly similar in the Rooted and student groups, the church devoted particular resources to the student programme with the aim, as Freddie described, of 'equipping and training' students in techniques that will form them as confident in their ability to hear God speak in the text of the Bible. Attending to the means by which students are 'trained' to listen helps clarify the habitus the leaders at St John's aim to reproduce. Over the course of an academic year, groups studied one book of the Bible in depth, following a programme written by the church leaders. There was an informal atmosphere at meetings, which followed a structure, beginning as members arrived and chatted over supper, often with music by bands such as Arcade Fire playing in the background. On one level, their music tastes were unremarkable for middle-class students. Yet on another level, the choice to play music by bands whose lyrics at times express sentiments that appear diametrically opposed to the teachings of the church,[5] indicates how everyday audio and media consumption becomes a means of fragmented auditory experience: while students carry sermons in their iPods and smartphones and seek to draw the words of these into themselves, they also carry other voices that jar with this.

At 8 p.m., the music was turned off, and one of the ministers addressed everyone from the stage and prayed a short prayer, asking 'that we would listen as you speak to us through your Word', constructing a boundary marking the turn of concentrated attention to the text as the most significant part of the meeting. One of the two appointed group leaders—trained by more senior church staff members—led the conversation, beginning by asking a member of the group to open in prayer, and then asking another member to read the set Bible passage aloud as everyone else followed in the church Bibles. The style of discussion in many ways resembled academic seminars. Group members were encouraged to focus on the text in front of them to develop an understanding of attentiveness to the *words* of the text as the means of hearing God speaking, and to spend time preparing for each meeting using set preparation questions.

Early in the academic year, students spend a weekend together at which newcomers are given a talk on the doctrine of revelation to help shape their understanding of the purpose of Bible reading. Freddie said they hoped that students would learn that it's possible to read the Bible 'and be hearing from God; it's possible to work out how to apply them [the scriptures] today, that while that needs to be done carefully . . . and read in context, it's still . . . a good thing to do, and not too difficult to do on your own'. Freddie said he told new group leaders that if you watched first year groups from the church's gallery, over the course of the year you could see a change in how students engage with the Bible. Earlier in the year, he said, students tended not to look at the text during meetings and gave answers from prior understanding, whereas by the

---

[5] See, for example, the lyrics of 'Antichrist Television Blues' (Arcade Fire n.d.).

end of the year, 'you've got much more looking down to see the answer, and . . . that's something we're trying to encourage and train'. Most students also engage in one-on-one weekly Bible study with an older member of the congregation to encourage this way of engaging with the text.

The group's discussions focused on comprehending the passage in its context, working out the structure of the argument, the author's intention, and which sections of the text are applicable today. Through these discussions, students learn to develop a particular temporal engagement with the text: for each passage they were asked to focus on discerning both the author's intentions and what God is trying to say to them as a church today through that passage. By listening to each other in conversation and helping each other to interpret what God might be saying in the text, students therefore learn to understand these discussions as a means by which they hear God address *them*, corporately and individually.

There was no discernible difference in the Rooted group's practices, although there was no need for leaders to reiterate the importance of focusing on the text, as individuals were used to attentiveness to the words of the text and had internalized the understanding that God addressed them through the Word. Lucy said to me as we chatted one evening, 'the longer you are a Christian, the more you realize how amazing it is that the Creator God has revealed Himself to us in this book'. She picked up a Bible from the seat next to her and hugged it: 'It's the way God *speaks* to us, the way we get to know Him.' Although there has been a shift away from focusing on 'meanings' in religious rituals, especially within anthropology, this practice of listening to the words of the Bible together in the group becomes dense with meaning as individuals learn to interpret this as the means by which God addresses them and asks them to respond to His teaching in their everyday lives. This understanding of these groups as a space of listening is inseparable from their also being a space of speaking, and church members describe their speaking in these groups as a form of 'witnessing' to each other. Their listening is therefore always bound up with other embodied practices: sitting, eating, and conversing with each other; and group members enjoy these interactions. Alan, who had previously attended a charismatic evangelical church, said one of the main reasons he preferred St John's was because the Rooted groups are 'so much fun'. He said his experience of London had been 'transformed' since joining St John's through his experience of 'church community', formed primarily through the Rooted group.

In Sunday services, listening to the Word was also positioned as central, indexed spatially through the positioning of musicians on the floor, the Bible reading given from the stage above that, and the sermon preached from the elaborately carved pulpit above that. The sacrality of the Bible was emphasized in every service, for example when David said to the congregation, before the Bible reading: 'we come now to the heart of our meeting, the reason why we're here, to hear God speak to us. It is, you might say, the high point, to hear God's Word as it is read to us and explained.' He usually asked the congregation to 'please take hold of any electronic device and switch it off so that no-one is disturbed while we're listening to God's Word', reinforcing the sense that *this* is the moment people have come to church for, and almost everyone I interviewed described the sermon as their favourite part of the service.

The leaders aimed to encourage particular techniques through which individuals could become better listeners. In one Sunday service, Pete interviewed Natalie, one of the church staff, about what being a good listener involves. She said, 'we are coming together as a family to hear God speak to us, as a family', and gave the congregation tips from her own practice about 'how to listen well', such as finding out what the passage will be in advance from the church website and reading it before the service, listening for 'three or four key themes' to remember later in the week, and writing notes during the sermon to return to later on in the week during 'quiet times'. All the seats of the church have Bibles placed on them in advance of the service, and during the Bible reading and sermon, the congregation follow the text and take notes on handouts or in notebooks. While other evangelical churches often use Power-Point slides during sermons, these are not used for sermons at St John's. This is a conscious decision to encourage people to focus on the ministers, who—all skilled orators—scarcely look at their notes while preaching, instead making eye contact with the congregation. While listening is discursively privileged, this is therefore bound up with a visual aesthetic, as the congregation look up to follow the expressive faces of the male preachers, look down at the words on the page, and jot notes on the handouts. Dress also plays a visual role in creating the church's ambience, and the church leaders are conscious of the semiotics of clothing: all the church staff are expected to wear suits at midweek meetings aimed at those working near the church, and the ministers wear suits or blazers and chinos for Sunday morning services, changing into jeans and jumpers, T-shirts, or rugby shirts for the more informal, youth-oriented evening services.[6]

The spatial arrangement of the congregation sitting to listen also functions as a visual marker, conveying shared dispositions of 'solemnity, respect, and submission to authority' (Morgan 2012: 176). As Morgan writes, 'Sitting in unison is no less important for mainstream Protestants than praying or singing together. The assembled congregation is consuming the Word of God together, as a single body, and this affirms its sense of what "church" is' (p. 176). The church interior is brightly lit, with white walls and utilitarian flexible seating, and these visual forms together emphasis the centrality of 'listening', performing in their plainness as 'sounding boards' to return the

---

[6] I never saw any of the ordained ministers wearing any form of clerical dress.

words to the hearer more effectively.[7] Thus the 'iconicity of the text' is underlined: 'bodies are disciplined to attune the ears to the prevailing soundscape and to predispose feelings to arise as if separate from the body; and spaces host sound and allow light to lift the eyes from objects and to illuminate the spaces and plain walls that reverberate with sound' (p. 167). Visuality and other forms of embodiment are at work, but they perform unobtrusively, 'all the better to turn words into pure content, delivered in an unadulterated, immaterial form' (p. 167). The body and material objects are not rendered irrelevant, but this aesthetic brings the words that are spoken and heard to the forefront of individuals' conscious attention, while the 'body is put to rest in order to augment hearing and make it a soul-receptacle like the church interior' (p. 171).

This focus on attentive listening as the means of relating to God constructs a boundary distinguishing 'authentic' Christianity as Word-based from other Christian traditions that place greater emphasis on ritual or emotion. David said in one sermon:

> Reformed Christianity is always challenged by Deformed Christianity . . . If somebody backslides from the Christian faith, they've been in a church like this, they very, very rarely completely throw over the whole boat. Normally what happens is you go into a deformed form of Christianity that isn't so focused on a final word and a finished work. And you start saying . . . I need something extra to give me assurance, I need a worship leader to lead me into the presence of God, or I need a priest, charismatic catholic. Now that's not to say that there aren't real, genuine, lovely Christians in those movements. But actually, a Christianity that starts to rely on the visual and the tangible, and to add to the final word and the finished work, I need something extra, a fresh word, an extra experience to assure me that I'm in the presence of God, that's deformed Christianity.

This distinction between 'authentic' and more emotional forms of Christianity was frequently articulated, both by leaders and members of the congregation. This conscious differentiation from other similar religious lifeworlds can be seen as a distinctive feature of piety movements in pluralist modern contexts, exemplified here in the cosmopolitan setting of London. Turner argues that piety in the contemporary world is about 'constructing definite and distinctive lifestyles involving new religious tastes and preferences. In short, piety or the pietisation of the everyday world, has these . . . characteristics of combining new elements to create a religious habitus that stands in competition with other possible combinations in a competitive religious context. These new combinations are then defined as the orthodox standard by which the worth of

---

[7] This is in contrast with some charismatic evangelical churches of comparable size I visited during fieldwork, which typically have the lights dimmed and musicians and preacher spotlighted, the congregation sitting on cushions and beanbags facing the musicians at the centre of the space.

a good Christian or a good Muslim or a good Jew could be measured' (2011: 285). Yet despite the anti-ritualist discourse at St John's, church members are nevertheless conscious that their formation as listeners depends on training of the body through specific techniques to develop a particular habitus that will enable them to hear God speak. One such technique is their engagement with music.

As many members of St John's have either previously attended or have friends who attend charismatic evangelical churches, they are especially con-scious of their distinctiveness from charismatics and how their acoustic sensibilities are tuned in ways that are intentionally different. This affects their understanding of music in church. Church members describe songs as functioning pedagogically rather than providing an opportunity to 'receive' the Holy Spirit as in charismatic churches, reinforcing the main listening event as the sermon. Rebecca, a twenty-two-year-old graduate, said singing is 'a medium by which the Word of God can dwell in you richly'. While 'the sermon should be expositing the Word of God', the next day, 'when I wake up, what I'll be remembering in the shower is the song; so the song should be so full of the words of God that actually it's almost like helping it to dwell richly in me'. She added that when she feels 'down and can't speak truth to myself, and ... forget all those unseen realities', what really helps is a song 'that speaks the words of God ... it helps it to get in'. She said singing is not about the individual before God, but is 'horizontal: we sing to each other so that the word of Christ dwells in us richly ... so that it's really embedded in my thoughts'. She also described internalizing the words of scripture by talking to friends as 'a further form of meditation, like chewing on God's Word and thinking, how can I just get this into my very short-sighted thick brain? I need people to tell me, I need to be reminded.'

Through this metaphor of Christ 'dwelling' in them as they draw His words into themselves, belief and body are connected by their discursive practices and they learn to understand their listening bodies as vessels for the divine. The metaphors of 'chewing', 'hunger', and the idea of the Word as 'holy food' that were frequently used in song lyrics can be connected with this.[8] De Certeau describes belief as knotting individuals into relations with others, like a sacrifice in the Durkheimian sense of establishing a society: 'by what it takes from individual self-sufficiency, it marks on what is proper to each (on the body or on goods) the existence of the other ...' (1985: 194). As listening to sermons is experienced as the most sacred moment in church services, so the metaphor of 'eating' to describe listening can be compared with the sacrament of the Eucharist: as they 'chew' on sacred words, their bodies are

---

[8] See, for example, the lyrics of 'Speak O Lord', from <http://www.gettymusic.com/hymns-speakolord.aspx> (accessed 22 September 2014).

marked with the existence of the other through receiving the 'food' of the Word and this marks their social collectivity (cf. Coleman 2000: 127–8).

Hirschkind describes Muslim practices of listening to sermons as a means of ethical self-formation, and sermons at St John's are also intended to address the conscience. Ministers pose questions throughout sermons, asking the congregation to consider their actions and attitudes in response to the ideals being outlined, and typically pose questions for them to ask each other afterwards. Through listening to such sermons, individuals learn to align their moral norms with the congregation's shared expectations and seek to fashion themselves as receptive to the words addressed to them by a God who, in the words of Pete, one of the curates, 'knows all and sees all and hears all', a kind of transcendent panopticon. This means of governing the self is achieved through orienting attention to a temporal framework that transcends mundane urban life in the act of listening. As David said in another sermon, 'As we come to Jesus then and sit at his feet and listen, we find salvation, light, life, wisdom, insight, eternity, peace, reconciliation.'

This ideal of attentive listening to the words of another might appear to threaten the independence of the individual subject and exemplify a form of moral heteronomy from which the Enlightenment emphasis on activity and autonomy recoiled. As David said, 'the trouble is, listening to his Word in the Bible like this can seem so un-experiential. I mean, you're just sitting there, and . . . it seems kind of just rather a passive thing'. Yet this understanding of listening is also interwoven with modern norms of autonomy and rationality. Let us consider how this takes shape.

LISTENING AS THE PRACTICE OF RATIONALITY

The centrality of rationality at St John's was brought home to me in my first meeting with David, when he recommended I read Stark and Finke's *Acts of Faith* (2000), which, in his words, 'argues that faith is entirely rational'. The emphasis on rationality at St John's meant that listening was understood as a process through which the listener is able to evaluate the preacher's interpretation of the Bible and look for 'evidence' in the text of the Bible to support their views. Freddie told me that the ministers 'try and show our working [in sermons] enough to enable someone to evaluate whether they agree with what's said in the pulpit, but also to enable someone to think, "I can apply that working method myself".' After sermons, there were often question and answer sessions for the congregation not only to ask the ministers questions of clarification and consider how to 'apply' the teachings of sermons to their lives, but also to allow for critique of the sermon, and questions were often raised that expressed disagreement with ministers' interpretations. An understanding of faith as based on rational evidence was also frequently emphasized in sermons; for example, Freddie stated in one sermon that 'on the basis of rational evidence, it is rational to be a Christian'.[9]

As many members of St John's work in highly rationalized professions, it is not surprising that this shapes their interactions in church. In my Rooted group, members' professions were in law, financial services, teaching, and medicine. When I asked Alistair, one of the group's leaders and himself a lawyer, why there were so many lawyers at St John's, he said he thought there was a homology between law and Protestantism, pointing out that Martin Luther had studied law before becoming a monk, and that Calvin had been a lawyer. 'So what do you think the similarities are?' I asked. 'Words,' he replied, 'words, structure, analysis . . . And also evidence.' He said he liked evidence, the tradition of British empiricism, and for things to be rational.

This privileging of rationality is a prominent cultural marker of not only St John's, but also other large conservative evangelical churches, bound up with the history of the social class background of this movement in Britain. As David said in one sermon, 'many of us are Stoics by upbringing . . . stiff upper-lipped'. The formation of this culture is bound up with the male, public-school habitus of key twentieth-century leaders of British conservative evangelicalism and the historical prioritizing of evangelism amongst boys at prominent public schools and elite universities, leading, as Pete Ward argues, to a privileging of reason over emotion (1997: 40). Members of St John's at times linked the emphasis on rational listening with the male leadership. One retired man told me he'd left his previous church because a new young minister had taken the church in a direction with 'too much emphasis on the charismatic, and other social nonsense'. I asked what he meant. He replied that there used to be young children allowed in throughout the whole service, because the mothers complained that if they took them out, they would not be able to hear the sermon, 'but of course they couldn't hear it anyway, and neither could anyone else'. He said that at St John's 'there is a tight male grip', which means that 'there is much more *discipline* in these areas'.

The intellectualized culture that has emerged within these large conservative evangelical churches means high levels of literacy are required to participate.[10] When I commented on this to Natalie, she said she thought that St John's was self-selecting in this sense, but that there was still an emphasis on seeking to 'study' the Bible in churches in more deprived areas. She said studying and learning are central to Christianity—'we wouldn't have the education system we

---

[9] The specific forms of evidence he was referring to here were the arguments in support of the Resurrection that are also used in the Alpha Course. See, for example, Alpha 2010.

[10] The church runs separate 'international' Bible study groups for those members whose first language is not English. One individual I interviewed criticized the fact that this made church membership difficult for those without the cultural capital of educational attainment, and contributed to the socio-economic polarization of urban space.

do if it wasn't for the influence of Christianity...If someone becomes a Christian, they will take that imperative to *study* God's word seriously.'[11] Despite the efforts of some members of the congregation to reach beyond socio-economic polarization through the Reaching the Unreached network, there is, as Natalie described, a self-selection of individuals who feel at home within this milieu. One Sunday evening, discussing 'standards of wisdom in the world' in his sermon, Freddie asked members of the congregation who have a degree to put their hands up. It felt as if everyone in the church responded. He then asked members of the congregation who have more than one degree, or a further professional postgraduate qualification, to put their hands up. I would guess that over a third of the congregation put their hands up. Freddie commented that 'the national average for such further qualifications is 20 per cent, so here at [St John's] we are bizarrely overeducated'. Freddie said he intended this to challenge the congregation to think about whether they are too concerned about what 'the world' thinks about them. Yet the performative effect of this seemed to objectify the evangelical subject as highly educated, reinforcing the sense that it is a space in which intellectualized approaches to faith are privileged. This shapes how members of the church characterize the church's culture. Alistair asked the Rooted group one evening how they'd describe St John's to their friends. Philip, another group leader, replied: 'We might talk about the excellent, intellectual preaching.'

'The witty illustrations,' Alan added.

'The intellectual, clear, rational, and witty sermons,' Alistair summarized. 'Anything else?'

'The smoked salmon sandwiches?' Lorna added. She was partly joking—she had brought smoked salmon for our group to celebrate the end of term that evening. Yet her comment draws attention to the exclusion of women from the privileged male role of preaching, and the significance of their roles in creating the conditions of conviviality.

This emphasis that St John's places on the rationality of faith is also linked with wider perceptions of evangelicalism as irrational and anti-intellectual (Noll 1994). The prominence of binaries promoted by celebrity atheists such as Dawkins that equate atheism with 'education, critical thinking and evidence-based understanding' and religion with 'fundamentalism, superstition, intolerance and suffering' might also partly underlie the particular emphasis on reason and evidence (Richard Dawkins Foundation For Reason and Science n.d.). Yet the roots of this emphasis on rational listening run deeper and are

---

[11] When I interviewed Gemma, after she left St John's to move to a suburban church after marrying, she said the focus on Bible study was still central in her new church—although adding that Bible study groups there felt different because they were organized in separate groups for men and women—but commented that she missed the intellectual challenge of sermons and study groups at St John's.

interrelated with a desire for a certain kind of 'public' culture. David expressed a sense of connection between forms of rational listening and civic life in a sermon on 2 Corinthians:

> Over the summer, we as a teaching team encouraged one another to read Neil Postman's book *Amusing Ourselves to Death*. It was written in 1985. And Postman's thesis was that with the arrival of television, methods of communication have changed radically. He suggests that we have entered a world—this is 1985, remember—where instant rather than permanent, impression rather than reason, entertainment rather than serious discourse are the norm. As you read the book...surely we have to say that Postman's thesis was right, that...we've entered a world of soundbite and spin, where politicians appear to be elected at least in part on looks and media appeal, newscasters are employed on the basis of their ability to look good in front of the camera, and where celebrity culture has taken over from an age of carefully reasoned, sustained logic in our public discourse.

David argued that this media logic has affected evangelicalism, leading to celebrity preachers whose 'teaching style is anecdotal, short on substance, light on logic, full of self-referencing stories that puff up the preacher, that do little to instruct the listener. And you have to conclude, when you look at it, they've deliberately put the beautiful people at the front, everybody seems to have perfect teeth that glisten white, they're part of the beautiful celebrity world.' He argued that as the Corinthian church had been open to 'false teaching' by being impressed by 'worldly preachers', so Christians today are also 'wide open to false teaching' because of the cult of the celebrity preacher. He described 'authentic Christian ministry' as characterized by 'failure', 'weakness', and 'frailty', and said:

> It's never nice to look around at other ministries, but Paul does...in order to guard the flock. Some of you will have come across, for example, Joel Osteen, *Your Best Life Now*, that has sold millions of copies around the world. Or here in London, Hillsong. There's no doubt that their message is different to the authentic message of the New Testament. You will not hear cross-shaped living: if any man would come after me, let him take up his cross daily and renounce self, deny self. You will hear: 'your best life now'. But because all of this is presented in a style that is so deeply attractive and deliberately apes the celebrity culture of our age, hundreds, thousands of people have been taken in by it.

David's critique of celebrity culture and his idealization of a rational public culture does not, however, straightforwardly reflect a 'modern' norm of autonomy. It is bound up in a conviction in both God's authoritative speaking in scripture and people's ability to use reason as they listen to discern 'authentic' Christian teaching.

Postman's book idealizes nineteenth-century civic culture in the United States, in which audiences had the capacity to concentrate on political speeches lasting a couple of hours. The articulated desire by the leadership at St John's for 'reasoned' public listening and discourse expresses dissatisfaction, like Postman, with the perceived triviality of contemporary public discourse and suggests a desire for forms of 'rational' public debate on 'non-trivial' issues in which religious voices resonate. In a sermon on secularism, David described the British public sphere as shaped by 'secularist fundamentalists' who 'ban[ned] from the public sphere the possibility of discussing and openly criticizing and weighing and condemning the relative value and truth claims and moral values as to what is good and bad in the different religions and no religion'. He stated that this 'make[s] it impossible for people to say, oh actually, we think that is wrong, sinful, bad for society, bad for people and untrue, and that is a very, very dangerous position for a culture to end up in'. While we saw in the previous chapter that members of St John's feel uncomfortable expressing moral positions possibly perceived as judgemental of others' moral behaviour, at the same time, they articulated a desire for public spaces in which speaking and listening to each other about faith is not felt as a taboo.

David's words, like Postman's, describe individuals' modes of listening as themselves affected by broader cultural shifts and new technologies. When I interviewed Mark, the church's head of media, he said it was important to be aware of how the media affects people's ability to listen, and said the church needs 'to reverse the trend of short attention spans. We need to educate people to listen, because the Christian message is a coherent message . . . The Bible—particularly the letters of Paul—is full of arguments, and you've got to learn to be able to follow an argument, and to *think*, and that is increasingly counter-cultural. And that's where I think we need to use all the modern tools of the web to draw people in and attract their interest, but actually the core business of what we're doing is getting people to *listen* very carefully, and to read carefully, and to pay attention.' He gave me a paper he'd written for the church's leaders, addressing how modern media 'affect our culture and particularly how they impact/should shape our preaching'. He wrote:

> Ease and speed of communication means recipients are potentially bombarded at all times of day and night by incoming information, mostly trivial. In the absence of sufficient self-discipline, recipients are easily and frequently distracted by incoming data . . . The tendency towards shorter attention spans, caused by the 24/7 bombardment, undermines people's capacity to think critically and coherently and to follow reasoned argument. Since much Christian teaching (not least in the letters of Paul) involves sustained argument, this is an important consideration.

Mark argued that while new media should be used to 'maximize scale of distribution through social networking sites etc.', the church should help develop and train attentiveness:

> If people have difficulty concentrating during a sermon, they need to *develop* the discipline and faculty of listening. Talk outlines (and notetaking) can help, but the

sermon should still be able to function without these aids ... If people cannot concentrate on a sermon, how will they be able to concentrate on reading the Bible for themselves? It is important to *develop* these skills rather than find a substitute genre ... It is the duty of the Church to encourage concentration and the appreciation of sustained argument, so that believers can benefit from sermons and personal Bible study. Just as the Reformation caused a huge growth in literacy in the past in the places they touched ... so too today's Church needs to counteract the short attention spans of the Internet age and foster an abiding appreciation of the written and spoken word of God. [*emphasis in original*]

Mark's words demonstrate that tuning the senses towards attentive listening is felt as countercultural within an age of fast-paced exchanges of communication and needs cultivation.

Although this emphasis on reason might appear in line with modernist norms of autonomy (and critical of a 'postmodern' fragmentation of meaning), the turn to the self implied in norms of rationality is bound together here with a heteronomous impulse to 'deny the self', in turning to attend to God as other. How, then, do these norms of 'public' listening relate to 'personal' listening in more private city spaces?

LISTENING PERSONALLY

The church leaders suggest a variety of techniques for 'personal' listening, enabling individuals' bodies to become vessels for the words they hear. These include writing out verses from the Bible reading and displaying them around the home, talking to and praying with others about the sermon, reading and 'praying through' Bible readings from the service later in the week, and writing out the notes taken during the sermon into a diary. Church members are encouraged to download audio files of the sermons and email them to friends, and play and discuss them with others in their workplace or university Christian unions, and many members of the congregation subscribe to the church's podcast channel. Predating these technologies, there is a history at St John's of recording sermons for circulation and repeated listening via CDs and cassettes, and the church's media department has sermons dating back to the mid 1960s stored, with 6500 of these available online.[12] Individuals who'd been members of the church for several years sometimes had favourite

---

[12] Mark stated that while one of the aims of putting the talks online was evangelistic, aiming to 'extend the reach' of St John's globally (he mentioned that talks had been downloaded in 136 different countries), but he also emphasized the pedagogical aim of facilitating attentive listening: 'The aim is ... to improve the quality of listening. When a person listens to a talk in church, within a few days you can only remember a fairly small portion of it. But if you listen to it again

sermons they listened to repeatedly. Jenny, an insurance worker, told me there was a talk on the Psalms that she listened to while ironing that 'just hits the spot and encourages you to keep going'. She said that now she has an iPhone 'I put the earphones on and listen to a talk in the middle of the night', and commented that she found this better than reading the Bible in the night because she does not have to put the light on and disturb her husband.

Reading the Bible in 'quiet times' is understood as the primary means of 'personal listening'.[13] Giving a talk to students about 'developing your relationship with God', Liz said, 'we need to give ourselves time in the day to let whatever we've been reading [from the Bible] sink into your heart'. She said that during her walk to work, she meditates on a passage, thinking through what it shows about God and what it might mean for her friends. She offered the students practical tips for their engagement with the Bible, suggesting they could 'put verses on the fridge, or on your desk' and memorize verses: 'a wonderful resource for times when you need to turn to them. I still know verses I learnt as a child.' Following her talk, students were asked to talk with each other about how to be more disciplined in their personal daily Bible study and shared their tips about what helps them focus in 'quiet times' when concentration wanders, and how they might better cultivate habits of attentiveness in their listening.

Some individuals at St John's were critical of this privileging of rationality, however. One student who'd recently started coming to St John's expressed her critique of the approach characterizing small group meetings: 'to understand everything in the context, you have to know so much history, and I think . . . it's too much emphasis on that'. She said she felt as if God was being 'made normal, kind of standardized and made quite scientific and . . . put in a box'. Hannah, who'd been at St John's for over twenty years, expressed a sense that through her time there she had lost a sense of emotional intimacy in her relationship with God. She said, 'I think sometimes we are *too* rational, and not emotional enough . . . I wouldn't ever want to take away from the rational side of [St John's], but sometimes I think we perhaps don't allow ourselves to love God enough.' John, who'd previously attended a charismatic church, said he found services at St John's 'quite dry . . . it's all stand up, sit down, hands in pockets'. In the Rooted group, individuals sometimes opened meetings by praying that the study 'would not just be intellectual, but Lord, that you would change our hearts and lives by your Word'. Despite the discursive

---

or a third time, your attention is very much greater, that is the beauty of recording, the fact that you can stop and go back if you didn't get a point. So it's extending the reach and also the depth of listening.'

[13] Almost all members of the church I interviewed said they were engaged in regular individual daily Bible reading, often using guidance notes or books that can be bought at the bookstall in church, with these 'quiet times' averaging between ten and forty-five minutes, although some members also said that they sometimes found this discipline a struggle.

privileging of rationality, individuals therefore still desired an experience of God that is both intellectual/rational and emotional/intimate.

The busyness and instrumentalized urban orientation towards time Simmel highlights can affect individual listening practices. When I interviewed Matthew, he described working in the city as 'like the Fritz Lang movie *Metropolis*: coming in, clocking in, doing their shift, clocking out, and there's very little left for life'. The long working hours of most members of St John's means finding time to listen in their daily routines is felt as a constant struggle. Describing her quiet times, Jenny said that on an average morning these would be fifteen minutes, and added: 'It depends on how panicky I am about work, whether I can actually get my act together to realize that this is more important . . . I try to pray about what I've read and learnt . . . but I must admit that I never spend as much time as I'd like, and I'm often conscious of the fact that I'm thinking, gosh, well, if I keep going till then, then I'll get to work by then.' Therefore although members of St John's develop a desire to listen and sense that this should be their priority, the actual practising of this can be felt to be an ongoing struggle, and the church leaders are aware of this, as exemplified in David's praying for the congregation one service:

> Thank you, our loving Lord, that you know everything about us. You know how busy we've made ourselves, you know the long lists of things we think we have to do, and we pray that it would become a joy to us to listen to the Lord Jesus day by day. Please put this discipline at the centre of our beings and as we listen, please enable us, we pray, by your Holy Spirit, to act on what you say.

In and through the performative effect of these words, we can see an understanding of the evangelical subject as divided within himself, aware he is distracted and divided in his attention, and labouring to come closer to the ideal of the attentive, undistracted listener. Thus while listening to God is felt as a means of directing attention to a transcendent voice beyond the busy times and spaces of the city, it also divides the subject, introducing a disposition and moral demands in tension with these, further contributing to the experience of subjective fragmentation.

Both 'public' and 'personal' listening practices are techniques of subjectivation, as individuals seek to form themselves as 'abiding in the words of Jesus'. Coleman analyses the importance of internalizing the words of scripture in Pentecostalism, in which the born-again believer does not interpret the words of the Bible, but rather receives them through the Holy Spirit (2000: 127). At St John's, there is this same emphasis on internalizing the words of the Bible as enabling access to an ultimate source of truth, but in contrast with Pentecostal culture, there is little emphasis on the Holy Spirit: one of the student group members joked that critics of St John's from other churches label its understanding of the Trinity as 'God: Father, Son, and Holy Scripture'. This indicates that it is not only members of St John's who are conscious of the particular habitus the church seeks to develop in distinction from others in a competitive urban religious marketplace, but that other churches are also aware of such differentiations. As members of St John's then seek to shape their thoughts, knowledge, and attitudes towards self and others through these embodied techniques of engaging with and internalizing these words, they seek to understand themselves as *subjects* obedient to and receiving their identity from the Spoken Word.

A complex picture of evangelical subjectivity emerges from these practices of internalizing sacred language, rational listening, and desire for intimate relationship with God. Although this emphasis on reason might appear in line with modern autonomy, this exceeds the boundaries of the autonomous subject of Enlightenment modernity: when the evangelical hears her own thoughts, she also hears God 'inside' herself in the words of the Bible she has internalized, and the meaning of this is only comprehensible through her being part of a community of believers, whose identity is configured as facing towards—and in tension with—the world. This intersubjective formation of the listener is captured in a passage from John's Gospel that the Rooted group were studying one evening. Jesus, addressing his disciples, says: 'Abide in me, and I in you . . . If you abide in me, and my words abide in you, ask whatever you wish, and it will be done for you' (John 15: 4–7, ESV). Being in relationship with Jesus is seen as having His words abiding *within* the individual's interiority, but this presented in terms of a choice: '*if* you abide in me and my words abide in you' (John 15: 4–7, ESV). The voice the evangelical subject learns to hear through listening to sermons in church, through listening to podcasts of these, or when reading the Bible in which it is one's own inner thought that is 'heard', is experienced as God speaking. As these sacred words are heard, taken up, and made the individual's *own*, the boundaries between self and other in the mediation of an evangelical identity are blurred, as God, objectified as Other, is experienced within the self.

Members of St John's form themselves as listeners through techniques of making the words of the Bible their own. Although this is presented as an individualizing choice, this is bound up with the ideal of obedient, disciplined subjection to the Word which members of the church hold, as Hugo described, as 'the Word of total wisdom and total authority', anchoring meaning and identity. Although there is a sense of human agency implied in the valuing of rationality, this is held together with a critique of autonomy, and David said that what stops people accepting God is 'that they don't want to submit to Him. When it comes down to it, they don't want someone else deciding how they should live, their autonomy is too important to them . . . This is what we call sin.'

Members of St John's are therefore 'un-modern' in the sense of their being marked by their relation to the spoken Word they strive to heed. Although their working to form themselves as listeners implies a sense of individual agency, this listening also reveals a desire to direct attention towards something that transcends the self, whose address, asking for their response, simultaneously individuates them. Jonathan, a young graduate, criticized charismatic evangelical songs because they 'make the focus the individual much more than God and who *He* is, what He's done for us, who we are in the light of Him . . . I used to turn up at church and . . . would be asked right off the back to sing a song that basically expressed what *I* felt about God and what *I* want to do for God . . . Then I arrived at [St John's], where . . . we'd start with singing songs about God and about Him and about His love rather than our love, and His grace rather than our goodness, and the focus is Him rather than us . . . And that reminds me of why I want my life to be about Him.'

The body pedagogic means of incorporation into the church in the act of listening is both a form of communion with others while also sowing the 'seeds of individualism' as their individual bodies become vessels of redemption through the choice to receive and submit to Jesus's words (Mellor and Shilling 2010: 32). This creates a sense of separation from those outside the church and connection with others in the church, while also indexing the inter- and intrasubjectivity of the evangelical in relation to God, who is felt as both Other and experienced within the self. Graham Ward articulates these central paradoxes of Christian faith through the metaphor of participation, which implies a 'relational ontology' that he sees summarized in Christ's words to his disciples, 'he dwells in me, and I in him' (John 6:56, KJV):

> In the conception of a Christian praxis, there is no room for a . . . modern notion of self-sufficiency. This already implicates us in a different construal of freedom than that operating in the notion of the liberal secular subject . . . This does not mean that Christians have no sense of their singularity, their uniqueness . . . In speaking . . . of a relational ontology in a Christian act in which the subject is always participating in that which transcends himself or herself—indeed, not only transcends but grounds any sense of there being a he or a she—I do not wish to implode notions of selfhood but to refigure them.
>
> (2009: 185)

Ward's theological exposition evokes central paradoxes implicated in the nature of subjectivity and agency that members of St John's listening practices also index. The nature of subjection implied in this notion of Christian agency can be interpreted as a means of expressing irreducible interconnections between self and other,[14] human agency and subjection, and experiences of power and powerlessness, drawing into question ideals of self-sufficiency and individualism.

---

[14] These interconnections are profoundly implicated in the very relationship between individual subjectivity and words, as 'our' words, which have always come from outside, are never only 'ours': 'when I listen to myself, to my words, to the sound of my voice, I can hear others: I hear others "inside" myself' (Levin, cited in Schmidt 2000: 35). See also Strhan 2012: 25–6.

CONCLUSION: '*THE STILL POINT*'

Western modernity can be seen as Janus-faced in the conceptions of self it promotes—a Kantian ascetic, disciplined self, and the expressive-affective mobile self, both of which we might see as derived from different Protestant cultures—Protestant asceticism, and the emotional effervescence of eighteenth- and nineteenth-century conversionist movements (Turner 2011). The culture of listening at St John's discursively privileges the ascetic, disciplined self, but this is held together with expressive-affective dispositions, as individuals seek to have their 'hearts and lives' changed by their listening. This aesthetic of listening constructs a boundary of separation from 'others' who do not hear God or who place emphasis on other means of connecting with the divine, most prominently charismatic evangelicals, shaping a distinctive institutional identity for St John's in comparison with other churches in London. It also constructs a distance marking God as Other, yet as they consume His words they experience this distance as transcended, and seek to discipline themselves to become better listeners and more attentive to the Spoken Word. Their seeking to internalize the words of God expresses their desire for their subjectivities to be shaped by a transcendent source of meaning, for *all* of their life, as Jonathan stated, to be about Him, rather than experiencing themselves as the authors of their own meanings, even if in practice, they are conscious that this is a struggle.

The urban soundscapes of members of St John's are fragmented as their modes of interaction are shaped by sounds, voices and other modes of practice that affect their listening to God. Jonathan compared the busyness and noise of London life with his rural upbringing:

> Though London has its beauty, it is in no way close to what we find in nature, and that [nature] reminds me of the gravity of the world we live in, and God's place in it, or over it . . . And the busyness, London is a very busy place to live . . . there are so many options of things you can do, it's a city that defines itself through busyness and work and experience, yeah, a sort of high-octane life, I guess . . . There isn't a lot of quiet . . . just peace and quiet is quite rare in London, in any urban environment, I guess, but in London especially.

Although their listening may be pressured through the relentless busyness of middle-class urban life, it can at the same time be seen as a means of constructing times within the week outside the hyperspeed of their globalized urban locations and finding a 'still small point of the turning world / . . . where past and future are gathered' (Eliot 1974: 191).

The idealization of rational 'public' listening David articulates on one level seems to correspond with norms of rationality in broader understandings of a modern 'public sphere' (Habermas 1989).[15] Yet, on another level, it might *also*

---

[15] Space here precludes discussion of the historical interrelation of evangelical Christianity and the norms of a public sphere and democratic life, themes which have been extensively

to a certain extent be conceptualized in terms of a 'counterpublic', cutting across such public/private distinctions. Hirschkind argues that the temporal frame of the Islamic *umma* mediated through listening to sermons encourages not only ethical self-formation but also critique of contemporary politics and calls for moral renewal (p. 118). At St John's, listening practices mediate, as we saw in Hugo's sermon, a temporal frame orientated towards a past history of God's relationship with His people and His future promises to make the faithless city holy. This likewise, therefore, encourages individuals to examine both their own everyday practices *and* broader moral and political norms in the light of these, shaping, for example, their critique of a broader culture of individualism. However, as we saw in the previous chapter, church members' willingness to express such critiques outside the church is inhibited by norms of privacy and reserve.

While this 'public' listening does shape members of the church's orientations towards their own moral formation and wider public and political life, this 'counterpublic' does not undercut notions of public and private to the extent Hirschkind outlines in Egypt. Furthermore, while Hirschkind's informants were 'critical of rationalist, academic approaches ... [that] succeeded in neither grabbing the attention of an audience nor stirring the pious passions' (2001: 630), at St John's, 'reason' is itself deemed a virtue, as the means of relating to God is understood as primarily a form of knowledge. As Luke, a postgraduate student, put this: '*feeling* God as present—I don't know what that feels like ... I *know*, I have knowledge, and ... I *believe* that God is always there watching over us, and that ... His love extends to all of us, in terms of actually caring about what we're doing all the time.' Yet although rationality is discursively privileged above emotion at St John's in a way that is distinctive from Hirschkind's informants' listening, individuals' desire is likewise to form themselves in obedience to a Spoken Word orienting them towards a transcendent beyond the fragmentation of the city.

De Certeau's narrative of a shift away from a 'listening' economy towards the authority of the individual in modernity captures how members of St John's locate both broader culture as shaped by ideals of autonomy and their descriptions of the dangers of idolizing the self. Their struggles to find time for 'personal' listening in their busy urban lives contributes to their consciousness of an internal fragmentation, which serves to deepen their sense of both difference from and dependence on God. Yet amid the frenetic, fragmented soundscapes of the city, their collective listening to long, intellectually challenging sermons and their listening to each other in Bible study groups demonstrates the tuning of their aesthetic sensibilities to resonate with the rhythms of past practices as they seek to become, in David's words, 'the people

---

debated in relation to the formative era of American politics and religion (see, for example, Hatch 1989; Jon Butler 1990; Porterfield 2012).

who give ourselves to listen to Him'. While in many ways their cultural locations are firmly in step with the logics of urban modernity, there is also something that resists total assimilation as their ambition to be 'aliens and strangers' is both performed in and shaped by their formation as listening subjects.

The focus on disciplined attention to the Word at St John's demonstrates a continuing function of 'listening' as an identity marker, objectifying conservative evangelicalism as different from other Christian traditions that place more emphasis on the visible manifestation of emotions or the bodily performance of rituals. Yet despite evangelicals' lack of discursive emphasis on the materiality of linguistic mediations, we have seen that they are nevertheless highly conscious of the embodied techniques by which they experience themselves as in relationship with God. Practices of attentive listening—to sermons, to each other, and to the words of internal thought when reading the Bible—are the aesthetic form through which the transcendent is experientially mediated in their bodies. This might be expressed in terms of John Donne's description of the church as an echo of the voice of God: 'The scriptures are God's voice, the church is His echo – a re-doubling, a repeating of some particular syllables and accents of the same voice' (cited in Winkett 2010: 142). For members of St John's, faith is embodied as their speaking and listening bodies become the means by which they learn to understand themselves as experiencing the voice of God echoing in a culture where this sound is felt as anomalous. Yet because of their simultaneous locations in the busyness of the city, this hearing is always interrupted, and introduces a further sense of fragmentation that is specific to their desire to be better disciples. Let us turn to explore how the personality of God towards which they seek to become oriented in this listening provides a means of finding coherence in response to this.

5

What Does God Want? Coherence, Love, and the Personality of God

'Which commandment is the most important of all?' Jesus answered, 'The most important is, "Hear, O Israel: The Lord our God, the Lord is one. And you shall love the Lord your God with all your heart and with all your mind and with all your strength." The second is this: "You shall love your neighbour as yourself." There is no other commandment greater than these."'

(Mark 12:28–31, ESV)

As members of St John's listen with each other, they are learning to listen to God. David said in one sermon, '*Why* is it that listening to Jesus is the one priority that really counts? . . . The answer of course . . . has to do with who He is and what He has come to do . . . [W]e should listen to Jesus because of who He is, and we should listen to Him because of what He has done. He has come down from God to earth, to declare to us the character, the concerns, the priorities of God . . . Without Jesus, no-one knows God. With Jesus, it is as if a great doorway has been opened into heaven, and we can see God, know God, relate to God, experience God, in this life.' Here David articulated a theological rationale for listening to Jesus's words: it is through these they can know God's character. But how does that character affect them? How does it shape who they are as subjects?

We have seen that as members of St John's formed themselves as listeners, they learnt to experience God as mediated *in* the words they hear. Although their modes of embodiment are important, these are pushed below conscious attention so that it is the *content* of the words they learn to focus on, conveying their experience of God. As the words of the Bible, and specifically the words of Jesus, are experienced as the means by which they know God, then, to borrow a phrase from W. J. T. Mitchell, what does God *want* of them? To understand everyday conservative evangelical experiences, we need to explore how God has His own life and loves within evangelicals' lives, which are irreducible to and transcend—yet also exert a pressure on—their immanent social relations. We have explored the role that modes of speaking and listening play in evangelical subject formation, yet the personality of God inscribed in these practices through cultural sediments predating modernity is also an actor, and what He is felt to desire shapes evangelicals' practices, desires, and the formation of their subjectivities.

In asking what God wants, I am not intending to offer a theological answer. When I introduced myself to church members and explained that I was exploring the difference their faith made to their everyday lives, several people told me that to answer that, I ought to read the Bible. I did not do that. Yet their advice, while perhaps influenced by evangelistic impulses, demonstrates their consciousness that one way they experience their lives as distinctive from those around them is shaped by their relationship with the Bible, and this is bound up with their conviction that through the Bible they experience God. Through their engagement with the Bible in different settings, they relate to a God whose character has specific contours and who wants certain things of them. The personality of this God then has a *social* agency, shaping who these subjects are as they seek to respond to the demands they experience Him making, which affects the binding and unbinding of their social relations with others.

There is a growing interest among anthropologists in how individuals relate to the divine or transcendental (e.g. Luhrmann 2012; Meyer 2008, 2010), and Chapman, Naguib, and Woodhead (2012) have examined how people's understanding of God is influenced by broader macro-level social changes such as individualization. They argue that within British evangelicalism and charismatic Christianity, God has become much closer to the individual, as an intimate, loving friend who supports a personal journey through life, a God who makes 'more sense of the demands and opportunities faced by middle-class Britons of the post-Thatcher era, and for black and ethnic minority Christians making their way within it' (2012: 179). They note that such a God also has political implications, which include embracing consumer capitalism and an openness to neoliberalism' (p. 190). This tracing of 'God-change' within British religious landscapes demonstrates the potential of attending to the specific contemporary and historical contours of sacred figures. Turning in this chapter to explore what God *wants* in evangelicals' experience raises questions not only about 'God-change', but makes the intersubjective space of the relationship between evangelical subject and God a field of investigation. My aim here is to orient analysis of evangelicalism towards everyday relations, processes, and affects, to consider not only 'what evangelicals want' (Smith 2000), but to reverse that question and consider how evangelicals understand themselves to be centrally concerned with what God wants of *them*. Before exploring this, let us briefly return to Simmel's thesis, which provides a model for investigating the social agency of a divine figure without entering into metaphysical speculation.

In 'The Personality of God', Simmel begins his analysis of God's personality through considering the nature of human personality. He argues that human personalities are formed as multiple unconscious psychic elements within us that are in a state of continuous interaction 'forge themselves into the unity we call personality' (1997h: 50). Human personality is not a stable, unified centre of the person, but always an interrelation of multiple parts as they adapt to, transfer and penetrate each other (p. 50). Simmel argues that there could only be 'perfect' personalities if this interaction between the personality's elements were part of a perfectly unified whole, but this is impossible, since '[o]ur psyche is as much enmeshed in a world external to itself as is our physical body; influences are at work within it that cannot be accounted for by our psyche alone' (p. 51). The structure of time also prevents psychic unity: temporal progression requires '"memory" of the past in order to bring its content into an ever fragmentary interaction', and this prevents 'any unity of all of its content' (p. 51).

It is only in God that the perfect personality of complete unity and coherence is found. God is 'the ultimate realization of personality', for He 'knows no "memory" in the human, temporal sense, which always assumes its opposite, the act of forgetting. For Him there is no past . . . The wholeness and unity of His being is not subject to the fragmentariness and incompleteness of temporal incoherence' (p. 51). The divine personality of atemporal coherence is transcendent, yet this absolute unity does not provide imaginative resources for the human mind to grasp, and immanent images, such as the Christian Trinity, are needed (pp. 52, 59).

Simmel suggests that Christianity first articulated the idea of a God who was both transcendent and 'at the same time a personal god, displaying the cohesive, unifying strength of this form in the unconditional breadth of His being and deeds' (p. 176). He argues that people draw on ideas to create a sense of life's meaning, and that God's perfection provides resources for people to order the fragments of their lives into a pattern of coherent meaning and purpose. To the person of faith, God embodies ideals of 'power, justice and perfection' (p. 61), and these stand above the relativity of our fragmented existence: 'He is the pure meaning from which our relative, imperfect, and impure lives gain their meaning and their form' (p. 61). While modernity—and, paradigmatically, the metropolis—leads to cultural and subjective fragmentation, this conveys more 'fully the unity of the object of our faith and our behavior toward it' (p. 38).

In contrast with the standard sociological view of fragmentation as leading to secularization, for Simmel, this coherent God offers resources to fashion a sense of coherence and unity out of the fragmentary conditions of modern life. This is only possible through God's transcendence: Simmel argues that the multiple concerns of individuals' lives converge as the object of faith 'in a sphere beyond the empirical world, because it would be impossible to reconcile our manifold and diverse spiritual concerns in an empirical context' (1997e: 37). He characterizes the nature of believers' relations with this transcendent as desire. Desire depends on a distance between the subject and the object of her desire, and the value of what we desire depends on its capacity to resist our possession. He argues that in the relation between person and God, internal senses of disharmony create the resistance needed for 'the power of religion to express itself and make itself felt', describing human desire for God as love (p. 38). He notes Plato's positing of love as a third condition between having and not having. Love 'means to have and not to have at one and the same time, an infinitely secure possession that nevertheless, each day and with untiring efforts, must be acquired anew, not merely preserved' (pp. 38–9). As love increases, its goal is always unattainable, and for this reason 'it is apt to speak of God as "Love" itself', as the relation with God is experienced in this state of having and not having that is love:

> In our feeling for God, the tension between having and not having reaches its ultimate climax; for whether this emotion remains finite in our love for finite beings or whether it merely hints vaguely and uncertainly at the infinite, both are directed toward Him, and therefore are truly infinite. The religious soul is bound to its God equally strongly by the bonds of having and those of not having; or rather one might say that its God comes into being at the point where these conflicting bonds, extended beyond the finite world, converge.
>
> (pp. 39–40)

God is experienced as both present and absent, and the promise of coherence that the personality of God offers is 'at every moment . . . unity and unity yet to be' (p. 43).

While religion provides resources for integrating the fragments of modern life and the self through developing an orientation towards a transcendent unity, at the same time it introduces a further form of fragmentation that divides the subject. This is because religion is itself a cultural form at odds with other cultural forms: 'it resolves the contradictions it finds outside itself as well as those which arise constantly between itself and the totality of the rest of life' (p. 43). And yet that sense of fragmentation, which provides resistance between the fragmented self and the coherence of God, increases the individual's desire for God. Thus religious faith is 'a never ending task, as a process of development in which each stage attained points infinitely beyond itself' (p. 44). Simmel therefore sees God's personality as having social agency in offering a promise of coherence and relief from internal contradictions, while simultaneously intensifying consciousness of subjective division as it leads us to become increasingly aware of internal divisions in contrast with this pure divine unity. At the same time, this orientation towards transcendence leads individuals to develop specific dispositions and desires in tension with broader cultural norms, and this process further contributes to the experience of cultural fragmentation.

To what extent does this interplay of coherence, fragmentation, and the effort to work on the self still hold in the experience of members of St John's today? Simmel's somewhat mystical approach towards religion is at some distance from conservative evangelicals' focus on knowledge, evidence, and rationality. Yet I will suggest that his emphasis on human desire for a God who is coherent and transcendent helps open up conservative evangelicals' experience of the character of God.

In tracing how members of St John's experience God's personality, I primarily address two characteristics: unity and desire. My focus on these is because they have particular agency in forming conservative evangelical subjectivities. My resources here are those forming the instauration of God in the lives of members of St John's: the Bible, sermons reflecting on Bible passages, the words of hymns and prayers, and particular creedal statements. I begin by focusing on the characteristic of unity central to monotheism, and then God's desire, and consider how these characteristics are mediated in the experience of church members, so that they experience God as asking certain things of them. I then describe how members of the church experience themselves as constantly falling short of these ideals, and show that their language of adultery, idolatry, and guilt enables them to construct a narrative unity that makes sense of their worldly attachments. The final section shows how their focus on Jesus's death and suffering body both intensifies and provides an emotional release from this sense of guilt, binding them in their sense of relationship with God and each other.

'THE LORD IS OUR GOD, THE LORD IS ONE'

Monotheism recognizes the existence of only one God, and this is central to how His character is articulated at St John's: the creator and ground of all that is, God is unity and integrity in person. The first of the Thirty-Nine Articles, which members of St John's see as an expression of Anglican orthodoxy, articulates this view:

> There is but one living and true God, everlasting, without body, parts or passions; of infinite power, wisdom, and goodness; the Maker, and Preserver of all things both visible and invisible. And in unity of this Godhead there be three Persons, of one substance, power, and eternity; the Father, the Son and the Holy Ghost.
>
> (cited in Church Society 2003)

This monotheism is *ethical* monotheism: God is not only understood as One, with the reality of all other gods denied, but is supremely concerned with morality and Himself possesses infinite moral virtue. In the biblical narratives that members of St John's engage with, God's goodness and power are portrayed as so infinitely greater than human characteristics that His people mostly cannot see them, and when they do, for example, in a vision, their difference from God becomes terrifyingly clear: Isaiah's response to his vision of the Lord seated on the throne was, 'Woe is me! For I am lost; for I am a man of unclean lips, and I dwell in the midst of a people of unclean lips; for my eyes have seen the King, the LORD of hosts!' (Isaiah 6:5, ESV). Preaching a sermon on this passage, Hugo emphasized that this is a *moral* difference, stating that the word 'holy' the seraphim repeat in Isaiah's vision 'is used to describe God in His total differentness from us. His otherness from His creation. It's used over 800 times about God in the Old Testament and it speaks of . . . His moral excellence and His perfection and His righteousness.' Hugo said that this holiness—the 'Godness' and 'goodness of God'—speaks of 'the essence of His nature, which is revealed in the outshining of His glory, filling the whole creation, the whole earth is full of it . . . God is *the* holiest that you could ever imagine. He is set apart from us . . . even the best of human beings cannot approach anywhere near to the righteous, awesome, exalted, omnipotent God.' Isaiah recognizes himself as sinful, a 'man of unclean lips', and Hugo described what the correct response to this vision of 'the expression of His perfect nature'—should be: not to be 'fearful before a powerful creator' but rather to 'to be sinners and recognize ourselves as such before a holy God'.

While members of St John's learn of this understanding of God's infinite moral goodness, power, and transcendent otherness through listening to such sermons and reading the Bible, at the same time, this God is described as intensely personal: contra the Thirty Nine Articles, He has passions and loves of His own and desires a relationship with His people. The creation narrative in Genesis, which was the focus of several sermons during my fieldwork, describes God as making man in His own image: He does not want to be alone. And, as Mitchell points out, this man, created in the divine image, also has his own desires and 'asks for a mate to love him in turn' (2005: 57). Thus we see that this God, although transcendent, is profoundly relational and makes beings who are likewise relational.

Although biblical narratives such as the Book of Isaiah characterize God's nature in terms of a sense of transcendent unity and otherness, conservative evangelicals, drawing on the relational language *also* used, have no hesitation using personal terms to convey His characteristics. One of St Paul's privileged soteriological tropes for God's relation to humans, frequently referred to at St John's, is 'reconciliation'. This, as Alister McGrath writes, implies 'that the transformation through faith of the relationship between God and sinful human beings is like the reconciliation of two persons – perhaps an alienated husband and wife' (1994: 207–8). In conservative evangelical teaching, what God *desires* is a relationship with His people, and as the Only God, He wants people to respond to Him alone in worship, obedience, and love. Yet despite this language of intimacy and love, this is held together with a sense of His otherness: Hugo preached in terms emphasizing a distinctiveness from charismatic evangelicals' emphasis on friendship with God, 'This God is not our buddy. He's not our best mate. I'm horrified when I hear even Christians talking about "the man upstairs", when we assume somehow that God is on a level with us. No; what the church needs today is this . . . overwhelming vision of holiness, of the greatness of God, that God shares His amazing mercy and grace with us but He doesn't indulge us: He isn't a Father Christmas in the sky figure.'

This understanding of God's character as Other is typically expected to lead to specific 'correct' responses: both a consciousness of one's own sinfulness in comparison with God, and to expressions of praise and adoration; for example, in a passage from 1 Chronicles that David referred to in a sermon: 'Blessed are you, O LORD, the God of Israel our father, for ever and ever. Yours, O LORD, is the greatness and the power and the glory and the victory and the majesty, for all that is in the heavens and in the earth is yours. Yours is the kingdom, O LORD, and you are exalted as head above all. Both riches and honour come from you, and you rule over all' (1 Chronicles 29:10–12, ESV).

As we saw in the previous chapter, members of St John's are encouraged by their leaders to focus in detail on specific passages as a means of hearing God speak and of learning of His character and the 'correct' responses to this. They also seek to locate these passages in the context of an understanding of the narrative of the whole Bible, and the third year of the church's Bible study programme involves reading the whole Bible over the course of a year in the small groups. Through this narrative framework and its explication in sermons and Bible study groups, the church leaders hope that members will develop a sense of temporal progression in God's dealings with His people in terms of, first, a covenant relationship established with Israel and then, second, a new covenant through the person of Jesus. In this interpretation, what God wants of His people was first objectified in the legal codes given to the Israelites, and in the first commandment of the legal code, God is concerned with His people's worship of Him only: He forbids the making of rival idols or images (Exodus 20: 1–6). As God spends more time on this commandment than others of the Decalogue, this prohibition on idolatry appears to be the one He deems most important, especially as the others can be suspended at times.[1] As Mitchell notes, we see God demanding the fidelity of His people, and He is jealous when they worship another. The golden calf the Israelites build in Exodus 'is a substitute for God, like a rival lover who moves in when the husband is away. The Israelites are "whoring after strange gods", and idolatry is a form of adultery' (2005: 133). This monotheistic prohibition on idolatry is still today a significant feature of how members of St John's

---

[1] For example, killing is allowed as a punishment for idolatry: an example of this is when God tells Moses and the Levites to kill those Israelites who had worshipped the golden calf.

understand and experience God's character and His expectations: God as One and the Lord of all asks, first of all, that His followers worship Him and Him alone. Yet, as biblical narratives convey a sense of God *wanting* His people to respond to Him in obedience and love, desire implies the absence of the thing desired, and members of St John's emphasize that the Bible is a story of people *not* relating to God in the ways He wants, turning away from Him towards other gods, such as the golden calf.

While the legal codes make it clear that God tolerates no rivals and wants His people to worship Him alone, these biblical narratives also set out moral obligations, requiring that His followers act with equity and justice. As conservative evangelicals experience God's personality as the expression of perfect goodness, wisdom, and justice, they understand Him as requiring that His people also exemplify these virtues. This expression of morality has been understood in broad terms as involving the curbing of human desires for wealth, power, and pleasure (Miles 1996: 111). But God's *desire* for His followers' morality, like His desire for their faithful devotion, indicates that this is often lacking: His people continually fail to meet the moral require-ments He sets out. At St John's, this was emphasized as leaders and members of the church repeatedly articulated not only a sense of their own individual sinfulness, but referred to a collective 'sinfulness' and 'rebellion' of God's people throughout history. This is how Jerusalem, for example, was described in the Bible reading that preceded Hugo's sermon discussed in the previous chapter:

> How the faithful city
> > has become a whore,
> > > she who was full of justice!
> Righteousness lodged in her,
> > but now murderers . . .
> Everyone loves a bribe
> > and runs after gifts.
> They do not bring justice to the fatherless,
> > and the widow's cause does not come to them.
>
> Therefore the Lord declares,
> > the Lord of hosts,
> > > the Mighty One of Israel . . .
> 'I will turn my hand against you
> > and will smelt away your dross as with lye . . .
> Afterward you shall be called the city of righteousness,
> > the faithful city.'
> > > > > (Isaiah 1: 21, 23–4, ESV)

God, as pure unity and coherence, is described as wanting His people to be devoted to Him only, and this is expressed through their obediently doing what He says.

Equally significant to conservative evangelical teaching on God's character is His expressing His love through forgiving His people when they fall short of His standards: He wants to be with them despite their constant turning away. This desire for reconciliation is seen as most powerfully expressed in the sacrificial death and resurrection of Jesus that is central to conservative evangelical theology. Jesus's suffering body offers the possibility of breaching the separation between God and humanity, a story showing God suffering, as the atemporal, transcendent God enters into space and time, in a sequence of descent and ascent. Evangelicals describe Jesus, as God incarnate, as providing new ways for His followers to relate to God, and what He asks, in terms of morality, exceeds the requirements of the legal code: 'You must therefore be perfect, even as your heavenly Father is perfect' (Matthew 6: 48, ESV).

In this very brief sketch of how God's personality is instaurated in conservative evangelical teaching as unified and as expressing desire, this character might appear to express paradoxical traits: He is both transcendent otherness *and* demonstrates intense, jealous concern for His people. And yet conservative evangelicals (mostly) do not feel this paradox as a contradiction, since the Bible, the authoritative Spoken Word, emphasizes that this God is One. As One, He also wants His people to be of one heart, mind, and strength in their love and devotion to Him. How then is this distinctive divine personality practically mediated in the experience of members of St John's? And what effect does this have in forming their subjectivities and shaping their social relations in the city?

DESIRING COHERENCE

The primary means through which members of the church learn to experience God as having a life and personality of His own within their lives are through learning to hear Him speak in the Bible, listening to sermons, discussions in Bible study groups, and the inculcation of habits of devotional Bible reading and prayer. Occasionally there are talks specifically focused on explicating His character. In the third year track of Bible study groups, for example, there was a series of talks on 'the Doctrine of God' at the groups' weekend away. These examined a selection of Bible passages, and the groups were also asked by the speaker to discuss Reformation creedal statements such as the Thirty-Nine Articles, the Belgic Confessions, and the Westminster Declaration of Faith. The speaker cited passages from the Bible that he said described God as 'pure Being', 'Light—searing moral purity', 'Truth—it is the essence of God that He tells the truth', and 'in His essence unchanging—the same yesterday, today, and forever'. He then asked group members to look up these passages together, and in the feedback session after this, he emphasized that God is 'absolutely certain, you can build your life on Him', and contrasted 'divine simplicity' with human 'multiplicity'—'God cannot be cut up into bits, you are made up of parts.' The groups' discussion of these passages emphasized God's immutability, atemporality, moral perfection, and His requiring moral purity from His followers.

Although here the personality of God was mediated in part through discussion of doctrinal statements, in the church members' everyday practices, God's personality emerged more through their interactions with the books of the Bible they were reading or listening to sermons about. During my fieldwork, the narratives members of the church were engaging with focused, for example, on God's actions in relation to Israel in the books of Isaiah and 1 and 2 Chronicles, on the person of Jesus in Mark and John's gospels, and on St Paul's discussion of God's redemption of His people in 1 and 2 Corinthians and Colossians, in their weekly Bible study group meetings. All these contributed to an understanding of God's personality in relational terms that was held together with ideas of His atemporal transcendence and immutability, contrasting with the rhythms of their busy middle-class metropolitan lives, as, for example, workers in global corporations in the city arrived at St John's from business meetings—sometimes having just flown in from other countries—just in time to lead their Rooted meetings.

In a sermon on 1 Chronicles, as part of a series focusing on the 'Unity of the Kingdom' in contrast with a 'Divided World', David emphasized that God's greatness requires 'wholehearted devotion and affection' from His followers. The Bible reading for that service included the expression of praise in the passage from 1 Chronicles cited earlier, and David discussed this in his sermon:

> Why should we give our undivided and wholehearted loyalty and service to God? Because He's worth it, because He'll never let us down . . . His is The Greatness. The Majesty. It was Muhammad Ali who some of you will remember used to say, 'I am the greatest' . . . and you know, Muhammad Ali, as you look at him now, you think, 'what a tragedy'. But of God we can say . . . 'Yours is The Greatness, the majesty'. But not just the greatness and the majesty, but also the power and the victory . . . At the centre of the five attributes, glory speaks of His moral, eternal, philosophical weightiness. Truth, purity, integrity, justice, love, compassion, severity, holiness. Why give God wholehearted service? Because He's worth it. And then the end of verse 11 is wonderful, isn't it, because it speaks of exclusive, personal power. Universal: 'yours is the kingdom, O Lord, and you are exalted as head above all'. Exclusive: '*yours* is the kingdom, O Lord'. Personal: 'yours is the kingdom, *O Lord*'.

We see in these words how the personality of God expressed by King David in this passage from 1 Chronicles, in which God is described as the perfection of human values, shaped David's expression of his understanding of God's personality in his sermon, and he understands this as entailing specific requirements for His followers.

This reflection on God's attributes forms a sense of human separation and distance from God, which is articulated in the following verses that David repeated in his sermon, in which King David contrasts God with the transience of human life: 'But who am I, and what is my people, that we should be able thus to offer willingly? For all things have come from you, and of your own have we given you. For we are strangers before you and sojourners, as all our fathers were. Our days on earth are like a shadow and there is no abiding' (1 Chronicles 29: 14–15, ESV). Addressing these verses to the congregation, David emphasized this sense of differentiation from God:

> 'There's no abiding'. You know, you think you're young...the world is your oyster, it's all lying ahead of you, you're in your thirties, maybe you're in your teens, or maybe in your forties, you think, 'yeah, I've got loads of time'. You're just a shadow. The Bible speaks of us as a breath on a cold winter's night. You breathe it out, it's there for a second, and it's gone. So says David, very conscious at the end of his life, maybe he's 65, 75, 'look, I'm just a fleeting shadow, and you've allowed *me* to give myself wholeheartedly to this project of yours, the building of [the temple], what a privilege. How could you ever have allowed someone like me?' And the sense of privilege. The innate worth, the undeserved privilege, and then the eternal purpose.

Through this passage in 1 Chronicles, and David's preaching about it, the distance between the sense of human life as fleeting and transient and God as the eternal perfection of human values is objectified. But a sense of God's relationality with humans is also expressed here, as David identifies King David's being asked by God to build a temple with God addressing members of the church today, subjectifying them as likewise receiving the 'undeserved privilege' of working on God's 'project'.

As God's characteristics of coherence and unity reverberate in Biblical narratives which are the focus of teaching at St John's, so also does the idea that these characteristics are required of His followers, for example in the commandment to love God 'with all your heart and with all your soul and with all your strength' (Mark 12: 29–30). David emphasized this demand for coherence in relation to this passage from 1 Chronicles and commented that in the passage, King David and the Israelites 'rejoiced because with a whole heart, they offered freely to the Lord'. He said that this is a 'wonderful' verse and worth memorizing, and went on:

> That word, 'wholehearted' means exactly what it says. It speaks of every part of me. The whole of me. The psalmist...speaks of 'Lord, give me an undivided heart', it's a wonderful verse, Psalm 119. 'Give me a whole heart' he could have put. And the idea is you know, there's not this little bit of my passion focused over here on my career, and you know, this that and the other, and then a little piece of

me over here focused on God, or one piece of me focused over here on my favourite sport, and another piece focused on my X-box, and then another piece focused on-, you know, that would be a *divided* heart, wouldn't it? And it always results in a miserable life.

So it's not as if God was the focus of their energy at the Christian Union, or at camp in the summer, or midweek Rooted, and the rest of the time actually their heart was somewhere else. Rather, 'the people rejoiced because they'd given willingly, for with a whole heart they had offered freely to the Lord. David, the king, also rejoiced greatly'. It's a great summary verse, isn't it?

While in the passage from 1 Chronicles, the Israelites' wholeheartedness related to their building of the temple, David said to the congregation that they needed to interpret their lives outside the church through this interpretative framework, aiming to view their everyday work lives in terms of wholehearted, willing service to the God who is 'worth it':

> My ultimate concern, even at work, if I'm there for sixty hours next week, or some of you even longer, yeah, there will be jobs to be done and to do it properly to the glory of God, honouring His name for the advance of His kingdom, but my ultimate, absolute concern will be for the building of His people. And at the weekend, this meeting will be of paramount importance, as we gather, and midweek, whenever we gather, will be of extreme importance, because actually I'm giving myself wholeheartedly, willingly.

David's interpretation of God's requiring coherence from His people does not entail building the temple, but rather the moral demand to serve God wholeheartedly, which means that they should see their 'absolute concern' in their everyday working lives as 'the building of His people', which translates, David said, to seeing attending Sunday and midweek meetings as a central moral imperative.

Simmel contrasted God's unity with human fragmentation, and David's sermon instaurates this. His preaching about wholehearted service constructs the sense that this ethic is something members of the church *should* desire—as something God asks of them—but that they have not realized it in practice. Reflection on this demand through the form of the sermon thus functions to make individuals conscious of ways in which their actions and desires do *not* reflect this ethic. After the sermon, there was a question and answer session in which the congregation were asked to write questions on slips of paper for David. Nick, the young curate leading the session, read the first question out: 'How can we ensure we are wholeheartedly devoted to God? Even though I know I should be, other things always seem to grab my attention.' This question indicates how the sermon, performing a moral address to the congregation, encourages individuals to reflect on their own practices in the light of the ideal of wholeheartedness, and this makes listeners conscious of their struggles to be wholehearted, with the question and answer session a space for shared acknowledgement of this sense of struggle. David replied that 'whole-heartedness comes from having my heart captured by the Lord. I was reading Psalm 119 this morning as part of my daily reading and it says, "Give me a whole heart"... So two things: the human side—meditate on God and His character—and there's the God side, ask Him to give it to you.' Reflecting on God's character in this Bible passage and in listening to the sermon is thus a technique of the self through which members of the congregation are encouraged to monitor their thoughts and motivations in response. As God's personality is held up as perfect, and the 'privilege' of wholehearted service is named as an ideal, church members interrogate their own attitudes towards this ideal, and want to find ways of disciplining their actions to exemplify this wholeheartedness.

This same desire for unity within the self, formed through reflection on God's character, was also encouraged in a sermon Pete preached on truthfulness. His sermon was part of a sermon series on the Sermon on the Mount, and focused on Matthew 5: 33-49, which begins:

> Again you have heard that it was said to those of old, 'You shall not swear falsely, but shall perform to the Lord what you have sworn.' But I say to you, Do not take an oath at all, either by heaven, for it is the throne of God, or by the earth, for it is his footstool, or by Jerusalem, for it is the city of the great King. And do not take an oath on your head, for you cannot make one hair white or black. Let what you say be simply 'Yes' or 'No'; anything more than this comes from evil.
>
> (Matthew 5: 33–6, ESV)

Pete began by describing the Sermon on the Mount as a light that is a 'brilliant light that draws me like a moth to a spotlight; but the light is so bright that it burns and sears', and he said these opening verses set out God's demand for truthfulness. He read verses 33–6 again to the congregation, and said, 'let's observe the way of the world, the way of fingers crossed, of forked tongue... We know in our society something of the cost of a culture of deceit, so wracked with lies is the public life of our nation that we take very little at face value any more... We hear a politician's statement, and the first thing the pundits report is not what was said, but what wasn't, because the truth only ever lies between the lines.' He went on: 'God wanted His people to be different. Very simply: to be men and women of their words. To mean what we say and say what we mean.'

Here we see how the sermon form mediates an understanding of God's desire for His people to act morally in terms of speaking the truth. Pete said that in Jesus's time, oaths were only binding if they were sworn by the gold of the temple in Jerusalem:

> Jesus is saying, 'God is the God of the whole world', so you can't go around swearing by things and imagine somehow this oath doesn't matter because you haven't mentioned God's name... We're talking about the living God, the God of

heaven and earth, the one who knows all and sees all and hears all. How dare you play games with his name? Instead, verse 37, this is the straight talking way of God's kingdom: let what you say be simply 'yes' or 'no'. To put it even more simply: Christian, be a man or woman of your word. Anything more than that comes from the evil one, and *the point is that words are a very valuable currency. Our God is a God who chose to reveal Himself in words. He's a God who cannot lie. He keeps all of His promises and His word will never pass away.* Our Father in heaven is a God of truth, and so Jesus's question for the crowds, when it comes to our attitude to truthfulness: are you perfectly truthful, like your perfect father in heaven? Or are you more like the father of lies himself? [*emphasis mine*]

Here we see that Pete describes God's demand for coherence and truthfulness as related to an understanding not only of His moral perfection and truthfulness but also of His omniscience, as one who 'knows all and sees all and hears all'.

Pete addressed the congregation in terms that encouraged them to identify with those addressed by Jesus in the narrative, and challenged them to compare their morality with that of the 'perfect Father'. Thus this understanding of God as perfect transcendent moral integrity has agency shaping Pete's articulation of a separation between God and humans. At the same time, the sermon expressed a desire for and means of connection with God, as individuals internalize an understanding of His standards as an ethic to guide their actions. The performance of the sermon thus signifies the interrelational figuration of the congregation as they sit and listen to Pete, who is understood as having the authority to interpret Jesus's words as he addresses them from the pulpit above them. As the congregation learn to listen to God, they are *together* subjectified as those addressed to be truthful in response to a divine command, which they are encouraged to perceive as differentiating them from those around them in the world.

Pete went on to contrast this demand for truthfulness with contemporary moral life. He cited research stating that '20 per cent of all ten-minute social conversations include a lie', and addressed ways members of the congregation might be untruthful in everyday life, though adding that they shouldn't 'get into the minutiae of ethical casuistry and ask, "so what am I meant to say when my wife asks...does my bum look big in this?"'. He said it was a moral *attitude* that mattered: 'Remember that Jesus is gunning for an attitude of the heart, a commitment to be a person of truth, saying "be like your father in heaven"...We claim to have the truth; we follow the one who said, "I am the truth," and so our first point then: no lying on our lips.' Pete then went on to discuss other moral challenges he interpreted as arising from the passage, such as turning the other cheek and self-sacrifice, which he said have significance as a form of witness to non-Christians:

There is no higher destiny than to be conformed to the likeness of God. And no greater ambition for which we can labour...As we Christians become more and more like our father in heaven, as we allow the good deeds of our truth-speaking and self-sacrificing and our love to shine before the people of London, there is every hope that the people on our streets, in our offices, in our classes, that they will see our good deeds and be so attracted by them that they will want to learn of the King of Love himself.

He ended with a prayer, as the congregation bowed their heads: 'We pray that, Our Father, you would help us not just to brush His word aside, but to allow it to sink deeply into our heart... Confident of your grace again this morning, we pray that you would indeed change us and help us to hunger and thirst for this deeper righteousness. And then please, by your spirit, would you help us to live in this way, for Jesus' sake.'

The service closed with an organ-accompanied hymn, followed by the customary silent pause before the pianist began to play softly, and members of the congregation started chatting with those around them. I was sitting with Lucy, Sarah, and Cathy, all in their forties, and they began talking about the sermon. Sarah said she found 'the area of white lies really challenging'. She said she'd been on the Tube the day before, and had been really tired but had offered to give her seat up for an elderly lady, who'd said to her, 'You must be really tired yourself.' Sarah said she'd replied that she wasn't, when she had been, and said she wasn't sure if that had been the right thing to do. Lucy said she thought this was 'a difficult area', and they talked about the difficulty of avoiding half-truths and white lies, discussing the example Pete had given of saying you can't attend something you've been invited to when really you are free. Cathy said she was relieved when she was able to offer a genuine excuse for not being able to make it to a particular event she was invited to, though Sarah said she needed to have one evening at home a week, and didn't have a problem with saying so in turning down an invitation. Such is the busyness of their lives.

Here we see that bringing God's personality as 'truth' and His demand for truthfulness to conscious attention through listening to the sermon encourages members of St John's to reflect on instances of their behaviour deviating from these norms through their informal discussions after the sermon. This also instaurates a social division, naming church members as called to be truthful and differentiated from the untruthful world. The particular importance of this ethic of truthfulness, bound up with language, can be linked with a norm of sincerity. Keane argues that it was through particular linguistic practices that Protestantism produced sincerity as a modern virtue. The performance of sincerity indexes a particular kind of subject: individual, but also relational, bound up with a particular orientation of obligation towards others, since in sincerity, I not only produce words indicating my interiority, 'but am producing them *for you*; I am making myself (as an inner self) available for you in the form of external, publicly available expressions' (2007: 211). Thus sincerity necessarily involves displaying to another a connection between the words that I speak and my interior state. Many of the Protestant linguistic practices Keane discusses, such as collectively reciting creeds and confessions, were in evidence at St John's, and demonstrate how the norm of sincerity is produced through specific modes of performance. In most services, for example, the congregation recite the Church of England prayer of confession. The curate leading the evening service often introduced this by saying that this prayer is 'not appropriate for everyone here this evening', but is for people who are Christians 'who believe that Jesus died for them and that through him they have forgiveness of their sins'. He then typically gave a minute's pause for the congregation 'to look over the words of the prayer and see if you can mean them, and if you can, then please join with us'. This moment for individual reflection on whether or not the individual agreed with the words of the prayer reinforced a sense of the importance of the sincerity of the individual speaking these words, that the words they spoke corporately together should reflect their own interior condition, which is taken as the mark of who *really* is a Christian.

While Keane shows how linguistic performances in Protestantism created a normative tilt towards sincerity, I want to suggest that the personality of God understood as pure coherence *also* plays an important part in the intersubjective formation of this ethics of sincerity and truthfulness. As outlined in the previous chapter, the listening practices of church members encourage them to focus on the content of sermons and Bible passages, which leads them to focus on God's character. The unity and coherence of this character exercises agency both in how members of the church learn to relate to Him and in their self-formation, as they seek to discipline their thoughts and bodies as unified according to the transcendent ideals they perceive God as addressing to them, shaping their sense of moral distinction from 'the world'. Yet these demands also divide evangelicals within their own subjectivities, and as they inevitably fail to attain these standards of moral perfection and become conscious of their internal divisions, this intensifies their desire for a God who offers the promise of coherence. This idiom of desire evokes a different texture of relationality than the rational listening discussed in the previous chapter. How, then, does this understanding of God's relational character contribute to evangelicals' desire for coherence and the tensions they live with in everyday experience?

LOVE, ADULTERY, AND IDOLATRY

It seems obvious—to the point of trite—to say that the God who emerges in conservative evangelical experience is one who loves them. While this God is pure coherence and unity, He is also a God who loves and requires fidelity from His beloved, for them to serve Him alone. The biblical narratives members of St John's focus on describe this God as offering the possibility of reconciliation to those who have turned their backs on Him, worshipping other gods. How was this aspect of God's personality mediated at St John's? Kevin Lewis O'Neill describes his Guatemalan Pentecostal participants' desire for God as 'a slippery object of study', more accessible through participant observation than formal interviews, because it often 'lingers below the surface of narrativity, altering in innocuous ways how people live their lives and govern their bodies' (2010b: 134). At St John's, God's desire for His church and their desire for Him was not always articulated in interviews, yet the image of God as lover and of Christians as formed in intimate relationship with the divine was never far below the surface.

A student supper illustrates this. After Sunday evening services, students hang around for a supper of jacket potatoes, bacon sandwiches, chocolate, fruit, and soft drinks, over which they chat and are given a talk on a particular theme by one of the leaders. During my fieldwork, there were a couple of talks on the theme of relationship with God, and for one of these, I was sitting with Gemma and Luke from my small group, Freddie (the student curate), Archie, and Becky. Timothy, a member of the church staff in his late forties who co-ordinates the church's 'apprentices' scheme, was giving the talk. Addressing the students in his quiet voice, he said 'a relationship with God is the greatest blessing we have', and is 'vital to what God is doing'. He gave a summary of a conservative evangelical narrative of God's interrelations with humans, beginning with the Fall, God's liberation of Israel and their disobedience, and then His 'rescue mission' and the 'new covenant relation' offered to those who have faith in Jesus. Timothy said that 'God promises that one day He will rescue His people; He promises a perfect relationship with God, when He will live with them.' He then read a verse from John's Gospel: 'Jesus answered him, "If anyone loves me, he will keep my word, and my Father will love him, and we will come to him and make our home with him"' (John 14: 23, ESV). Timothy said: 'Jesus brings us into this Trinitarian relationship', and emphasized it is God who initiates this relationship: '*He* made it happen because *we* are weak and helpless.' He spoke of the relationship with God as 'a relationship of great intimacy and depth, of father and child, husband and wife, bridegroom and bride, an amazing relation of intimacy'.

Timothy then asked what 'relationship' actually means. He said that most people would tend to answer this, 'reading the Bible and praying', and said that these 'are crucial, but are *how* the relationship happens, not what it *is* ... Communication is central, but what do we expect from communication?' He said, 'our relationship with God gives us our identity ... God wants our involvement; we should be concerned with His concerns.' He added 'we should love God because He loves us and wants us to love Him ... But what does it mean to love God? Obedience? Loving each other? ... Neither of these is enough.' He said that loving God must mean 'desiring Him, feeling passionate about Him, trusting God'.

Timothy set two questions for each table to discuss: 'What does it mean to trust God? What does it mean to love God?' On our table, Gemma and Becky both said they found it hard to trust God when thinking about their future careers, which they felt anxious about. Their comments indicated their normative understanding that this sense of trust *should* have an emotional impact, leading them to feel calm in their thinking about their futures, while demonstrating their consciousness that their own emotional responses—shaped by broader conditions of economic uncertainty for young people in London and elsewhere—did not match this expectation. Becky then said that trust 'isn't just about the future, it's about the present, how we spend our time now'. She was in the middle of her finals, and said she felt she should always be revising, and had shortened her quiet times, and her flatmate had asked her whether she really needed quiet times at all. She said she'd responded, 'having quiet times is an act of trusting; spending time with God is really important'. Moving on to discuss what loving God means, Gemma said that when she tried to explain who God is to non-Christian friends, she tended to explain 'in quite abstract terms, whereas the right response should be to want them to know Him, because He's just, like, am*a*zing'.

Comments during the groups' shared feedback demonstrated how these students didn't always think of their relationship with God with the passion Timothy had described as the 'right' response. One student said, 'sometimes it's hard to love God because it's hard to know how to go about it'. Timothy responded, 'loving God means getting to know Him', and commented that cultivating the 'right' attitude is important: 'it shouldn't be a matter of reading the Bible because we're supposed to, but of reading the Bible to find out more, because He's so wonderful. Likewise, prayer shouldn't feel like a duty.' Becky then said to the whole group: 'it's easy to feel passionate about God when I've just got back from New Word Alive,[2] but I don't feel like that all the time'. Timothy responded with the analogy of marriage: 'sometimes we may not always be thinking about the fact that we are married, and we aren't necessarily always excited about being married, but the fact would remain that we *are* married, and it is likewise in our relationship with God . . . Emotion has its right place: neither too big nor too small.'

This idea of God as a bridegroom or lover and the church as given its identity in response to His love was frequently repeated in song lyrics that also reinforced this sentiment, and these were another means of mediating this understanding of God as desiring an intimate love relationship with His people. At St John's, songs were a mix of contemporary evangelical songs

---

[2] New Word Alive is an annual conference organized by British evangelical organizations such as UCCF and Keswick Ministries.

with traditional hymns (often organ-accompanied), a cultural style further marking a distinction from the dominance of contemporary songs in charismatic evangelicalism. In both the contemporary and traditional songs at St John's, lyrics often specifically linked the idea of God's love with images of Jesus's crucifixion, so that the individual singing was performatively enacting a response affirming commitment to this idea of God as faithful lover. The final two verses of one of the most frequently sung hymns during my fieldwork, 'A Debtor to Mercy Alone', by Augustus Montague Toplady (1740–78) demonstrate this:

> The work which his goodness began,
> the arm of his strength will complete;
> his promise is 'Yes' and 'Amen',
> and never was forfeited yet:
> things future, nor things that are now,
> now all things below or above,
> can make him his purpose forgo,
> or sever my soul from his love.
> Eternity will not erase
> my name from the palm of his hands;
> in marks of indelible grace
> impressed on his heart it remains:
> yes, I to the end shall endure,
> as sure as the promise is given;
> more happy and yet more secure,
> the glorified spirits in Heaven.

In these words, we see the idea of God as an agentive lover, and the Christian as responding to *His* love and *His* promises. This image of God's 'strength' was often used in reference to God, but less often in relation to the person of Jesus, whose physical vulnerability was more often a focus, while songs also evoked the idea of Jesus as lover. The song 'His Forever,' for example, describes how Jesus 'loved me 'ere I knew him' and 'drew me with his cords of love, tightly bound me to him' (Sovereign Grace Worship 2003).

While Pentecostal and charismatic song lyrics often use language conveying the idea of evangelicals' desire for God and *their* agency in this relationship (O'Neill 2010b: 144), songs at St John's focused more on God's agency as lover, as in these words.

An understanding of God as desiring His people affected how church members felt they should relate to the Bible, with different overtones from their focus on rational practice. The man leading the prayers one Sunday morning spoke of how they as a church should 'love God's Word like a bride loves letters from her groom'. This way of relating to God shaped individuals' personal Bible reading in spaces outside the church. Louisa, a postgraduate student, described her daily Bible reading and prayer using this language of intimacy. She said that after having broken up with a non-Christian boyfriend, 'I feel so much more intimate with God, really, as father, even as lover...I'd say, you've got to have X-rated prayers with God if you really want to know Him.' She said she found the psalms helpful when 'I might feel quite close to Him; they're quite intimate, they're intimate prayers, so occasionally I'll just take one, they're praise, almost like love letters to God...and I just take one for my own and write it in my diary and feed it into my own prayers'. Naomi, in her late forties, described her relationship with God as like a marriage. She said that as a single person, she had not especially appreciated other women in her previous church trying to set her up with men, and had told them, 'I've already *got* a man. Jesus.'[3]

In addition to these images of God and Jesus as a lover/bridegroom who binds His evangelical subject to Him, Old Testament descriptions of God as a lover who requires fidelity of His beloved also exercised agency on how members of St John's interpreted their relations with Him and how they learnt to monitor their values. A sermon series on the Book of Hosea played on the theme of sexual infidelity, with the image accompanying the series showing a woman's eyes cast guiltily down, evoking a sense of illicit encounter. In Hosea, Israel's adultery is her worship of other idols. When God speaks through Hosea, He says to 'the children of Judah and the children of Israel':

> Now I will uncover her lewdness
>   in the sight of her lovers,
>   and no one shall rescue her out of
>   my hand...
> And I will punish her for the feast days
>   of the Baals
>   when she burned offerings to them
>   and adorned herself with her ring and jewellery,
>   and went after her lovers,
>   and forgot me, declares the LORD.
>   (Hosea 2: 10, 13, ESV)

The punishment of this adulterous idolatry, however, is followed by a new union between God and Israel in the Hosea narrative:

> 'Therefore, behold, I will allure her,
>   and bring her into the wilderness,
>   and speak tenderly to her...

---

[3] Diane Austin-Broos's study of Jamaican Pentecostals found that women used metaphors of sexual intimacy to describe their relationship with God, whereas the terms used by men were more formalized (1997: 151–2). At St John's, in contrast, both men and women used idioms of sexual intimacy to convey their sense of relationship with God, most frequently the bride/bridegroom trope.

'And in that day, declares the LORD, you will call me "My Husband"... For I will remove the names of the Baals from her mouth, and they shall be remembered by my name no more... And I will betroth you to me for ever. I will betroth you to me in righteousness and in justice, in steadfast love and in mercy. I will betroth you to me in faithfulness. And you shall know the LORD.'

(Hosea 2: 14, 16–17, 19–20, ESV)

Such Old Testament prohibitions of idolatry refer to concrete acts of destroying idols so that Israel would return to faithful worship of the One God. Listening to sermons on these passages encourages church members to identify with the adulterous/idolatrous nation of Israel. Yet, as they do not literally build other objects of worship, and there is no physical act of destroying images, as individuals listen to these passages, they are encouraged to monitor their thoughts and actions and interpret desires they experience as in tension with the moral demands of God as the means of their adultery. Thus, through conservative evangelicals' listening practices, God's character as a jealous lover becomes a subjectivizing force on evangelicals: the naming of the ideal subject who loves her bridegroom God with wholehearted devotion divides the evangelical subject, leading her to *desire* this wholehearted love relationship, while becoming increasingly aware of her own 'infidelity', the ways her desires and practices wander from what God wants of her.

This interlinked trope of idolatry/adultery was used in myriad contexts to narrativize the inevitable internal fragmentation members of the church experience as their focus on God as coherent leads them to become conscious of their practices and desires associated with *other* forms of life they simultaneously inhabit in the metropolis. Four women in their early twenties from the church—Emma, Lana, Lisa, and Jo—invited me to their home for supper one evening, and exemplified this consciousness in their discussion. Walking to their house from an earlier interview at St John's, I walked through an area of London with a large Muslim population, past the East London mosque and lots of fast-food outlets selling Halal meat. There was a large billboard advertising Lurpak butter with the words 'Salvation is not found in a garage pasty', illustrated with an image of a bacon sandwich behind, and it struck me that the advertisers did not have much grasp of the local variations in the London market. The area was a mix of large 1960s council estates and some older Georgian buildings, and Emma, Lana, Lisa, and Jo lived in a cosy Ikea-furnished house, in a square of smaller local authority and ex-local authority houses. Conversation flowed easily throughout the evening, and as we talked over glasses of red wine and the spaghetti bolognese Lisa had cooked for us, both Jo and Lisa said that they didn't have quiet times every day. Jo said, 'I was speaking with Rhiannon[4] the other day... about the images that the Bible uses

---

[4] Rhiannon is another woman in her twenties from the church.

for the things we put above the Lord, and how He speaks of us as adulterers, like He talks of Israel in her adultery . . . And I was like, gosh, who have I slept with—in inverted commas—this week, like before the Lord? And it's been, you know, sleep, and er, YouTube videos, it's too embarrassing to say.' She eventually admitted—to much laughter from the others—that her 'adultery' has been watching falconry videos on YouTube, rather than reading the Bible. She said, 'They were really boring videos. These are the kind of things I put above the Lord, and I think that's shameful and horrid.'

Thus, as God warns of the lure of graven images in the Decalogue, so Jo's 'confession' of her 'adultery' shows that her internalization of her identity as God's beloved leads her to feel guilty about the seductions of the banal distractions of contemporary visual media. While not always carrying these overtones of adultery, this language of idolatry to describe a sense of falling short of the ideal of 'wholehearted' service was a means through which individuals learnt to narrativize their consciousness of their internal fragmentation and compartmentalization. This enabled them to construct a coherent narrative that made sense of the force of differing moral norms experienced in everyday urban life, interpreted in this language of (inevitable) idolatry. In this narrative, they have agency, but God is ultimately in control.

This language of idolatry reinterpreted from the context of idol worship in Old Testament narratives to encompass humans' ethical orientations towards different sources of meaning was exemplified in a lunchtime talk on Faith, Ethics, and the Workplace that Clara invited me to at her firm early on in my fieldwork. On the way to her office through the city on a sunny, summer Thursday, office workers—the majority, predictably, men in suits—were walking quickly through the city streets to get their lunches, many checking their smartphones while walking. I felt conscious, as I waited for Clara in the building's expansive atrium with a massive modern sculpture towering above me, of how the architecture smelt differently of money and power than most buildings I find myself in on an everyday basis. This was the first time I had met Clara at her workplace: she was wearing a pencil skirt, purple blouse, and high heels, and I was glad I hadn't turned up in jeans.

The event had been organized by one of the firm's partners, who had invited Tom (one of the cleanly shaven thirty-something ministers from St John's), a rabbi, and an imam to speak. The meeting was in the top floor of the building, in the 'client entertainment suite', with far-reaching views over the city. With all the seats full and people standing at the back of the room, Clara was pleased so many of her colleagues had shown up. All the speakers chose to address the topic of the place of faith and values in the workplace through discussing the issue of compartmentalization. The imam spoke of how important it is 'not to leave your values at the glass revolving doors when entering the building'. Tom, speaking next, said there are 'two main dangers at work . . . The first is idolizing work . . . seeing our work as that which gives us security . . . when that should come from God.' The second he described as 'despising work—seeing it as the means to our own ends, rather than God's ends'. He said he thought there was a temptation for 'the firm to become God', so that individuals saw their primary responsibilities as to the firm, rather than to 'serving the wider community', and he emphasized that business must not be seen as separate from life outside work: 'What we do in work should be connected with the rest of life, with what we do in our relationships. This is why it does matter what leaders do with their expenses, if they are unfaithful in their marriages . . . Integrity should extend to all areas of life', adding that 'Only Jesus can set us free from meaninglessness.' Rabbi Levin, speaking after Tom, addressed the commonalities between their perspectives, and emphasized that 'faith is what gives life meaning, enabling us to see that life is precious . . . Faith gives core perspective and meaning to our lives.' Here we can see that this idea of faith as offering a sense of coherence, and the difficulties of the everyday experience of negotiating different moral spheres, are not the unique concern of evangelicals, but it was only Tom who explicitly narrativized this in terms of idolatry.

Ministers at St John's use this language of idolatry to describe anything that distracts from devotion to God and offers a rival source of meaning. Pete said in a talk at one of the Bible study groups that an idol is 'anything [other than God] you put your security in'. Contemporary 'idols' described in sermons were the self/self-reliance, materialism, money, families and aspirations for one's family, humanity, romantic relationships, greed, strength, political leaders (including Barack 'Messiah' Obama), one's spouse, and 'all ethnic religions of the world'. In a question and answer session after a sermon on monotheism, one of the questions addressed to Freddie was whether fashion and gadgets can become idols. He said, 'almost anything can become an idol', but in determining whether or not it has become an idol, 'you need to think about how much time and money you spend on it, and whether it's where you get your comfort from . . . If you were having a bad week, would you be comforted by knowing that you were dressed OK? If it is becoming your idol, then flee from it . . . not that we want to say that Christians have to be dowdy.' Church members learn to use this language of idolatry to describe anything 'competing' with God to be a source of security and the self. At one of the evening sessions training members of the church in how to speak about their faith, Pete asked everyone to suggest what non-Christians follow as idols, and people called out 'money', 'themselves', 'pleasure', 'the well-being of future generations', 'happiness', and 'football'. Pete said to them that these things 'are not in themselves bad, but they are bad when they are placed as more important than Jesus'.

Through these discussions, we see the importance placed on the idea that God be seen and felt as the overriding source of coherence and meaning, with 'idols' representing alternative rivals. While idols in the Old Testament narratives were external objects, and God is portrayed as asking for the literal destruction of these, here the clearing of idols and images takes place through the monitoring of the self for rival sources of meaning and pleasure. The pervasiveness of this rhetoric of idolatry indicates the awareness of church members that it is easy in the fragmented spaces of the city—in which the voice of God does not necessarily resound in most of the everyday spaces they move between—for alternative sources of value to rival God. One of the most frequently mentioned idols was materialism/money. In one sermon David described the location of the church as located 'right in the middle of the Temple of Western idolatry, the city, where the idol of the West is materialism', and Matthew, the minister in charge of city ministry, described members of the church as slaves to a system in which money is the prime value:

> it's slavery . . . you're not in control of your circumstances. The boss says 'jump' and you jump . . . Because so much of it is professional services, so there is this slavery/idolatry battle . . . Part of the battle for the Christian is to keep reminding them that they are valued not because of what people think about them or because of the number of noughts on the end of a salary, or the size of their Queen Anne mansion . . . They are valued because they are God's children.

Church members often used this rhetoric of money/materialism as idolatry to indicate how they interpreted *others'* values as idolatrous, rather than to describe their own struggles, often referring to themselves as 'downwardly mobile' in contrast with their non-Christian friends, marked by their regular giving of money to the church.[5] Occasionally individuals talked about financial decisions they made on the basis of their faith, but they did not generally describe this in terms of struggle, but rather posited it as a marker of their moral distinction from non-Christians. At one of the Rooted groups, Hannah, for example, spoke about how when her husband, Philip, had become a director at the organization where he worked, several of their friends had suggested that they move out of central London to a mansion in Surrey. She said that their decision to remain in an area of urban deprivation in the inner city— admittedly living in a large Georgian house, albeit not a mansion—was motivated by their commitment to St John's. In comparison with many corporate directors of comparable organizations in an era of seven figure bonuses, their lifestyles are unshowy:[6] their preferred holiday destination is a rented cottage in Devon, they do not drive an expensive car or have a second home, and Hannah—a Cambridge graduate—works as a volunteer for an educational charity. In a discussion about what their non-Christian friends valued, Philip said, 'I often wonder, why would people want to spend all that money on a

---

[5] The church encourages its members to give generously to the church—tithing being the minimum expectation—and the majority do.

[6] See Dorling 2011: 191.

Ferrari or whatever? I was saying that to someone at work, and then said, "oh yes, and you've got an Aston Martin haven't you".' Edward, a banker in his early thirties, then said, 'I think people should be able to see the difference in our lives, that we're living differently, that it isn't those things that are making us happy.' As members of St John's discussed together their sense that how they spend their money was 'different' from their non-Christian friends and colleagues, expressing such narratives of others' idolatry became a practice that reinforced their sense of distinction from non-Christians. Their discussions demonstrate that they perceived a fragmentation between the values of the church and a broader cultural valuing of wealth, and they described those outside the church as worshipping at the altar of materialism. This forms part of the narrative explaining why individuals reject God: the alternate idol they are worshipping is money.

This language of idolatry/adultery shows how members of St John's learn to interpret God's personality as requiring the devotion of the beloved and not tolerating rivals, which operates as a subjectivizing force. As they pray, listen to sermons, and discuss biblical narratives together, they are formed as subjects reflexively conscious not only of their sense of being divided from others, but of internal divisions and disorientations, aware of other potential lures in the city distracting from wholehearted devotion. Thus the Christian life is experienced as an ongoing struggle between these contradictory forces at work in the self and society, and individuals learn to describe these different forces they perceive at work in themselves and others through the morally polarizing logic of sin/devotion, good/evil. Alistair said to me over coffee one morning that 'the divide between good and evil' is one that goes 'right through every human heart', and in a sermon, David described the tension between the desire 'to enjoy the fleeting pleasures of sin' and the desire 'to be mistreated with the people of God' as 'a battle that goes on right in the heart of every Christian believer'. In another sermon, he said that to prevent 'half-hearted, divided Christianity, where you're just torn in three directions, five directions...' requires 'taking the knife out, metaphorically, and sticking it into something. Some treasured desire that is producing a divided heart... Some desire for something that the Lord hasn't given me, but that I'm hankering after, and is actually dividing my heart.'

The prevalence of this language of struggle—and the narrativization of this as sin—that ministers articulated was constantly reiterated by church members in their discussions in small groups, and Clara told me 'it is something *every* Christian lives with' and becomes 'more conscious of' through personal devotional practices. She said that as individuals become more self-aware through practices of praying, confessing, and reading the Bible, they become '*more* aware of what their own particular temptations are'. She described the areas of her life she felt as her own 'struggles' as tendencies towards over-competitiveness and her longing for a boyfriend. Older members of the church often talked about how the longer they had been Christians, the more aware they felt of their 'sinfulness', and this learned self-understanding as 'sinful' is foregrounded when ministers often publicly described themselves in sermons as conscious of their own sinfulness and internal conflicts, David for example, describing himself as 'today just as sinful as I ever have been'.

Robbins describes how Pentecostals in Papua New Guinea learnt to understand themselves as sinful through practices of confession, and this learning of a sinful identity is also evident at St John's. Robbins argues that his informants experience a sense of fragmentation between the focus on community life associated with their old Urapmin ways of life and the individualistic emphasis of Pentecostalism, and that they learn to recognize behaviour from their old way of life as sin. For members of St John's, the temporal order of this tension is reversed: they narrate Christianity as becoming culturally outdated in Britain as the moral norms they experience outside the church 'career away', in David's words, from the values they associate with their faith. Yet their narratives of idolatry/adultery demonstrate that they are reflexively aware that their own modes of behaviour are shaped by both evangelical and wider cultural values in tension with these. While Robbins demonstrates how it is through particular practices that individuals develop their identification as sinful, this is also an intersubjective process, which at St John's includes particular experiences of the personality of God, who, understood as perfect, demands that His people also embody perfection. As individuals *inevitably* fail at this, they scrutinize their behaviour to discipline themselves to come closer to the bar God sets of whole-hearted devotion and love. Thus the unity and desire of God have agency on members of St John's, leading them to name those attitudes and aspects of their own and others' behaviour that are discordant with this. They are both separate from and connected with others whom they objectify as separated from God through their turning away from Him, and they describe this sense of moral separation in terms of guilt.

Having considered the significance of narratives of idolatry/adultery, let us consider how, bound up with this consciousness of internal fragmentation, this sense of guilt serves to bind members of the church more closely in their relationship with God and each other.

GUILT AND TRANSCENDENCE

Foucault describes how Christian practices of confession constructed a particular form of the subject, responsible for their actions and divided within themselves as they sought to purify themselves from polluting thoughts (1978: 58–63; 1988: 40–6). At St John's, practices such as reciting the Church of

England Prayer Book confession and singing hymns produce the evangelical as a guilty sinner, with a sense, as Hugo described, of her difference from a holy God. This narrative of the subject as divided and guilty for her idolatry/ adultery is bound up with the promise of an ultimate coherence posited in the future identity of the sinner who repents of her sinfulness and believes in Jesus's redemption as saved. This understanding of Jesus' death as sacrificial atonement for their sins is central to conservative evangelicals' self-under-standing, constituting a dividing marker of identity within contemporary British evangelicalism, with more charismatic and 'open' evangelicals and liberal Anglicans often rejecting this emphasis (Wood 2011).

It is difficult to overstate the centrality at St John's of this understanding of Jesus's death as an atonement. Unlike Calvinist theology, there is a doctrine of assurance, and church members—if they doubt their salvation—are taught to 'return to the cross' to feel assured of God's forgiveness. 'Meditation on the cross' and explicit focus on Jesus's sufferings are encouraged through various means, reinforcing an emotional response of guilt and a sense of dependence on Jesus. A sermon Freddie preached on the 'suffering servant' passages from Isaiah illustrates how members of the church learn to understand a sense of their guilt as related to the violence of Jesus' death. Freddie talked about the brutality of YouTube footage of a lynching in Lebanon, emphasizing that the death of the suffering servant in the biblical narrative was similarly brutal, similarly real: 'This is a *real* death we're reading about tonight.' Freddie described what happened to the man in Lebanon, and said that in the suffering servant passage, the servant is beaten up beyond all recognition. He used language evoking visceral images to drive home the physical violence of Jesus's death as a 'bleeding lump of meat'.

Freddie said that Isaiah was seeing a video flash before his eyes of Jesus's death, and described the suffering servant passage as the video to a song: 'There are two people in this song: Him and us . . . We are in the video, but not in the way we expected . . . We walk into the picture with our sins and our guilt, and we walk away empty-handed, with peace.' Freddie emphasized the idea of Jesus 'carrying the burden' of sin: 'this death carried our guilt, our shame, our responsibility . . . Imagine everything we ever did wrong, piled on top of us as a heap. The simple answer is that the servant carried this for us.' He asked the congregation to draw two columns on their handouts, and to write the following words under each of the headings 'Us' and 'Him', as in the following table:

Us	Him
Guilt	He didn't complain and went forward like a sheep to be sheared
Sin	By oppression and judgment he was killed
Strain	An innocent man picking up our guilt

As well as drawing these columns, the young woman sitting next to me scrawled in biro by this passage in her Bible 'GUILT', underlined and capitalized. Freddie went on, 'The problem with humanity is that there are no goodies. This servant finds a way to turn baddies into goodies.' He turned this into a personal question addressed to the congregation: 'What do *you* make of Him? What do you make of God and His plan? Was it just a hot day with a brutal death, or was it the most wonderful day?' He told the congregation to make another two columns on their handouts, and under a column with the individual's own name, to list 'all your sins and transgressions, and in the other column, write "sinless", "blameless", and see if you can believe that He would swap places with you'. The sermon was followed by two songs, which George, leading the service, said that the congregation should sing 'as a prayer and encouragement to each other'. The words of these described a sense of union with Jesus achieved through His death:

> Before the throne of God above
> I have a strong and perfect plea
> a great high priest whose name is Love,
> who ever lives and pleads for me.
> My name is graven on his hands,
> my name is written on his heart...
>
> One in Himself, I cannot die:
> my soul is purchased by his blood,
> my life is hid with Christ on high,
> with Christ, my Saviour and my God.[7]

The evangelical tradition—and Protestantism more broadly—is often seen as individualistic, and it is possible to view these lyrics as individuating the subject whose high priest pleads for her. Yet it is also possible to see the orientation towards God expressed in focusing on Jesus's death as also exceeding this, revealing a sense of self-transcendence in desire.

As church members learn to relate to God as a lover, so we might interpret *their* desire for God as a form of eroticism. Social theorists have conceptualized 'eroticism' in a variety of ways. By using the term to intimate desire, I do not intend to limit this to sexuality,[8] but to express Weber's sense of eroticism

---

[7] The words of this hymn are by Charitie Lees De Chenez (1841–1923), online from <http://www.hymnary.org/text/before_the_throne_of_god_above_i_have_a_> (accessed 9 December 2014).

[8] I am intending the term to carry with it broad meanings that within Christian theology have traditionally been associated with desire for God. As Ward notes, 'Divine eros, the love of God, and human eros, the love of human beings for God possess far greater dynamics, operating across far greater domains, than just sexuality. But since the nineteenth century, the development of medicine, and the increasing erotification of our culture post-Freud, eros and sexuality have come to mean the same thing' (2000: 76). In his theological anthropology, Ward seeks to 'undo...the knot that tied eros to sexuality, and hopefully rescue...the idea that Christians

as an 'embodied creative power' and 'boundless giving of oneself... [in] opposition to all functionality, rationality, and generality' (1948: 347) and Bataille's treatment of eroticism as '"an exuberance of life"... in which the boundaries associated with the "discontinuity" of individual existence are dissolved', which can take the form of physical eroticism, emotional eroticism and religious eroticism (Shilling and Mellor 2010: 440–1). Bataille argues, as Shilling and Mellor note, that with religious eroticism, there is an eroticism of spirit in forms of religious sacrifice where individuality 'is violated by an act that fuses the sacrifices and other participants together with their victim. The victim dies and the spectators share in what that death reveals... There is always a violation of individuality in eroticism, reaching beyond the present in search of transcendent meaning' (p. 441).

In these songs' words, the language of union with Jesus through his death can be interpreted as articulating a religious eroticism. In this, there is a longing for a transcendent meaning beyond the present and the self, which offers an escape from discontinuity and subjective fragmentation. While we might discern an individualist emphasis in the songs' 'I' words and church members being asked to write down *their* sins, this individuation is expressed simultaneously with a desire for the communion of *all* church members together with Jesus. At another service, the congregation recited together:

> George: This is love:
> Congregation: Not that we loved God
> but that he loved us
> and sent his son
> to be the propitiation for our sins.

George then prayed a short prayer thanking God 'that we will be part of the most intimate, most permanent relationship that the world has ever known'. After the sermon, the congregation sang a hymn with words articulating the idea that as His body they would be 'joined in intimate communion / Two made one—like man and wife'. Hugo's preaching on Isaiah also emphasized this idea of the church, rather than the individual, experiencing this union. Describing how 'the faithless city will be transformed into the holy city', he stated that the canopy image in Isaiah 4, denoting a future relationship between God and the purified city, intimates the idea of a 'a marriage chamber'. He said that the relationship between bride and groom evoked through this is 'an Old Testament hint of that image of intimacy and love and faithfulness... The whole people of God are under the bridal canopy.'

This construction of the communal identity of the church as guilty and sinful, united in, and yearning for a transcendent relation with God achieved

---

are also governed by desire, that desire is fundamental to our nature as human beings as God created us'.

through Jesus's death, might appear a difficult emotional load for the individual to bear, with the violence of Jesus's death described as not only related to shared guilt but also specifically to *their* individual guilt. Individuals are encouraged to focus on the cross in such ways that these feelings of guilt help develop their sense of intimacy with God. In a question and answer session, David said that 'real love for Jesus is nurtured by reflecting on who He is and what He's done for us', and encouraged 'meditating on His character and the kind of things that make us love Him'. 'What Jesus has done' is used at St John's as a euphemism for Jesus's death; for example, Luke, a postgraduate student, told me he sometimes cried at home when meditating on Jesus 'and what He has done'. In group Bible studies, individuals are encouraged to identify with characters in biblical narratives who reject Jesus, acknowledge their guilt, and are forgiven. Individuals often spoke of how moving they found it that Jesus forgave characters such as Peter, likening Peter's denial of Jesus to their sense that they repeatedly turn away from God in their everyday actions.

Through these individual and communal practices of reading, discussion, prayer, singing, and imaginative contemplation, over time members of the church develop an 'emotional regime' (Riis and Woodhead 2010: 185) in which guilt serves as a form of binding to God, moving through emotions of sadness, wonder, and gratitude, as individuals learn an understanding of Jesus's suffering and death as motivated by His love for them. While they feel a sense of connectedness with God through this, in their specific reflection on Jesus's death they experience Him as other. In one of the student group's discussions on the passion narrative in Luke's Gospel, Patrick, Luke, Chris, and Gemma all commented that they find it difficult, in Patrick's words, to 'get my head round the fact that Jesus was willing to go through all of this for me'. Luke said, 'I know I'm a Christian and going to heaven, but I'm still scared of death. But Jesus was willing to go through this. And He's God, which makes the story even more amazing . . . And it's my sins that put Him there.' Older members of the church, habituated in techniques of focusing on Jesus's death in prayer or meditating on Bible passages, spoke of how over time their increased consciousness of their own 'sinfulness' made them 'more aware of God's grace'. As mentoring relationships between older and younger Christians are encouraged, older church members stressed to younger members, for example Liz speaking to the student group, that they 'should not dwell on their guilt', but after confessing their sins, they should feel confident that these have been 'dealt with at the Cross'. These intergenerational relationships provide a means of modelling the 'right' way of handling guilt, although as we will see in the following chapter, individuals, especially younger church members, still expressed doubts that they had been forgiven.

Through focusing on violent images of the cross and developing an understanding of Jesus as a 'sacrificial lamb', members of the church interpret Jesus's death as the sign of God's love for them, through which their subjective divisions are ultimately reconciled. Hugo described this understanding of relationality with God effected through Jesus's death as both present and moving towards a future consummation in his sermon on Isaiah 4:

> The city in Revelation is the bride of Christ... Here is the eternal kingdom to which we're moving... No more threats, nothing to undercut the security He gives His people. Nothing that threatens to destroy, no more idols that divert our attention and delude us into thinking that something that we have made is going to satisfy us. No; everything that man longs for and has tried to construct in independence from God down through human history, it's all to be found in the branch[9] and in His glorious, fruitful city, where He keeps and preserves His people in total security and utter joy, for there the Lord will create His presence.

Thus we see that despite the rhetoric of the evangelical subject as a rational listener, their focus on God's personality also objectifies them as loved objects of God's desire, mediated not only through words but also visual images members of the church imagine while listening. Although 'public' listening is dominated by more rationalized modes of engaging with these words, it is in communal singing, prayer, and individual devotional practice that this sense of self-transcending intimacy with God comes more to the fore. Some are aware of this as an emotional disjunction, but this is not always so.

CONCLUSION: THE LIVES AND LOVES OF GOD IN THE LIVES AND LOVES OF PEOPLE

Members of St John's desire for coherence, truthfulness, and wholeheartedness in their own actions accords with Keane's focus on how Protestant practices effected a normative tilt towards sincerity, with a matching of words and the subject's interiority. This chapter has explored how it is not only habituated practices that are significant in forming ethical norms such as truthfulness; these are also related to individuals' experiences of God's personality mediated through these practices. As this character is felt as both transcendent unity, wholly Other, and as a lover who demands fidelity from His beloved, these differing characteristics have agency on how members of St John's learn to relate to both God and their own subjectivities: they are divided within themselves and from others as they strive 'to be perfect' as their 'father in heaven is perfect'. Marx argued that with Protestantism there was 'no longer a question of the struggle of the layman with the priest outside himself, but

---

[9] Earlier in the sermon Hugo had described 'the branch' in this passage as a Messianic reference to Jesus.

rather of his struggle with his own inner priest' (1975: 250–1), and we have considered the intersubjective formation of this internal sense of struggle, and how for members of St John's this is bound up with specific ways of relating to God's character.

Jack Miles argues that historians of religion have overlooked the psychological impact that monotheism has. His biography of God draws attention to the different personalities that co-exist within the unity of God and he contrasts the effects of this with polytheism: 'Other things being equal, protracted exposure to a God in whom several personalities coexist and alongside whom no other god is ever portrayed even for the folkloric fun of it must foster a way of thinking of the self as similarly composite and similarly alone' (1996: 407). While members of St John's relate to different elements of God's personality at different times, there is a discursive emphasis that His character is ultimately unified. Their focus on God as coherent leads them to desire coherence in their own lives, and they understand this as a struggle, as their attention to this characteristic of God and His demand for wholeheartedness leads them to be aware of the ways in which they compartmentalize their faith and are distracted from God in their everyday lives. Their focus on monotheistic narratives warning against idolatry provide them with narrative resources to make sense of this internal division as their own 'infidelity'. This leads them both to be increasingly self-conscious of specific ways their lives are fragmented and to see the lives of others as shaped through worship of idols that their lives are also shaped by. Sennett argues that the master image of God in early Christianity was pure Word and Light, and it was the ritual practices of Christianity that introduced a sense of the subject turned outwards towards others (2002b: 371). However, conservative evangelical understanding of God's character includes *both* a sense of His unity and transcendence *and* a sense that He is turned outwards in desire towards what is felt as other than Him, a God who loves and suffers for His people.

To return to Simmel's thesis, members of St John's experience God as coherent, and this responds to their desire for coherence in their own lives. But the distinctive emphasis on God's desire for His people and the moral demands He makes, bound up with narratives of adultery, intensify individuals' consciousness of their fragmentation and their struggles 'to be perfect' to a greater degree than in Simmel's account. This is bound up with the intensified cultural fragmentation members of St John's experience, as they negotiate myriad moral meanings and feel the demands of their faith as increasingly countercultural. In this context, their focus on Jesus's suffering and death enables them to deal with their sense of guilt at falling short of the ideal of wholehearted service, and this binds them in their sense of relationship with God. Their attention to Jesus's death both individuates them and increases their desire for God and a desire for self-transcendence, as they experience a sense of connection and communion with *all* those—past and present—they believe will likewise be united with Christ in a future consummation of their relationship. Their focus on God in this grand theological narrative and their desire to be obedient forms them—counterculturally—as desiring subjection, although conscious of their agency in being able to turn either towards or away from what God wants. Evangelicals are stereotypically seen as moralizing, intolerant, and judgemental, and their focus on God's moral demands leads them to differentiate between themselves, as seeking to be obedient, and others, who serve other idols. Yet their emphasis on themselves as sinners and sense that they too are idolatrous complicates this narrative of distance, as they recognize themselves as likewise shaped by the same moral currents as those they seek to be different from. In this context, the lines marking them out as different are fragile, and this encourages evangelical leaders to clearly stake out symbolic moral boundaries of distinctiveness that enable individuals to understand themselves as aliens and strangers.

Tanya Luhrmann (2004, 2012) argues that her Chicago charismatic evangelicals' experience of intimate relationship with God is bound up with the thinning of social life and association in the USA. My informants' self-differentiation from charismatics means that they are critical of Christians who, in Timothy's words, 'make the relationship too matey . . . they make God like a teddy bear'. Yet they do speak of a sense of intimacy with God, and understand God as wanting their love. In contrast with Luhrmann's evangelicals, my informants have busy social lives, socializing with friends from within and outside St John's, participating in sports teams, choirs, and other leisure pursuits, the busyness of which can make them feel guilty for squeezing out time for God. I would argue that their desire for God is more bound up with their system of religious intersubjectivity, in which the sense of coherence they experience God as offering transcends and gives meaning to the fragments of their lives as they move through different spaces that address them in different ways.

This allure of coherence is bound up with a sense of God's transcendence, and therefore forming an orientation towards God means developing an orientation towards transcendence, which necessarily implies absence and leads to experiences of doubt. In the final chapter, I explore how contrary to interpretations of evangelicalism that posit its global success in terms of the certainty it offers, members of St John's live with and find strategies for dealing with doubt and uncertainty that deepen their sense of interdependence on each other.

6

Of Time, the Body, and the City

Belief, Absence, and Incompleteness

On my bed by night
I sought him whom my soul loves;
    I sought him, but found him not.
I will rise now and go about the city,
    in the streets and in the squares;
I will seek him whom my soul loves.
    I sought him, but found him not.
The watchmen found me
    as they went about in the city.
'Have you seen him whom my soul loves?'
Scarcely had I passed them
    when I found him whom my soul loves.
I held him, and would not let him go
    until I had brought him into my mother's house,
and into the chamber of her who conceived me.

(Song of Solomon 3: 1–4, ESV)

Religious faith is often described as a psychological crutch, numbing suffering, deadening existential anxieties, and making pain and loss easier to bear. Is it a crutch? At St John's, people seemed at times to express a sense that their faith was a comfort that helped them through life, and at other times resisted this explanation. Preaching on the passage in the Sermon on the Mount in which Jesus tells his disciples that 'the gate is narrow and the way is hard that leads to life' (Matthew 7: 14, ESV), David said that 'some naïve atheists suggest that people become Christians as some sort of psychological crutch. But it's the Christian who's swimming upstream, against the current.' He described the Christian life as 'countercultural, in every generation and every stage of life: as you follow the teaching of Jesus ... you find yourself swimming against the current'. He said that Jesus's words in these verses 'explain so much about the

Christian life . . . It explains why the Christian life is not easy.' He described his own sense of struggle:

> The longer I go on as a Christian, I think the harder I find it . . . It was our friend John Chapman who when asked what his experience of the Christian life was replied, 'I never realized just how wonderful it would be and I never realized how hard it would be.' And almost in the same breath, he said, encouragingly, 'Don't worry. The first fifty years are the hardest.' So I picture a marathon runner approaching the Olympic stadium. I'm rather hoping that when I get into the closing years, as it were, in the stadium, doing the last three laps, the picture of the finishing line will cause me to take fresh heart, and to run with my head up. And I remember the early years of the marathon in one's twenties and thirties, where the battles were there, but one was full of enthusiasm and energy. I wonder if in the fifties and sixties, a man or woman is running the hard yards through the pain barrier of the wall.

Church members frequently expressed this sense of struggle, of the difficulties of the life of faith, that trying to live in a way that puts desire for and obedience to God at the centre of their motivation and everyday actions was hard work. Yet in the Rooted group one evening, while discussing the costs of being a Christian and how to talk about these to non-Christians, Alan said impatiently, 'Look, I'm sorry, all of this is good standard evangelical doctrine. But what about the other side of this? What about the Jesus who says, "Come to me all you who are heavy laden and I will give you rest . . . Take my yoke, for my burden is light"? What about if we have a friend who's really been through a difficult time? Do we *really* say to them that this is all about the struggle?' Alan's interruption of the discussion indicates that as well as the standard evangelical emphasis on the 'costs' of faith, these are held together with the emotional comfort faith offers. On another evening, Lorna said to the group, 'Non-Christians think our faith is just a crutch.'

'Is that necessarily a bad thing?' Alistair asked.

'It *is* a crutch,' Hannah said.

'And perhaps thinking like that is necessary to understanding what it is to be Christians,' Emily said, 'because being a Christian is about dependence, so you have to learn that God *does* become a crutch.'

'I had a master at school who was a Christian,' Alistair said, 'and he was a war hero, and everyone looked up to him. And I remember someone saying to him that his faith was just a crutch. And he replied, "Of course it is. And if I need a crutch, you certainly do."'

In these interactions we see that the experience of faith for members of St John's both does and does not make their lives easier: the relationship with God they experience as central to their religious lives has, as Orsi describes, 'all the complexities – all the hopes, evasions, love, fear, denial, projections, misunderstandings, and so on – of relationships between humans' (2005: 2).

Church members repeatedly emphasized that their faith was both a comfort and a struggle, that they were human and got things 'wrong' in their faith, felt they let God down, and at times, questioned where He was. In the previous chapter, we saw that as they learn to relate to God's character, they want to do what they understand Him asking, yet are conscious that they continually fail to meet His demands. This leads them to be conscious of their guilt and binds them closer in their sense of relationship with, comfort in, and dependence on Jesus. In this chapter, I explore how it is not only seeking to be obedient that makes the Christian life 'hard'. They also experience doubts in their faith, and these are felt as a state of unease.

There is a tendency in writing about evangelicals to posit them as religious fundamentalists, their faith—in response to the uncertainties caused by the increasing scale and abstraction of modern life—offering a sense of certainty, their view of revelation one which 're-establishes truth, realigns words and things' and anchors shifting meanings (Comaroff 2010: 29). While members of St John's do speak of God as offering certain truth and meaning, under- standing the fine textures of their lives means reading between the lines and noticing the tears and fissures in this, which mean that although they *long* for a God of whom they are more sure than themselves, in practice many struggle at times with uncertainty, and all are conscious that maintaining their faith requires discipline and struggle. Standard academic focus on evangelicals has not drawn attention to this complex dialectical interrelation of having and not-having, belief and unbelief, that many members of St John's experi- ence as an everyday tension in their religious lives.

The structure of conservative evangelicals' faith is based on an orientation towards God as transcendent and is bound up with His absence, and in this chapter I address how their word-based practices can contribute to forms of doubt, and how they develop and improvise strategies which respond to this and help them persevere in their belief. I begin by outlining the significance of absence within Christianity, and draw on de Certeau's writing on the structure of belief to illuminate the relation between self and other, present and future, implicated in this. I then describe how an orientation to the future is intro- duced at St John's, which entails a consciousness of Jesus's present absence and an understanding of faith as learning to trust in His promises for the future. I show how members of St John's can find it hard work to maintain that future orientation, and outline the techniques they use to respond to doubt and uncertainty. I argue that communal practices play a vital role in main- taining individuals as believers in the face of uncertainties arising from the negotiation of conflicting norms associated with the different urban spaces they traverse. These develop a strong sense of connection with other members of St John's and their collective identification as a church 'family', while reinforcing their orientation to transcendence and a sense of individual insufficiency and social interdependence, orientations contributing to their sense of being 'in but not of the world'.

ABSENCE, BELIEF, WORDS

Simmel argues that God's ultimate coherence is only possible through His being transcendent and physically absent in the immanent world. Christian reflection on the material absence of God is deeply rooted in the earliest fabric of the faith, in particular the life and death of Jesus and expectation of His future return. Throughout Christian history, Christians have looked back in remembrance of Jesus's life and death and forwards to His future return and the coming of His kingdom in ritualized form. By the time St Paul wrote his first letter to the Corinthians, the earliest form of what became the Eucharist already expressed this remembrance and expectation:

> the Lord Jesus on the night when he was betrayed took bread, and when he had given thanks, he broke it and said, 'This is my body which is given for you. Do this in remembrance of me.' In the same way also he took the cup, after supper, saying, 'This cup is the new covenant in my blood. Do this, as often as you drink it, in remembrance of me.' For as often as you eat this bread and drink the cup, you proclaim the Lord's death until he comes.
>
> (1 Corinthians 11:23–6, ESV)

In this ritual, we see Christianity marked from its earliest history by awareness of Jesus's absence. As de Certeau expresses this, 'Christianity was founded upon the *loss of a body* – the loss of the body of Jesus Christ, compounded with the loss of the "body" of Israel, of a "nation" and its genealogy. A founding disappearance indeed' (1992: 81). While biblical narratives draw attention to God's transcendence, the writing of the New Testament and the performance of the Eucharist are predicated on both Jesus's absence and the promise of His presence, beginning with Mary Magdalene's statement before the empty tomb: 'They have taken away my Lord and I do not know where they have laid him' (John 20: 13, ESV). In John's Gospel, Jesus's '"being there" is the paradox of "having been" here previously, of remaining inaccessible elsewhere and of "coming back" later. His body is structured by dissemination, like a text. Since that time, the believers have continued to wonder: "Where art thou?"' (de Certeau 1992: 82). The structure of the Christian relationship with the divine is therefore, as Simmel argued, a form of desire, depending on this condition of having and not-having, as Jesus is both absent yet at the same time invites His disciples to abide in His love, telling them that if they keep His commandments they will abide in His love (John 15:10).

This pathos of being, as St Paul describes, 'away from the Lord' (2 Corinthians 5:6, ESV), and the centrality of Christ's absence to the Christian experience has been a central preoccupation in theology.[1] Within the anthropology of Christianity, Matthew Engelke first addressed this 'problem of presence' in his evocative study (2007) of the Masowe weChishanu Church in Zimbabwe, exploring the uncertainties attendant in embracing material signs of God's presence. Within studies of evangelicalism, the question of how God becomes present as an intimate friend in the life of charismatic evangelicals has been taken up by Tanya Luhrmann (2012). The central tropes of belief, faith, and desire, by which members of St John's describe their forms of relationship with God, all imply a sense of absence and incompleteness in the present, which will be fulfilled by God, as Other, in a future consummation of that relationship, a point that de Certeau articulates in analysing the nature of belief. While there has been a shift away from examining 'belief' in the study of religion, because of its centrality in the self-understanding of members of St John's, focusing on how this modality of belief is formed and maintained, and the interplay of presence and absence bound up in this, helps illuminate their everyday experiences, comforts, and struggles. De Certeau's work helps draw attention to the intersubjective dimensions of this.

In 'What We Do When We Believe', de Certeau argues that belief entails 'the recognition of an alterity' (1985: 192). We saw in the previous chapter that God's character is constructed as Other through emphasis on His moral purity, transcendence, and immutability, which members of St John's contrast with their sinfulness, fragmentation, and transience, although their criteria to create that difference demonstrate a connection with God and His standards, so that this mediation of an alterity is complex. De Certeau describes belief as establishing a contract with one who has been recognized as other. This requires bringing the future into the present: the 'believer' must give up a 'present advantage, or some of its claims, to give credit to a receiver' (p. 193). Doing this means creating a sense of insufficiency in the self, as the believer 'hollows out a void in himself relative to the time of the other', and in doing so creates a deficit whereby his future interests and the future actions of the other are introduced into the present (p. 193).

De Certeau argues that belief depends on the coincidence of absence and presence, as belief in the other names an absence in the self, while also producing 'this "other" presumed to insure against what it is losing' (p. 201). Belief and time always remain linked, as this practice of difference, in which there is a *deferred* restitution by the other, 'endows "delay" with all its social pertinency. It is by this "deferred" that believing is separated from seeing' (p. 201). These relations are established in a social field in which a plurality

---

[1] See, for example, Augustine 1961; Milbank 1996; Ward 2000. See also Engelke 2007: 13–16.

guarantees the guarantor, and thus a plurality and a history are knotted into the act of believing, as these guarantors 'enable' believing. As earlier noted, De Certeau describes belief as operating socially like sacrifice in the Durkheimian sense, taking from individual self-sufficiency and marking on the self the existence of the other:

> the code of social exchange inscribed on individual nature, while mutilating it, transforms it into a blazon of sociality ... In the order of (re)cognition, believing would be the equivalent of what sacrifice is in the order of religious practices. It carves the mark of the other within an autonomy; it loses a present for a future; it 'sacrifices', in other words, 'makes sense' (*sacer-facere*), by substituting a debit for a credit.
>
> (1985: 194)

We have seen that communal practices of listening at St John's can be interpreted in these terms: as the congregation listen and consume the words of the Bible together, this takes from individual self-sufficiency by marking on them a dependence on God and each other. As they come to carry these words in their bodies, this forms them as believing subjects. But their sense of God's transcendence and Jesus's physical absence also constructs the incompleteness of the subject, who is constituted in a desire for what always exceeds her.

De Certeau argues that speech enjoys a privileged relation with belief: words state the absence of what they represent (p. 194). As conservative evangelicals are encouraged to focus on the object of belief as the Word, a particular consciousness of God's transcendence and material absence is mediated. Throughout the history of Christianity, Christians have sought to engage in practices whereby a historicity and a future with God are knotted into the present, effecting differentiating relations with God and marking Him and others who act as guarantors of their belief within their autonomy. How then is this temporal orientation, through which the material absence of God as transcendent is rendered present to consciousness in the act of believing, created at St John's?

'AS WE LOOK TO ... THINGS UNSEEN'

A discussion at one of the Rooted groups indicated the conservative evangelical understanding that becoming a believer is achieved through introducing the future of their relationship with Jesus into the present, and the central significance of words in this process. As it was our group's turn to wash up that evening after all the groups had finished eating their dinner of roast chicken and potatoes, our discussion was curtailed from the usual hour and a quarter to forty minutes. Janet, a barrister in her forties, was leading the discussion, which was focused on a passage from 2 Corinthians. Following the usual pattern of meetings, Janet began by asking group members to read the passage aloud, a couple of verses each:

> Since we have the same spirit of faith according to what has been written, 'I believed, and so I spoke,' we also believe, and so we also speak, knowing that he who raised the Lord Jesus will raise us also with Jesus and bring you into his presence. For it is all for your sake, so that as grace extends to more and more people it may increase thanksgiving, to the glory of God.
>
> So we do not lose heart. Though our outer self is wasting away, our inner self is being renewed day by day. For this light momentary affliction is preparing for us an eternal weight of glory beyond all comparison, as we look not to the things that are seen but to the things that are unseen. For the things that are seen are transient, but the things that are unseen are eternal.
>
> (2 Corinthians 4:13–18, ESV)

Janet then asked the group to talk about how they saw the structure of the passage and what they thought Paul meant when he described Christians as 'jars of clay'. She split the group into threes, and instructed us to arrange some slips of paper she had prepared in a logical order that would make sense of verses 13–15. I was with Alan and Sheila, and I spread the slips of paper out so that the words on them were visible. Alan silently moved the pieces of paper so that the words on them were arranged in the following order: Have Spirit/ Have faith/As written/Believe/Speak/Know will be raised/Brought into his presence/Grace extends/Thanksgiving/Glory.

When everyone had finished, Janet asked Alan to explain his ordering, and everyone agreed that this was correct. Hannah said she found the order interesting, commenting, 'in some explanations of the workings of faith, you would have this order of ideas, but often the idea of speaking would be missed out . . . Here it's emphasized that if you *believe* in God, you will also speak.' Lucy agreed that speaking was fundamental. Alan said it reminded him of the passage in Romans where Paul speaks of confessing with the mouth, and he recited this from memory, pointing out to everyone that he'd learnt it from the Authorized Version: 'The word is nigh thee, even in thy mouth, and in thy heart: that is, the word of faith, which we preach; that if thou confess with thy mouth the Lord Jesus, and shalt believe in thine heart that God hath raised him from the dead, thou shalt be saved. For with the heart man believeth unto righteousness; and with the mouth confession is made unto salvation.' He spoke these words quickly and quietly, and afterwards, Janet agreed that it was important that 'belief' entails speaking of the words they had 'received'.

In this interaction, we see the stated conservative evangelical understanding of 'belief', entailing believing in what is written, speaking/confessing, knowing, with the result that 'the Lord Jesus will bring you into his presence'. This helps establish a normative understanding of a 'contract' between the believer and God, predicated on the alterity of God and guaranteed by the witness of the Bible and other members of the church (past and present), with the promise of a future with Him knotted into the present. As the group discussed the verses following this, they showed how their focus on the Bible in these study groups brought the future to their present consciousness. Janet put on the table a small cast-iron set of scales she had brought from work with a sheet of paper with scales drawn on it. She asked Lucy to scribe, and then asked the group to compare 'the present' with 'the future' described in these verses. Alistair said, 'we have light and momentary affliction' in the present, but the future 'will be the weight of glory beyond all comparison'. Lucy emphasized, 'it's an *eternal* weight of glory'. Hannah said that in the present, 'we are wasting away, but our inner self is being renewed'. Alistair added that 'at present, we look to things seen, and the contrast for the other column is "things unseen"'. Lorna, her voice strained, as if keeping back tears, said that when her husband was dying, 'it was so clear, he could *really* see the glory of what was unseen; he could see the passing of this life'.

Simmel describes the person of faith as drawing a contrast between the ephemerality of human lives and the eternity of God. Here we see how the Rooted group's habituated discursive practices encouraged them to draw this contrast and objectify the present as transient, marked by suffering, and of less significance than their future life with God. We also see the central place of *words* in forming a belief in the future: in this understanding of belief, the subject has received *words* of faith articulating a promise of what God will do (and has done in the past), through which they believe (and speak), and it is through the credit she grants to God's words and her passing these on as she speaks to others that she is incorporated into the body of the saved.

This interlinking of belief and an orientation towards time was created in various ways at St John's: through focusing on Bible passages, prayers, sermons, and the repetitive singing of song lyrics expressing, for example, a longing to dwell in a place of unending praise.[2] One of the most popular songs, 'By Faith', exemplified this knotting together of historicity and the future in the present as the lyrics expressed how 'our fathers' looked forward to a promise of a holy city in which peace and justice reign, and longed for the coming of the Messiah.[3] As the congregation sang of this desire for the long-awaited Messiah, all the musicians except the drummer dropped out, and the congregation sang to a rolling drum beat of the moment of the Messiah's coming being both foretold and remembered, creating a sense of the sacrality of this.

[2] See, for example, the lyrics of 'Beautiful Savior', from <http://www.lyricsmode.com/lyrics/m/matt_redman/beautiful_savior_all_my_days.html> (accessed 22 September 2014).

[3] See <http://www.gettymusic.com/hymns-byfaith.aspx> (accessed 22 September 2014).

Church members described this focus on God's promises for the future as central to their faith; for example, an economist who told me that time was crucial to their faith: 'since Abraham onwards, we've been looking forwards'. While Abraham in Genesis sets out for an unknown land, trusting in God's promise of that land and his future descendants, practices of looking forwards at St John's mostly do not entail a sense of God's promises being fulfilled in the near future, but rather after their death. The church taught a dispensationalist understanding of salvation history,[4] but the eschaton was not figured as imminent, and members often said that they found it difficult to keep their focus on Jesus's coming again.

The church leaders therefore encouraged individuals to work on themselves to develop this future focus. At a 'Summertime' discussion group,[5] one of the evenings focused on the idea of Jesus's return. I was sitting with members of the student group, and the passage was Revelation 2: 20: 'He who testifies to these things, says, "Surely I am coming soon." Amen. Come, Lord Jesus!' (ESV). The minister speaking that evening, in his thirties, tall, dark haired, wearing an open-necked white shirt and jeans, said, 'the message that Jesus is coming back is not popular in contemporary culture', and commented that if people were to shadow him for a couple of weeks, 'they wouldn't get a strong sense Jesus was coming back'. He posed the question: 'what is it about living in London in 2010 that distracts us from Jesus's return?', and set three questions for the group to discuss around the tables:

1. How frequently do you think/talk about Jesus's return?
2. Why is it often the case that this truth gets neglected?
3. What are the dangers to us as Christians if this truth gets neglected?

Here we see how the study groups' discursive practices encourage reflexivity and the monitoring of thoughts and words in the light of the sense that one *should* be thinking about Jesus's return. On our table, Chris, one of the student leaders, asked Jeff, a quiet American maths postgraduate, wearing a buttoned-up polo shirt and chinos, to read the questions. Jeff read the first question out, and Steve, the young man sitting next to him, said he *thought* about Jesus's return more than he talked about it. Gemma said she didn't think about it that much, and Chris said he didn't either, 'because things are comfortable in this world . . . it's easy to think you can be completely satisfied by things in this world'.

---

[4] This was evident when one of the ministers preaching at the Rooted weekend away about the Book of Joel offered a summary of church teaching on salvation-time. He asked his audience to imagine a time line, 'and on that time line is the event of the Lord Jesus . . . The Jesus event is God sorting out the world . . . God's coming is part of that same event, but they are stretched apart, by, at the moment, about two thousand years, like elastic.'

[5] The Bible study groups programme runs only during the academic year; and over summer, all groups met together for 'Summertime' group studies in the church.

Jeff, who'd assumed the role of leading the discussion, said Chris's comments linked with the second question. He said that in the US, people tend to think of those who talk lots about the end of the world as 'crazy, like people who read *Left Behind* books; you wouldn't want to be associated with them'. Patrick said when he heard someone 'shouting something about the end of the world' on the street or on the Tube, 'you might *know* what they're saying is true, but you're still embarrassed by them'. When there was a pause in conversation, I asked the group why they thought that some cultures emphasize Jesus's return more than others. Jim, a tall blond engineering student with a soft Yorkshire accent, said that when he'd been in Ghana, Christians there placed more emphasis on Jesus's return, and he linked this with their experiencing material hardships. The rest of the group agreed that it was harder to focus on Jesus's return when the material comforts of their lives in London appear to offer, as Chris said, 'many ways to satisfaction'.

After ten minutes' discussion, the minister told everyone to wrap up, and said, 'we don't know exactly what Jesus meant when he said he was coming "soon", but as Christians, we should *learn* to love that promise'. Presenting ideals of how individuals might learn that love, he said that two of the church's mission partners in Belgium 'begin every day meditating on Christ's return. This is oxygen to the Christian soul.' He said Christians should focus on the *person* who is going to come, rather than thinking of Jesus's return as an event: 'the Lord I *now* depend on is the one who will come, so we need to build on our relationship with Him, grow in that relationship'. He said they needed to 'keep pointing each other to the words of Jesus . . . As we meet together, we are preparing each other for Jesus's return . . . No wonder we shouldn't add any words to this or take them away [referring to the passage in Revelation]: His words are perfect.' The group discussed how 'to learn to love that promise', and Jeff commented, 'as our lives now are finite, it doesn't matter whether that promise won't be fulfilled for several thousand years'. At the evening's close, as the group prayed, individuals said thanks to God for His promise of Jesus's return, and they prayed they would learn to be more focused on this.

Through this discussion, we can see that it is through practices of attending to the text of the Bible that this future element of belief is introduced into the present. A future orientation is present in most books of the Bible, from the promises made to Abraham and Moses, the prophets' expectation of God's judgement on Israel, to the imminent future eschatology of the New Testament authors who believed that the end of the world was nigh. But while apocalyptic expectations were not uncommon in the first century, members of St John's experience these teachings as profoundly at odds with the temporal orientations of the world around them. While there is a tendency to posit a return of apocalyptic thinking, religious and secular, in the wake of the financial crisis of 2008, this discussion shows that members of St John's feel that they *should* be thinking and speaking about Jesus's return, but that the comforts and satisfactions of this world make that difficult. And their friendships with each other—marked by their shared middle-class tastes—contribute to these comforts and satisfactions: the pleasure of a leisurely Sunday lunch served with wines expertly chosen by Alistair, in Lorna's dining room in her north London Georgian townhouse, looking out onto an autumnal garden as late afternoon turned to dusk, Lorna chatting excitedly about her upcoming fundraising Himalayan trek, with Philip putting effort into staying awake, exhausted after a week of long-haul business travel, or Lorna and Janet enjoying visits to the Proms or to the opera together.

This tension of *wanting* to be oriented to the future and the difficulty of maintaining this orientation was evident in many discussions. In one of the student group meetings, focusing on an apocalyptic passage in Luke's Gospel, Gemma asked, 'If we know that Jesus is coming back, and could come back any day, why don't we wake up in the morning and go, "wa-hey, Jesus is coming back today"?' Luke said he thought 'it's because we're too attached to the world. It's very easy to feel at home in the world.' Louise, a more senior student leader, commented, 'we are, in fact, aliens and strangers in the world'. Luke replied, 'it's like we're on vacation in the world, but we will be going home . . . I was talking about this the other day with Freddie, and was thinking about what I would do if I knew Jesus was coming tomorrow . . . I guess I would be like, those friends who I was waiting to get to know better before I mentioned Jesus, well, I'd make sure I got on with it.' He added, 'Wesley, when he was asked that, said he wouldn't change anything. Man, that man was godly.' Luke's comment that they're 'on vacation' in the world, in contrast with Louise's emphasis on being 'aliens and strangers', suggests that he has to a certain extent internalized this normative construction but nevertheless has a sense of enjoying the world.

The aim to discipline the self to be mindful of a future salvation was often bound up with focusing on mortality. Thus, as de Certeau described believing as involving the calculation of a future interest, the promise of eternal life they are encouraged to believe God offers is felt to be worth the 'costs' of faith, as they become habituated to contemplating their own mortality through listening to sermons focusing on this theme. Freddie, in a sermon on 2 Timothy, said: 'Paul wants us to be focused on the life to come, so you can take the shame. Be like a soldier who will endure anything as he looks forward to his commanding officer coming home.' He asked the congregation to turn to a particular passage, and read out St Paul's words:

> For I am already being poured out as a drink offering, and the time of my departure has come. I have fought the good fight, I have finished the race, I have kept the faith. Henceforth is laid up for me the crown of righteousness, which the Lord, the righteous judge, will award to me on that Day, and not only to me, but also to all who have loved his appearing.
>
> (2 Timothy 4: 6–8, ESV)

Freddie said Paul 'had made his choice' to endure and 'take the shame', and therefore approached his death 'with joy'. He asked the congregation, 'as individuals, have *we* made that choice?', demonstrating how bringing the future into the present entails asking the congregation to reflect on both God's judgement and their own mortality. Frank Kermode notes that Augustine saw that 'anxieties about the end are, in the end, anxieties about one's own end; he was long before me in suggesting that apocalypse, once imaginable as imminent, had the capacity to become immanent instead' (2000: 186). This is what it does at John's.

While church members strive to focus on the future, maintaining this focus is felt as a struggle: Pete said at the start of a sermon, 'what causes us to doubt the certainty of heaven?', and in another sermon, Hugo said, 'What keeps us from wanting the heavenly city?' As their orientation towards the future arises through focusing on the words of the Bible, it is also, we will see, partly their focus on words that leads to doubts and uncertainties about whether or not God is really present in their lives.

'LORD, I BELIEVE; HELP MY UNBELIEF'

Members of St John's express a conviction, as the Rooted group discussed in a study on 2 Corinthians, that while they are 'at home in the body . . . [they are] away from the Lord'. It is, they are taught, through words that God's character is mediated and they can experience a relationship with Him as they speak and listen. This presence and absence of God as the structure of faith was clearly articulated as the Rooted group discussed the phrase St Paul uses in 2 Corinthians, 'we walk by faith, not by sight'. Hannah, leading the discussion, asked what the phrase means. Edward, in a serious tone of voice, said, 'I think it means that we live by what we *know* is true, from what God has said in the Bible . . . But it's not the same as having a tangible face-to-face encounter with God . . . It's like if a parent were away from their child, and communicating by email. Our relationship depends on our listening to what He is saying and responding in obedience.' He reiterated: 'it's not the same as having the physical presence of the father there . . . the relationship can break down'.

We saw in Chapter 4 that emphasis on listening is a practice differentiating conservative evangelicalism from other Christian groups whose practices are characterized by visible forms of emotion or traditional ritualized practices. To repeat David's words: 'A Christianity that starts to rely on the visual . . . I need . . . an extra experience to assure me that I'm in the presence of God, that's deformed Christianity.' Some church members who had come from charismatic backgrounds experienced the lack of focus on emotions as experientially limiting. One student, John—who spent most of his interview criticizing aspects of St John's when we met up for lunch in a studenty café on The Strand—described services at St John's, as already mentioned in Chapter 4, as 'quite dry . . . I find it's all stand up, sit down, hands in pockets'. A few months after ending my fieldwork, John emailed me to ask how I was getting on, and commented that he'd started going to a new church.

This mistrust of emotions is linked not only to the historical emphasis on the Word in Reformed Christianity, but also, as already noted, to the male public school habitus of British conservative evangelicalism's key twentieth-century leaders (Ward 1997: 30), and it is possible to see class and evangelical identity continuing to co-constitute each other in the habitus they produce at St John's. When I interviewed Freddie, he expressed consciousness of this, acknowledging that the church was shaped by its post-war leaders being 'public-school educated, with a low value on expressing your emotions publicly, and it's probably fair to say that the leadership at [St John's] is still significantly drawn from that group'. He talked about the effect of 'the growth of the charismatic movement . . . the older generation at [St John's] remember that as a split, and remember defining themselves not as charismatics . . . And that's a really interesting question: to what extent we are in reaction to charismatics rather than actually true to the theological principles where we want to be.'

Freddie explained the theological rationale for privileging knowledge over emotionality as linked to emotions' instability in contrast with the unchanging constancy of God's truth: 'If you're walking on the wall, if you look at truth or reason and you walk along the wall and emotion follows after, if you turn around and look at emotion and try and walk along the wall, then you'd probably fall off.' He explained that emotions are important to being fully human, but that they should 'follow what you *believe* to be true. So if you believe that Jesus loves you . . . it would be strange not to have the emotional response that's appropriate to you as a person.' He said that if someone relies on emotions to determine beliefs, 'then if you're feeling depressed or . . . stressed, you will make wrong deductions about your Christian life'. This mistrust of emotions is bound up not only with a differentiation between human instability and the unchanging coherence of God, but also with the temporal orientation of conservative evangelicalism, differentiated from charismatic evangelicalism. At one of the Rooted groups' weekends away, the minister leading said, 'although there are many good things about the charismatic movement, it's based on heresies', saying that charismatics are 'too focused on enjoying the gifts of heaven now, and therefore not focused on the future'.

As we saw in this previous chapter, this emphasis on knowledge as the marker of faith does not mean evangelical life is *un*emotional. The God in whom they believe is both a transcendent unity *and* a jealous lover demanding their fidelity. These characteristics, as we have seen, have agency in naming evangelical subjects as guilty sinners, as their reflection on God's character both divides the subject and increases her desire for wholehearted devotion and coherence. However, their learnt focus on the future, this idea of belief as *knowledge*, and emphasis on the biblical text as the only reliable mediator of the transcendent God together have particular effects on conservative evangelical subjectivities, making the maintenance of their sense of relationship with God precarious.

A sermon David preached on John 14: 8–21 illustrates how this focus on words can produce a sense of uncertainty about whether the individual has *really* experienced God. The passage begins with the disciple Philip saying, 'Lord, show us the Father, and it is enough for us.' Jesus replies, 'Have I been with you so long, and you still do not know me, Philip? Whoever has seen me has seen the Father' (John 14: 8–9, ESV). David said the issue he was going to address was 'the wait between the departure of Jesus and His return some time in the future, and what it looks like for you and me to have a genuine experience of God today'. He said Philip's words can be interpreted as a request: 'please, give us a full-bodied, face-to-face physical encounter with God the Father, and that will be enough to answer all our questions as we wait for your return, Jesus'. He went on to state that this consciousness of Jesus's physical absence is common to all Christians:

> We are . . . looking at an issue . . . that puts into words a longing which every one of us will be familiar with. There will, I hope, be many here this evening who are investigating the Christian faith . . . you're very welcome here . . . But I can easily hear you saying, 'well, if only I could just *see* God, if only He'd make Himself known, face-to-face, then I could believe'. And then there will be plenty of us who perhaps have been following the Lord Jesus for longer, who long to see God face to face. We know enough of God to know that on the last day when Jesus returns it will be a glorious thing. And so we say to ourselves, 'Lord, won't you just know yourself to us, may we not see you, that will be enough?'

The sermon was characteristically predicated on the conviction that Jesus/God continues to speak through the Bible. The contemporary audience are imagined as posing a question—why can't God reveal Himself?—which Jesus answers through the medium of the text, so that engagement with the text is constructed and experienced as a conversation with God. The answer Jesus provides, David states, linking this to the passage from John, is: 'look at me, says Jesus, and you see God. Listen to me, says Jesus, you hear God. Touch me and you've touched God. Walk with me and you've walked with God.'

David said that although in listening to Jesus's words the individual experiences God, all Christians would at times, however, experience God's remoteness:

> There will come a time, if not now, then at some future point when you find in your Christian life that everything seems just a bit dry and dusty. God seems oh so

remote. How is it that I have a living experience of God? Once I had a vibrant, active, energetic, vivid experience of God, those years ago. But from time to time you will find yourself just a little bit out of sorts in your experience of God. The psalmist calls it like being a wine skin in the smoke. Now, personally, I've never been a wine skin in smoke, but one can imagine the feeling as the wine skin dries out and becomes brittle and dry and dusty. And elsewhere, the psalmist calls it like being in the desert. How is it then that I experience and regain that living walk, vibrant experience of God?

He emphasized that God works 'through the *words* of Jesus', and said that Jesus's miracles were evidence of the power of God's word, as, with turning water into wine, the raising of Lazarus, feeding the five thousand, 'Jesus *spoke* and it happened'. David said someone might object: 'it all seems so academic, all we're doing is just sitting, listening to the Bible; you want me to come on a Wednesday night to study God's Word and sit round a table with a group of other people and read a dry, old, dusty book?' He said Jesus would respond: 'that is how God works'. He asked the congregation to visualize a red traffic sign that instead of 'men at work' reads 'God at work', and to 'imagine that sign, every time you walk in the doors of [St John's] to hear God's Word: God at work. Every time you set yourself the discipline of daily reading of God's Word: God at work. When you set out on a Tuesday, a Wednesday evening to come and read the Bible, I'm coming to God at work.'

Describing a period in his life when he felt 'a period of great isolation, and I have to say real discouragement . . . I felt a very, very long way from God, and a very, very long way from any experience of God,' David said he used to play Christian music to try and recreate the atmosphere of his university Christian Union. He described this as wrong because it did not 'take the *words* of Jesus seriously', and highlighted other technologies of religious subject formation that he considered inadequate:

> My question was just the same as Philip's question, 'Lord, show me the Father, allow me to grow in Christian experience.' But the answer of coming to know Jesus does not come from a mystical experience on a mountaintop . . . nor does it come from some sort of sacramental encounter in a religious ceremony . . . Nor does it come from manufacturing moving moments with a worship group that lifts me to the heights and brings me down, or a preacher who makes me laugh and cry and moves my emotions. It comes through the powerful words of Jesus . . .
>
> I wish I had something slightly more exciting, something with more sort of rrmmph to it . . . You sort of think, well, surely there's some sort of technique, some sort of conference I can go to in the Outer Hebrides, surely there's somebody we can go and see and have special advice, or hands laid on us . . . and we'll have an experience of God. 'No,' says Jesus, 'look at me, listen to me, speak to me.' It's Sunday school, isn't it? It's what you were taught—if you were brought up in a Christian home—on your mother and father's knee. If you want an

experience, a genuine experience, of the living God, wonderfully, it's as simple as that...You don't have to travel off on pilgrimage to Lourdes or something...You've got it right here, everything you need. Look. Listen. Speak.

David touched on the idea of love as also what Jesus commanded, saying that those who love Jesus obey His commandments, and that this makes the church a 'family' united with Jesus and the Father. He said, 'Jesus Himself will come and dwell in us, with us, by His Holy Spirit', and asked members of the church, 'tomorrow morning, when you're putting on your make-up or shaving in front of the mirror...can I ask you to look at yourself in the mirror and say to yourself, if you're somebody who loves the Lord Jesus, "God [*pause*] dwells [*pause*] in [*pause*] me [*pause*]. In me."' He closed by emphasizing a distinction from their 'authentic' modes of relating to God and charismatic evangelicals' understanding of the Holy Spirit:

> The point is not that...I do the...dry, dull and academic study of God's Word and then, yes, ah *now* the Holy Spirit is going to come and work powerfully...Sometimes you go to a church like that where you hear the sermon and then the vicar gets down out of the pulpit [*David walks down the steps of the pulpit*] and he says, 'well, now we're going to ask the Holy Spirit to come and move powerfully in our midst', and the music strikes up, and everybody starts to feel all wobbly and stuff...[*David walks back up into the pulpit*]. That's the first time I've ever done that, and I won't do it again [*the congregation laugh*]. We used to be tied by the pulpit to one of these [*he gestures to an electric cable*].[6] But sometimes you hear people do that in church; it is almost blasphemous. It is almost blasphemous because it suggests that God the Holy Spirit is somehow separate from God the Son and His Word and work. No: it is *as* we are listening to God speak through His Word that God the Holy Spirit is at work in us. It's a wonderful thing, teaching, training, building, correcting, drawing near to us, enabling us to love the Lord Jesus.

This sermon is striking because David's acknowledgement that *all* Christians feel God's absence acutely from time to time contradicts impressions of conservative evangelicals as always confident in their faith. Here we see that the temporal delay implied in belief is imbued with pertinency, as individuals not only ask 'where art thou?' but can lose their sense of certainty in what the words of faith index.

While consciousness of Jesus's absence is an ineradicable element of Christianity, as ritual traditions and the text of the Bible are predicated on His death and the expectation of His return, this sermon suggests that in contexts in which there are no obvious *visible* experiential signs, such as speaking in tongues, crying, laughing, 'going a bit wobbly', or rituals such as the Eucharist, that *mark* the Christian as incorporated into the body of Christ, individuals

---

[6] Ministers at St John's use wireless headset microphones when preaching.

can doubt that God really *is* at work in them. David aims to act here as a guarantor of belief, himself looking to the text of the Bible as a guarantor, and he seeks to reinforce amongst the congregation a faith that they really *are* experiencing God when they come to church, read the Bible, and pray, while modelling how to interpret and deal with experiences of God's absence. As a minister, he thereby encourages church members to persevere in the disciplined repetition of practices of reading, listening, and praying, delegitimating other Christian traditions' practices that are perceived as taking away from the centrality of scripture. This is not a Protestant 'fantasy of immediacy' (Engelke 2010b: 812): we see clear acknowledgement of the importance of the text and practices of listening, looking, praying, and meeting together as the embodied forms by which individuals become oriented to a mediated transcendent. But we also see acknowledgement of the precariousness of these practices, which is bound up with their material form as words.

Merleau-Ponty describes language as a material form that has a tendency to disappear:

> The wonderful thing about language is that it promotes its own oblivion: my eyes follow the lines on the paper, and from the moment I am caught up in their meaning, I lose sight of them. The paper, the letters on it, my eyes and body are there only as the minimum setting of some invisible operation. Expression fades out before what is expressed, and this is why its mediating role may pass unnoticed, and why Descartes nowhere mentions it.
>
> (2002: 466)

Any human experience of language is always embodied. Listening depends on the vibration of sounding bodies and the training of the ear to attend to particular sounds. Reading and writing involve the eye scanning, interpreting, and reproducing words, a process which, as Harvey notes, abstracts properties, persons, and things from the flux of experience and fixes them spatially, with writing as 'a set of tiny marks marching in a neat line, like armies of insects, across pages and pages of white paper' (1989: 206), or today more likely across computer, phone, and tablet screens. Yet attentiveness to words rather than the embodied means of experiencing them can push 'the body below the threshold of consciousness' (Morgan 2012: 171), most famously leading Descartes to doubt the reality of the body itself. It might be expected that conservative evangelicals' focus on a transcendent God mediated through words would lead to an almost absent body. Yet David's acknowledgement of his doubting religious experience shows how the nature of embodiment itself complicates this: his emphasis that listening to the words of the Bible *is* experiencing God demonstrates a consciousness *both* that it is only through material practices of looking, listening, and so on that individuals can have a relationship with God *and* that embodied humans crave an interaction with the sacred that is felt as somehow *more* than this.

The precariousness of belief in this context, I want to suggest, is bound up with the interconnection of three threads of conservative evangelical experience outlined in the preceding chapters. First, as Eliot describes words as 'slipping, sliding', and as language tends, as Merleau-Ponty writes, to efface itself, in a broader cultural context in which sensuous experiences of the body are valued, it is easy for what is mediated by words to seem less real than forms of religion that mark the body as more visibly having experienced God, for example, through heightened states of emotion. Second, as God is transcendent and Jesus is physically absent, it is easy, in the everyday busyness of modern middle-class life, to forget Him. As Emma, a student, said, 'yeah, thinking about God and eternity, it's just hard when we're so wrapped up in the day-to-day and the here-and-now, and sometimes it's just hard to remind ourselves of Him, because He's not immediately present'. Third, as the subjectivities of church members are simultaneously formed in secular urban spaces encouraging modes of desire and practice that pull against those encouraged at St John's, this can lead to emotional uncertainty, especially when the 'future interest' calculated in the act of believing appears less attractive than what must be sacrificed for that. This was exemplified by people who said they'd experienced extended periods of questioning their faith when dating non-Christians (not encouraged at St John's); student leaders said relationships with non-Christians were one of the main reasons for students leaving the church.

Charles Sanders Peirce describes doubt as 'an uneasy and dissatisfied state from which we struggle to free ourselves', in contrast with belief as 'a calm, satisfactory state' (cited in Morgan 2010: 3). Peirce writes that because of the emotional disturbance doubt causes, 'we cling tenaciously not merely to believing, but to believing just what we do believe' (p. 3). Matthew, in charge of city ministry, articulated his understanding of the ongoing necessity of disciplined practices in terms resonant with this:

> the default position for all of us as Christians is drift. We don't have to do anything to drift; if we don't do anything, we do drift, but we've got to make an effort to keep going, to continue . . . The old line people used to say to me, 'read your Bible and pray every day' . . . when you chat to somebody about why they've drifted into all sorts of mess, almost invariably you can trace it back to, 'well, I was in a busy patch and my Bible reading and prayer went out the window'.

Individuals spoke of doubt as an uneasy state. Lucy said she had made a conscious choice to be a Christian at university, 'but then afterwards, I found myself thinking, well, is this just a nice idea?' and said she had experienced a more extended subsequent period of doubt: 'I remember standing there, at the station, and there was this huge black hole of, is it really true?' As the church leaders acknowledged doubt as part of the life of faith, they encouraged particular techniques to 'keep going'. At an Easter Sunday service, Stevie,

preaching on John's Gospel said, 'there are times for all of us that we doubt
... It could be that coming to church, you had a fleeting question: what if it's
not true? It might be that those doubts are more deep-seated than that. John
would say that the evidence is true. When those doubts spring up in my mind,
I turn back to the resurrection.' This statement that 'all of us' experience doubt
enables the evangelical who experiences doubt to interpret this as not unusual:
they are still included in the 'us'. At one of the Rooted weekends away, a
member of one of the groups asked about feelings of despair. Pete replied that
Martin Luther had made the grounds of belief 'Not how *I* feel . . . but the cross',
and said 'a good routine Christian prayer is, "Lord, I believe; help my
unbelief."'

As words can be experienced as slipping, cracking, the church staff and
older church members encourage younger members to use techniques to
enable them to persevere in their belief, and model how to respond to doubts.
Several people talked about how when they experienced doubt, they found it
helpful to focus on the resurrection, and the church leaders encouraged this
technique, with the Bible taken as a 'guarantor' of Jesus. Stevie stated, 'John
has written his whole Gospel so we would believe', and he said that there was
'rock solid evidence' for the resurrection: 'let this iron evidence strengthen
your belief'. In a question and answer session, one of the questions Freddie
read out for David asked, 'Is doubt of such things as foundations, God's future,
His promises, on an almost daily basis, is that part of the normal Christian
experience?' David's response emphasized the importance of work on the
self—by oneself and with friends—as important in overcoming doubt, and
characterized this as an ongoing task:

> Some people find their whole Christian life plagued by doubt. And that is part of
> the battle of the Christian life . . . And it is a battle. You think of Jesus in the
> Garden of Gethsemane, on His knees, praying to the Lord. I was thinking about
> this just this morning actually in my own prayers, you know, I must realize when
> temptation comes, that's what it is: a battle. And then put on the armour of faith
> and preach the gospel to yourself again. Tell your friends that you really struggle
> in this area and ask them to pray with you to remind you of the great gospel
> truths. And don't stop meeting together . . . but encourage each other all the more
> as you see the day draw near.

Several individuals spoke of dealing with doubts using this idiom of 'preaching
the gospel to yourself'. Steph said it was important to acknowledge doubts, 'to
have integrity but work things through . . . So, talk to yourself, preach to
yourself, and reason from the scriptures to yourself. And I think that meeting
up with another person can just be helpful with that.' Others talked of how
they referred to passages in the Bible where others experienced doubt, so that
they could identify with these authors. Louisa said the Psalms had become
'very personal' to her 'through difficult and struggling times . . . because they're

just honest as prayers before God, you know: Where are you? Where is your faithfulness? When will you come? Please don't delay.' Others talked about how when suffering led them to doubt God's faithfulness, they, like Jesus in Gethsemane, addressed their doubts—and sometimes anger—to God. Hannah, whose father was ill for most of the period I was conducting fieldwork, and who visited him every week as his condition deteriorated, said she found herself getting angry at God about this, and asked other Rooted group members to pray for her in managing this.

Sermons consistently emphasized God's constancy and fidelity to His people to encourage belief in spite of consciousness of His material absence or indications of His inaction, with the Bible instaurated as guarantor of this. Freddie, for example, opened a sermon on Isaiah 49 with the question 'Has God forgotten us?' and considered this in relation to verse 16, in which God says: 'I have engraved you on the palm of my hands'. Freddie said, 'God in the tattoo parlour is the image here . . . God is less likely to forget us than a mother is to forget her infant . . . God feels for us *more* than a nursing mother.' Sermons focusing on God's faithfulness and credibility were one of the most common themes during fieldwork, and these were invariably followed by prayers and songs expressing these ideas; for example, the hymn following this sermon was 'Great is thy faithfulness', which George introduced, saying, 'this is a song that reminds us that God cannot and will not abandon us'. Individuals singing these songs and saying these prayers together instilled a normative tilt to trust in these future promises and in God's presence, as the words of the following song articulated a conviction that 'Our God is with us now'.

The act of believing entails for members of St John's the developing of a trust that God *will* act to bring them into His presence *and* a conviction that they *have* been redeemed and forgiven and that He is with them. Yet individuals also articulated doubts that this. Weber highlighted uncertainty over salvation as a pre-eminent concern for Puritans (2001: 65ff), and despite the doctrine of assurance that is explicitly promoted at the church, members of the church—especially younger members—often expressed doubts that they really had been saved. Steph talked about a friend who 'would say things like, "I just don't know if God loves me", that kind of thing'. Sermons like Freddie's aim to counteract this by describing the certainty of God's love, and the individual techniques ministers encouraged to counteract doubts about salvation involved 'returning to the cross'. As discussed in the previous chapter, focus on Jesus's death produces an emotional response in church members, and despite leaders' discursive emphasis that emotions should not be taken as markers of their salvation, this orientation to Jesus's death produces an emotional response which helps individuals persevere in the light of their uncertainties.

Older church members occasionally spoke of doubts about their salvation. Lucy, who'd been coming to St John's for twenty-five years, said, 'you do *occasionally* think, you know, this is so wonderful, can it be true? I mean, it's like a fairytale, isn't it? It is; it's happily ever after.' David said in a sermon that sometimes he worried if he got angry with his children that he was 'not numbered among God's people', but said that he interpreted the fact that he worried about this as showing that he was 'in the land of blessing rather than curse'. However, most older church members said that as they got older, they learnt over time to trust they were forgiven. Liz said, 'Once you're middle-aged, you realize you're just a sinner, and you get used to the fact that you'll keep getting things wrong.'

Individuals are conscious of using these techniques of the self to form their knowledge, emotions, and desires as coherent, and Gemma described it as 'bringing her emotions in line with reason'. Thus as we saw that consciousness of failure to meet God's standards for wholeheartedness embed the believing subject into relationship with Him through producing them as guilty and leading to a sense of dependence on Jesus, so also the uneasy experience of doubt encourages techniques that reassure them of God's faithfulness to and love for them. Because God is physically absent and, as Matthew described, the natural state for Christians is 'drift', church members are conscious that maintaining the credibility of a transcendent Other can be hard work, and that clinging to belief and persisting in a temporal orientation to the future He promises requires effort and discipline. While their individual strategies of dealing with doubt help re-orient them towards belief, it is the ongoing practice of their habituated communal interactions with each other that ultimately keeps them knotted in relations that maintain their believing in God's presence and future.

INDIVIDUALITY, INCOMPLETENESS, AND INSUFFICIENCY

De Certeau describes how belief requires others' guarantees: 'It is because others (or many) believe it that an individual can take his debtor to be faithful and trust him. A plurality guarantees the guarantor' (1985: 201). At St John's, it is collective practices in the church that establish the credibility not only of God but of other believers and the Bible that help individuals 'keep going'. De Certeau argues that belief entails hollowing out a void in the self, taking from individual self-sufficiency as the existence of the other is marked on the self (p. 195). The practices that maintain members of St John's as believers are a means of forming subjects conscious of their individual insufficiencies and orienting them outwards. As individuals desire to turn beyond the self, *through* the self, to God, and learn to orient themselves towards past and future, they seek to cultivate themselves (individually and collectively) as not at home in and different from the world through their shared practices.

The different listening practices cultivated in the church and Bible study groups are understood as vital in enabling people to 'keep going' as believers. Gemma said that when she doubted that God loves her, she found it helpful to listen to a sermon that 'speaks the truth to me'. Leaders are conscious that it would be easy, in a large urban church, for individuals to drift in and out of church attendance, and instaurate the significance of Sunday services and small group meetings as the time in the week when they experience 'God at work'. They encourage the congregation to text or email friends if they haven't seen them at church for a while, and to invite newcomers to supper after services and to look out for and chat to them, so they quickly feel welcome. Church members do this: after I stopped attending services at the end of fieldwork, although I had made the endpoint of my study clear to those I had got to know, I nevertheless received emails from people asking when I was next going to be at church. Individuals thus knot each other into relationships of accountability, so they feel there are people who expect and want to see them at church.

This accountability was a particular feature of small groups, as members learn to narrate their participation in these groups as a form of 'serving' each other, with an expectation of reciprocity. When Emily was rarely present at the Rooted group during my second year of fieldwork because of netball practice, others in the group described her absence with a sense that she was letting them down. One student said to me, 'I don't know any other church with such strong accountability, through the small groups, with your leaders. If I miss a [Bible study] session, I'll get a text from my leader asking if I'm ok . . . Yeah, there's lots of accountability.' Mostly, however, it is the friendships they develop with each other that mean they *want* to keep attending the groups, and enjoy them. One woman told me she looked forward to her study group 'with delight . . . I've never missed it, in fact, all last year, I turned up for all of them, and this year, I thought I wasn't going to make it one week, because I had [a problem with her eye], but they put a patch on my eye . . . and somebody walked me to the station. I haven't missed one yet.'

As members make themselves accountable to each other and to God, they form themselves as obliged to give their time to each other. The details of their practices as they listen to sermons, read the Bible, listen to, talk, and eat with each other orients them towards listening to God, seeking to hear Him speak and learn of His character, and to become themselves as 'aliens and strangers' looking forward to God's promises for the future. As they seek to draw closer to Him, they likewise want to be 'other', different from those around, but are conscious that maintaining that distinctiveness is an ongoing struggle. As Pete said in a sermon, for Christians, 'there will always be areas of your life that set you apart . . . If your identity is rooted in the approval of people rather than God, there will always be a temptation to conform to the standards of the world.' He encouraged the congregation to think of alternative sources of value as insignificant compared with the meaning promised by God, citing Tolstoy as saying, 'Is there any meaning in life that would not be annihilated by the certainty of my death?' He said: 'Life is futile unless God has ransomed us from futility. From that moment on, every moment is flooded with meaning and value, as we fulfil God's purposes, in every second . . . Everything else in the world will perish. Jesus alone is the one who can save, the unblemished, spotless, Passover lamb. God has given us a faith and a hope that cannot disappoint.' He then encouraged members of the church to consider their identities in the light of this: 'At my core: who do I think I am? Where do I find my identity and my security?' He said that Christians should be 'living for Him . . . wanting to be like Him,' and referred to the 'danger facing the Western church of going "spiritually native" . . . Be different, so we can make a difference in this world.'

As church members seek to develop this collective orientation towards the world as ultimately futile and God as the sole source of their identity and security, we have seen throughout this book that this is experienced as a struggle. The pressures and rhythms of everyday middle-class metropolitan life make it easy to forget about God, and the moral milieu individuals inhabit outside the church encourage norms of interaction that are in tension with what they understand God as asking of them. Questions like those Pete addresses lead them to reflect on their internal divisions, conscious of alternative sources of value that mean they *do* care about the approval of others, as for example, they do not want to speak about the church's teachings on issues such as sexuality. Their listening practices in the space of the church are thus a means of evangelical subject formation that draw boundaries separating them from those outside the church while also dividing the subject within herself, heightening her consciousness of her internal fragmentation, as the demands to be holy are set out in ways that she is aware she falls short of.

The small groups are to a certain extent constructed as a space where these boundaries of who is inside and outside can be established, monitored, and controlled, with members' behaviour deemed important for what it signifies about the church's morality to others in the city. In a sermon on Joshua, David said, 'we live in a very atomized and individualized society, and we can find it hard to think about our connectedness to each other', and he said the message of Joshua is that church members' lives are interconnected: what they do with their private lives 'has an effect on others in the church'. Although this did not happen with those I observed, the small groups can be a site where church leaders police symbolic boundaries in areas that locate the church as morally distinctive from wider culture, for example, over issues of sexual morality. In a sermon focusing on the church's teaching on sex, Freddie said that the church had excluded unmarried cohabiting individuals from the church, by asking them to leave their Bible study groups, and one of the minister's hesitations about allowing me to be a participant-observer in one of the Bible study programme tracks was, he said, because perceived as a non-Christian and yet participating in the Bible study, my behaviour might be 'confusing' to the group.

However, this policing and boundary-controlling function was not evident in the groups I observed. Although members formed friendships with each other, they didn't necessarily lay all their private lives open to scrutiny in the contexts of the groups, and their disciplining of selves and each other was formed less through the shared exposure of their 'private' lives than through their repetitive focus on reading, listening, and talking about the Bible together as they sought to shape their thinking in line with the words of the text. Liz commented that one of the problems of being a Christian in the city compared with a small town is that it is easy to only present a certain side of oneself to others. Jan, a retired doctor and one of the quieter members of the Rooted group, said to me that she thought I wouldn't necessarily observe what really mattered to people through the small groups, indicating her sense that members wouldn't necessarily discuss the most intimate concerns of their lives in these spaces. Individuals did, however, form close friendships with other church members with whom they felt more comfortable talking about more intimate matters elsewhere, demonstrating how the felt boundaries of 'private' and 'public' shaped what they were comfortable speaking about across different spaces. The fact that small group members didn't lay bare their private lives to each other in this 'public' setting suggests their modes of interaction are shaped partly through their internalization of an ethic of non-interference and partly through the fact their discussions in the group were in practice dominated, following the church's set Bible study programme, by textual exegesis and discussion of the ethical implications of these texts.

Thus while the logic of the desire for wholeheartedness might appear to tilt towards establishing forms of accountability in which individuals expose their moral lives to each other, their collective practices are in practice shaped by an urban ethic of civility, and they respect each others' rights to privacy in the church and in small groups. While they routinely acknowledged aspects of the struggles of living out their faith together—admitting they found it hard to evangelize to friends or family, and collectively identifying a sense of their 'sinfulness' that reinforced their shared identity as a church—the small groups were not where these issues were addressed at length. Yet their modes of accountability to each other nevertheless encouraged them to keep meeting together, embedding them in the practice of belief through keeping them in forms of relationship that drew them back to the church to keep listening to God. As individuals became habituated in forms of practice that afforded them pleasure in the give and take of their interactions, they learned to act, together with their leaders and the characters in the narratives that are the object of their study, as guarantors of the credibility of the Bible, and in doing so helped reinforce in each other their desires and ambitions to be disciples.

CONCLUSION

Narratives of selfhood and identity are, as Alasdair MacIntyre describes, relationally formed as individuals give and ask for accounts of themselves and their actions: 'I am part of their story, as they are part of mine. The narrative of any one life is part of an interlocking set of narratives. Moreover this asking for and giving an account itself plays an important part in constituting narratives' (2007: 218). As individuals experience themselves as accountable to others and develop a sense that these others depend on them, this forms an ethic of self-constancy. Paul Ricoeur describes how accountability and an ethic of responsibility are interlinked: 'Because someone is counting on me, I am *accountable for* my actions before another. The term "responsibility" unites both meanings: "counting on" and "being responsible for." It unites them, adding to them the idea of a *response* to the question "Where are you?" asked by another who needs me' (1992: 165). As members of St John's make themselves accountable, asking 'where are you?' of each other, they make themselves 'responsible' to each other, weaving themselves into relationships of mutual obligation. They learn to narrate their collective practices as a means of 'serving' each other and God, and form a shared identity as the body of Christ, seeking to listen to Him and working together to enable themselves to keep going as believers.

In this intersubjective fashioning of their collective identity as the body of Christ, they not only ask 'where are you?' of each other, but also experience God asking this of them, and they also ask this of Him. Sennett argues that flexibility and mobility in the labour market led to capitalist conditions of time marked by short-termism, flux, and disjointedness, threatening people's ability 'to form their characters into sustained narratives' as they lack long-term witnesses of their lives (1998: 31). As most members of St John's have moved to London for work and typically change jobs several times in their working lives, their urban experiences are likewise marked by this flux. In this context, they work to make themselves accountable not only to each other, but to God, who is a long-term witness, demanding their self-constancy. They understand God as a coherent unity who wants *their* self-constancy and coherence, and this leads them to be conscious of their internal fragmentation, narrated as sinfulness, and embeds them in their sense of dependence on a God who offers ultimate coherence in the person of Jesus. Yet as transcendent, God is never materially present. Thus contrary to narratives of evangelical certainty, many members of the church ask, as Louisa and the psalmist did, 'where are you?' and want to be reassured of God's constancy. They are conscious of these doubts, which they experience as an uneasy state, and work on themselves and each other to keep going in their belief, summoning each other, the Bible, and the characters in it to act as witnesses guaranteeing their confidence in God's faithfulness and love. As they acknowledge doubts and share techniques for dealing with these, their identifications with characters in the Bible who doubt enable them to locate such experiences of disjunction as part of an overarching, coherent narrative. This encourages them to work hard to trust not in their own emotions, but to develop a sense of trust in the knowledge of God and His character that they understand the Bible as revealing.

As they seek to shape their focus as looking forward to a future, heavenly city, and God's presence with them, they are conscious of the extent to which they are rooted in the immanent, earthly city, which makes their focus on a transcendent, materially absent divine and their discipleship 'wobbly', as Hugo described. As he asked, 'what keeps us from wanting the heavenly city? What makes it seem remote and distant to us?', he expressed consciousness that more 'immediate and pressing' everyday concerns can easily 'take over from God at the heart of our lives' and become 'idols'. This consciousness, as we saw in the previous chapter, forms evangelicals' self-understanding as sinful standing before a coherent, transcendent God, experienced as Other. Yet while 'idolatry' is understood as a 'rebellious' construction of alternative sources of value, so that the technique of dealing with this is cultivating a desire for obedience, the experience of doubt is not described as due to wilful rejection of God. It is rather seen as inherent to the structure of a faith mediated in words and oriented towards God's transcendence. Thus individuals collectively reassure themselves that in listening to the words of Jesus in the Bible, they *are* listening to God. Conscious that their natural state is 'drift', in their coming together they work to discipline their desires and actions to be oriented towards a future, aware that maintaining this focus is a struggle as God's speaking and His promises of a future simultaneously index His present absence. As they seek to discipline their thoughts and desires so that they *do* want the heavenly city, their knotting each other into forms of accountability plays an important role in their forming each other as witnesses to each other and to God. Despite their discursive emphasis that it is *words* that matter, members of St John's are conscious that embodied forms of co-presence, through which they learn to focus on words, are what encourage them to keep clinging to their beliefs. It is only together, conscious not only of their dependence on God but on each other, that they can become disciples.

Conclusion

The Conflict and Tragedy of Culture

VLADIMIR: Was I sleeping while the others suffered? Am I sleeping now? Tomorrow, when I wake, or think I do, what shall I say of today? That with Estragon my friend, at this place, until the fall of night, I waited for Godot? That Pozzo passed, with his carrier, and that he spoke to us? Probably. But in all that what truth will there be? [ESTRAGON, *having struggled with his boots in vain, is dozing off again.* VLADIMIR *stares at him.*] He'll know nothing. He'll tell me about the blows he received and I'll give him a carrot. [*Pause.*] Astride of a grave and a difficult birth. Down in the hole, lingeringly, the grave digger puts on the forceps. We have time to grow old. The air is full of our cries. [*He listens.*] But habit is a great deadener. [*He looks again at* ESTRAGON.] At me too someone is looking, of me too someone is saying, He is sleeping, he knows nothing, let him sleep on. [*PAUSE.*] I can't go on! What have I said?

(Beckett 2006: 179–81)

DISAPPOINTMENT AND ITS AVOIDANCE

Perhaps life is ultimately disappointing. The unavoidable truth is that we will all die, but does the time between our births and the grave have meaning? Are our lives banal, deadened by purposeless habits, as Vladimir suggests? How *do* we go on? How do we live with experiences of meaninglessness, with frustrated and unfulfilled hopes and desires, with our shared and most singular disappointments, with society, with injustices in the world, with ourselves? Do we hide from the tragic tensions of life, as part of a 'cult of optimism' by striving to 'think positively'? Do we try to find solutions that direct our focus away from failures, away from the existential uncertainties and mess of life, away from our own human limitations? Or do we acknowledge that the good in life also entails the bad? That to grow, to love, and to cherish always ultimately entails pain and loss; that the decisions we make must always be impinged on by the needs and acts of others; that we are simultaneously inhabited by multiple, often contradictory, needs, wills, and desires; that 'the light gleams an instant, then it's night once more' (Beckett 2006: 177).

Religion is often seen as a response to life's inevitable disappointments, to injustice, to the fact of our mortality, a response offering meaning and hope in the face of meaninglessness and hopelessness; to a famous critic, an opiate enabling us to tolerate the pains of existence rather than seeking to change the unjust social conditions that cause these pains. We see that desire for meaning in Pete's words as he preached one Sunday: 'Life is futile unless God has ransomed us from futility. From that moment on, every moment is flooded with meaning and value ... Everything else in the world will perish ... God has given us a faith and a hope that cannot disappoint.' Questions of meaning and meaninglessness might seem to be perennial existential themes, but there is much about contemporary life that heightens feelings of disappointment and disjunction, as both internal and external fragmentation are intensified through processes of individualization and social and structural differentiation. While there have always been individuals and problems, these, as Ian Craib notes, might once have been seen as moral choices in the context of a community or as struggles with forces of destiny (1994: 98). The change, he argues, has been to start 'seeing them in terms of individual morality with individual solutions', as conceptions of the modern autonomous individual became increasingly isolated from the wider society (pp. 98–9).

Urbanization was an important aspect of this change. In his account of metropolitan modernity, Simmel argued that the only way we can deal with the constant sensory bombardment of everyday urban life is through rationalization and constant monitoring, cultivating our sense of individual distance as we engage with many mostly unknown others in our day-to-day mundane interactions in instrumental, one-sided ways. The bombardments from different stimuli that people face today in contemporary urban environments (and elsewhere) is greater than in Simmel's time, as the number of events and concerns we have seems endless, while the number of roles we are expected to play increases. In an account of an ordinary day in one of my informants' lives, such as Hannah's, we can see a few central roles: wife, mother, teacher, colleague, friend, Bible study group leader. And, as Craib notes of his own experience, each social role we inhabit can in itself be broken down further:

> As a husband, I am friend, colleague, lover, and an enemy, and presenter of problems for my wife to overcome. Each of these roles draws on some different part of my personality and that part must remain dominant for most of the time I am playing the role ...

> It is very difficult for me not to think of myself as made up of different parts, manipulating them as I move through the day; there is nowhere in the day where they all come together as a whole person. I might like to think that this happens with my family, but if I started to try to...lecture my son, I would soon be in trouble (and rightly so). Home is certainly the place where I experience my strongest emotions, whether of love or hatred, but they disrupt my other activities; I know a number of colleagues who feel relieved every Monday morning, when they can get away from the messy emotions of the weekend and 'be themselves', although, of course, they are no more themselves at work than they are at home.
>
> (Craib 1994: 101)

Craib's account was written before the new rush of information in our digitally mediated age that threatens, perhaps, to overwhelm us with constant streams of news, unmanageable inboxes, and social media feeds on our different screens 24/7, encouraging a particular kind of polyconscious fragmentation. Conditions of globalization can also intensify vertiginous senses of instability and insecurity, as labour and capital flow at ever-faster speeds across transnational markets, and impersonal, instrumentalizing logics of commodification increasingly shape all areas of life. Yet despite the impetus of late modernity towards the fragmentation of self and society, we struggle in our contemporary age, as Craib argues, to tolerate the failure of our plans and our experiences of fragmentation. Popular psychology and self-help guides offer the secular fantasy of an omnipotent, self-constructing, and self-governing human subject who is resolved to manage himself better to avoid future failures and disappointments, as if this could solve something, could reconcile the disorder and internal divisions that are an unavoidable part of the human condition (Burkeman 2012; Craib 1994: 170; Rose 1990).

EVANGELICALISM, FRAGMENTATION, AND THE CITY

Social scientists have typically portrayed evangelicalism as offering a response to fragmentation by holding out a promise of certainty, predicated on an understanding of divine revelation as an event out of time: its 'white heat re-establishes truth, realigns words of things, stems semiotic drift', anchoring meaning in an order and coherence beyond the self (Comaroff 2010: 29). It is also seen as a way of trying to avoid the inevitability of death, disappointment, and conditions of suffering and injustice through projecting a transcendent City of God that will compensate for dissatisfactions with the present, disordered, immanent city. And in one sense, this corresponds with the story I have told in this book: faith *does* offer the promise of an overarching order, a future without suffering, and an image of wholeness in the personality of God and the Kingdom He promises. But this story is also, as we have seen, too simple. The experiences of members of St John's that I have described here show them acknowledging both internal and external fragmentation. Their narrative practices further intensify this consciousness of internal division and their dissatisfactions with the messiness of urban modernity and the self-sufficient individualism they perceive around them, while increasing their longing for the coherence they feel God offering in contrast. We have also seen their awareness of the precariousness of these practices, the inevitability of the divisions and disorder they experience within self and society, and of the struggle required to maintain their orientation to a transcendent Other who imparts a sense of order to their everyday lives.

Although intensified in contemporary urban cityscapes, the interplay of experiences of fragmentation, limitation, and impotence, and images of wholeness are themes that reverberate throughout the history of both cities and Christianity. The history of the Western city tells the story of a long struggle between 'the effort to create power as well as pleasure through master images of wholeness' and the possibility of humans acknowledging their incompleteness, as cities and civilization confront us, 'in all our frailty, with contradictory experiences which cannot be pushed away, and which make us feel therefore incomplete' (Sennett 2002b: 372). Sennett argues that it is in the state of being aware of our incompleteness and difference that 'human beings begin to focus on, to attend to, and to explore, and to become engaged in the realm where the pleasure of wholeness is impossible' (p. 372).

In Sennett's narrative, the master image of the body in the history of the Judeo-Christian tradition was that of a spiritual wanderer who 'returned home to the urban center where his suffering body became a reason for submission and weakness' (p. 373). Yet he argues that this legacy, like that of Athenians and pagan Romans, carried deep internal contradictions:

> when early Christianity took root in the city, it reconciled its relation to this visual and geographic tyranny so antithetical to the spiritual condition of the wandering people of the Judeo-Christian Word and Light. Christianity reconciled itself to the powers of the urban center by dividing its own visual imagination in two, inner and outer, spirit and power . . .
>
> (p. 373)

The early urban Christians worked hard to sever their attachments to place through rituals and forms of collective practice that would keep their focus on the Word and Light. These rituals that drew them together aroused in them a sense of discomfort in the body, which turned people outwards towards each other as they sought to turn towards God and away from the city.

Seeking to be 'pilgrims through time' journeying towards the Celestial city today, members of St John's likewise work on themselves and each other to form themselves as exiles, to be different from those around them in the city. Their conversion to God entails their turning away from the securities, pleasures, and comforts they experience in London life, learning to view the world as transient and ultimately disappointing, the secular values of the city as potential lures into idolatry, and their own bodies as frail and dying. As David put it in his sermon on 1 Chronicles that we considered in Chapter 5, 'you think you're young . . . the world is your oyster, it's all lying ahead of you, you're in your thirties, maybe you're in your teens, or maybe in your forties, you think, "yeah, I've got loads of time". You're just a shadow. The Bible speaks of us as a breath on a cold winter's night. You breathe it out, it's there for a second, and it's gone.' Yet this process of conversion is a turning away from the world that can never be completed, and individuals are conscious that their attachments to place make it difficult to focus on what transcends time and space.

The division of the imagination between the earthly and the spiritual city still then reverberates in the lives of conservative evangelicals today. Yet the interweaving of a master image of coherence and experiences of contradiction and dissonance is somewhat different in the modern metropolis from how it was in early Christian experience. The personality of God on whom members of St John's learn to focus is both Word and Light, impassive, ultimate unity and power, yet simultaneously a God who desires them, who suffers, and jealously wants their wholehearted devotion. The transcendence of this divine enables them to understand God as a fully coherent One, these seeming contradictions posited as a mystery beyond the reach of limited human minds. At the same time, these paradoxical characteristics provide imaginative resources for them to orient themselves towards this transcendent source of coherence, whom they trust—though sometimes doubt—has called and loves them. They seek to draw Him into their own bodies as they internalize the words of the Bible and learn to focus on images and narratives of Jesus's death and resurrection.

Through these practices they are marked as part of the body of Christ, and this creates a sense of their dependence on and desire for God and each other. As desire, like belief, is always predicated on a sense of absence, the narrative of Christ's resurrection and ascent formed Christianity as a faith constituted in an awareness of a displacement, insufficiency, and incompleteness within the immanent social order, as the absent physical body of Jesus became transposed into the church as His body (Ward 2000). This narrative of incompleteness shapes how members of St John's come to understand and experience both self and the world as ultimately insufficient in themselves, desiring a transcendent God who is materially absent and desires them. As they seek to be dependent on and obedient to Him rather than the self, this obedience marks them as part of the body of Christ, an ethic they experience as at odds with modernizing ideals of self-determination and autonomy.

Sennett describes the master image of the body that shapes contemporary Western urban imaginaries as that of a body drawn into an increasingly solitary rest, through the development of modern comforts such as armchairs, air conditioning, and central heating, which meant that people no longer sought to be with each other in public spaces (2002b). One of the main ways that members of St John's interpret their lives as different from what they see as an individualized, atomized society around them is through the modes of sociality and connections with each other they form through the church. As Hannah said, her life would be 'much more lonely' if it were not for St John's. Yet they are also conscious of the material comforts of their lives in the city and the extent to which this interrupts their focus on the future and desire to sever their attachments to place, and this leads them to experience doubts and uncertainties. The uneasiness of doubt encourages them to keep drawing to each other in collective practices, as they seek to cling to what they believe through their connections with and established accountabilities to each other and to God. Through these collective and individual disciplines, they acknowledge uncertainty, struggle, and their own sense of guilt and sinfulness, which then serves to bind them more closely in their desire for a God who relieves these tensions; and they narrativize these doubts and struggles as an 'ordinary' part of Christian experience.

The forms of practice internalized through their participation in church life mean that they have a strong sense of belonging to a bounded community and of the symbolic lines of division marking out the boundaries of their belonging. This emerges through their consciousness of the need to craft forms of mutual accountability in a large urban church and through their strategies of differentiation from charismatic evangelical churches, the latter of which leads them to emphasize the importance of their collective listening to a physically present minister. Like the Swedish charismatics that Coleman describes, members of St John's seek to internalize sacred words and circulate them to others. Their interpretation of their mundane conversations with others in the city around them as a potential means of this circulation (even if in practice this is a struggle) enables a pietization of everyday life, in which the pious are distinguished from those to whom they seek to witness (Turner 2011: 291). While Pentecostals' minds are 'colonised by the transcendent world of the Spirit' (Coleman 2000: 127), members of St John's seek to have their minds shaped through internalizing and submitting to the words of scripture addressed to them by a transcendent God who speaks. Yet through their focusing on the Word rather than 'experience' as marking their relationship with God, members of the church can also experience doubts and uncertainties that they really have been saved, or that they really have experienced God, and this means that forms of relationship with each other draw and mostly keep them together.

This focus on words does lead them, as Keane (2007) describes, to be concerned with sincerity, truthfulness, and belief, and to have a sense of the agency of the rational self who is individuated in their choice to respond in obedience to the will of God. Yet theirs is not a simple individualized notion of modern autonomy. Their narrative emphases on the agency of forms of mass media, of 'enslaving' expectations of corporate capitalist workplaces, of the pull of broader cultural practices and values, and of each other, are a way of articulating the complexity of relations between body, self, other, and society. Yet also exercising agency here is the personality of God. His coherence leads them to desire their own coherence, while increasing their awareness of their moral fragmentation as they move between incommensurable practices in the metropolis, as, for example, their subjectivities are formed through both norms of tolerance and privacy *and* the desire to speak of their faith in public ways that resist the 'ethic' of indifference.

As the roots of the evangelical movement emerged during Enlightenment modernity, and spread in public gatherings, so the forms of public listening and speaking it encouraged are recognized as formative in the creation of American civic life, and these bear their traces in the expressed desire for public listening and speaking at St John's today. Yet, as the teachings of the church rub up in increasing tension with modern norms of equality and members of the church become increasingly conscious of their being labelled intolerant and judgemental, they struggle to speak, as they are simultaneously shaped as modern, secular subjects, valuing norms of privacy and tolerance. Understanding how evangelical subjectivities can be both secular *and* religious challenges stereotypical understandings of evangelicalism as a culture that seeks to impose conditions of order on societies in response to the uncertainties and insecurities of inhabiting an increasingly fluid and fragmented world. While members of St John's learn to desire coherence and instil a sense of personal discipline within their own lives, and they desire to 'witness' to those around them, their secular sensibilities inhibit any desire to impose this order on others and limit the extent to which they choose to speak about their faith with others.

Through their focus on God's personality as coherent, members of St John's become increasingly conscious of the sense of shame and embarrassment that inhibits their speaking as a form of internal division, which they narrate in idioms of sin and idolatry. This consciousness of their own fragmentation increases their sense of separation from and desire for God as the pure coherent reconciliation of the tensions and contradictions of life in the present. Despite their learnt orientation towards the transcendence of God, maintaining attention on one who is materially absent is a constant struggle, and this introduces, as Simmel describes, a further form of fragmentation, specific to their faith, into their everyday lives. Their bodies then become the location of immanent/transcendent tensions as they seek to form themselves through particular techniques as subjects oriented to doing what they experience God as asking of them. Their developing consciousness of their own mortality and fragility framed in relation to a God who offers coherence and a transcendent order provides the mundane details of their lives both with a heightened sense of meaning and a means of acknowledging experiences of failure and of the ultimate recalcitrance of the world, even if, as they acknowledge, in the busyness of their everyday lives they can often lose sight of this.

Simmel describes the human being as 'the connecting creature who must always separate, and who cannot connect without separating...And the human being is likewise the bordering creature who has no borders' (1997a: 174). We have seen that members of St John's engage in interactions through which they seek to separate themselves from others, as 'exiles', forming themselves as oriented towards different values than those they describe as dominant in wider society. The public statements of conservative evangelical leaders articulating a tension between universalizing modern processes and traditionalist moral positions reinforce this narrative of a distinctive moral identity, their sense of being 'aliens and strangers' and increasingly counter-cultural. Yet we have also seen that this distance from 'others' can be hard work to maintain, as members of the church simultaneously live within, are shaped by, and find comfort in these same secular spaces. Their subjectivities are the site where they are at times conscious of how these connections and separations can rub up against each other.

My aim in this book has been to move away from simplistic portraits of evangelicals that arise through either sensationalizing exposé or apologetic homages that circulate in the media and influence wider public understandings. I have shown how members of St John's experience and find, within the immanent city, ways of negotiating human vulnerabilities, sensitivities, needs, and anxieties that shape social life more broadly, and have explored the specific effects of their faith in this process. My account challenges stereotypical understandings of evangelical certainty, missionary zeal, and intolerance, showing how the interactions of members of St John's are shaped by an urban ethic that makes them reticent about articulating their faith publicly: they do not want to express views that might be interpreted as an attempt to impose their moral teachings on others. Yet, their subjectivities are also shaped through the *desire* (even if unrealized in practice) that their faith will shape all of their everyday interactions, and that they would be 'other' from those around them and 'witnesses' for Jesus across all the moral milieu they inhabit.

Orsi describes the study of religion as constructing moralizing figures of 'otherness' that have fortified the difference between the liberal academic self and particular religious 'others', but examining conservative evangelicals' practices across different spaces in the city troubles this impulse. The subjectivities of these urban dwellers are formed through the complex intersection of a sense of relationship with God and each other, their being addressed by traditionalist moral teachings, including those on issues such as gender,

sexuality, and other religions in tension with secular modernity, and a simultaneous inhabiting of liberal, pluralist spaces outside the church that lead them
to experience these teachings as a cultural taboo that they are, in most of the
everyday spaces they inhabit, unwilling to transgress. Their consciousness of
these tensions, narrativized as sin and idolatry, increases their desire for God.
This God is experienced as other, differentiated through objectifying contrasts
between His coherence and their fragmentation. Yet He is also experienced
as within, shaping, and troubling the boundaries of the self, even while
remaining, as transcendent, always infinitely Other and physically absent.
For conservative evangelicals, believing in Him requires learning to look
through the present city to a vision of an eternal city beyond time. To do
this, they must connect with each other, and this provides a means of being
both at home and an exile within the city.

Analysing speaking and listening as forms of practice and their enactment
over time helps, then, to reveal the entanglements of evangelicals' forms of
simultaneous connection with and separation from others in everyday social
life. We have seen how they experience a sense of relationship with God
through specific modes of speaking and listening, and how these are bound
up with a particular moral logic and motivation to form the self as an ethical
subject. This opens up future possibilities for exploring the extent to which
other forms of religious practice are bound up with desires for coherence and
moral projects to form the self. Focusing on the personality of God and the
effects this has on the formation of evangelical subjectivities in particular leads
to further questions about the specific agency of monotheistic instaurations of
the divine. But the extent to which other techniques of the self provide means
of either acknowledging or avoiding conditions of disappointment and the
messiness of life might also be questions for research on other non-religious
and spiritual practices, for example in therapy, self-help, or New Age cultures,
opening up questions about the political implications and the orientations to
the social order these promote. And these questions that might also perhaps be
posed to scientific, philosophical, and other 'secular' academic practices and
enterprises.

My focus on urban religious piety shows how, in a pluralist environment,
religious actors differentiate themselves from and delegitimate the practices of
others (both religious and non-religious), while also revealing the fragility of
these boundaries of distinctiveness and the effort required to sustain them.
Focusing not only on what evangelicals say but on their speaking practices and
struggles to speak demonstrates the complex interrelation of 'public' and
'private' in religious experience, complicating narratives of the privatization
or de-privatization of faith as straightforward linear processes, and revealing
differences between evangelical leaders' emphasis on the need for 'public'
expressions of faith and the practices of ordinary congregants. These interrelations between 'public' constructions of religion by leaders and the media

and the everyday lives of members of religious groups are important areas to explore further in developing more nuanced understandings of the increasingly complex ways in which religion is located, negotiated, and contested across different and interlinked social spaces in the contemporary world.

INTERSUBJECTIVITY, ETHICS, AND THE TALE OF TWO CITIES

Examining experiences of what it is to live within and across these interlinked social spaces, my analysis has drawn on scholarship arguing for the importance of taking sacred figures seriously as part of these social worlds, opening up more expansive conceptions of everyday relationality. It is possible to explore the conditions of evangelical faith through a mode of sociological analysis that has typically constructed binaries of power relationships in terms of oppressor/oppressed, a variation of the Hegelian master–slave dialectic. The faith of members of St John's, as we have seen, expresses a sense of disappointment in the conditions of late capitalist modernity—as well as in wider tragedies of the human condition—even if to most spectators, many members of the church would appear to be richly rewarded by those conditions. Yet while we need to acknowledge the structuring force of conditions of social and economic inequality, a story focused solely on the power play of oppositional strategies and tactics does not do justice to my informants' experiences of spiritual and material relatedness, intensities, conflicts, and desires, which exist within and simultaneously exceed dialectical logics (cf. Singh 2014). Building on literature that examines how the transcendent is experienced through material and emotional practices (Engelke 2007; Meyer 2008, 2010; Morgan 2012), there is potential to develop richer, intersubjective portraits of religious lives to deepen insight into forms of spiritual relationality and striving, how divine personalities are experienced as making demands on individuals through particular practices, and the social agency of these personalities in shaping subjectivities. This contributes to literature in the anthropology of ethics, as well as the sociology of everyday life and religion. The rapidly growing interest in 'the moral' as a modality of social life is opening up avenues for empirically attending to fundamental existential questions about what it is to live a good life, and how this is negotiated within the concrete limits of everyday social existence. This has the potential to stimulate the study of religion to deeper engagement with central questions of meaning, value, and the moral imaginations shaping how people treat each other and how they feel they *ought* to treat each other, questions deeply rooted in the history of the discipline of sociology.

Much of the growing body of anthropological literature on ethics has drawn on Aristotle's discussion of *phronēsis* and Foucault's approach to techniques of the self (e.g. Faubion 2011; Laidlaw 2002; Lambek 2010; Robbins 2004), and I have also drawn on Foucault. The approach to everyday ethics I have taken here has also explored how relationships with sacred figures are important aspects of ethical formation within evangelicalism. One could analyse the formation of members of St John's as ethical subjects purely through focusing on their disciplines of introspection, confession, prayer, and Bible reading, in the Foucauldian and Aristotelian sense of the development of specific virtues and orientations to the self. Yet, following Latour and drawing on Levinas's approach to ethical subjectivity, developing a *realist*, empirical account that engages with the lived textures of these subjects' experience requires engaging with all their social relationships and the specificities of how these have agency in shaping who they are. The desire of members of St John's to do what God wants stems from their learnt sense of Him as 'searing moral purity', whose teaching 'draws me like a moth to the light', and their consciousness of God as One who *wants* their love, devotion, and trust. The naming of the ideals of moral purity, unity, and coherence in the personality of God thus has social effects in introducing into the evangelical subject an excessive demand to respond to Him through seeking to 'be perfect', a demand she can never fully meet. Narrating this in terms of guilt serves to bind the evangelical subject not only in her sense of relationship with God but also in her sense of relationship with other 'sinners'.

Aristotelian and Foucauldian understandings of the making of moral life imply a sense of people developing ethical orientations and virtues, individually and with others. God and other sacred figures are therefore important 'others' to consider as actors in this process. Future work on the everyday experience of evangelicals' and other groups' negotiation of their moral lives and meanings might, in addition to focusing on techniques of the self, give further attention to how modes of intersubjectivity are a significant part of this, how the lives and loves of sacred figures act within their social worlds, making people do and desire certain things, binding and unbinding particular kinds of relationship in space and time.

Conservative evangelicals' desire to form themselves to be better listeners and speakers is bound up with their affective experiences of being addressed by God and asked to respond to Him, in modes of interaction that pull against their being simultaneously addressed by multiple others who ask other things of them. These multiple and contradictory modes of address shape the conditions of the formation of their subjectivities. This experience of a divine address divides the evangelical within herself and encourages her to work on herself to come closer to the ideals of moral perfection she perceives God as asking of her. Dwelling within the fragmented cityscapes of late modernity, she is also multiply divided by the overwhelming quantity of cultural forms and sensations she has to negotiate in everyday urban life. Reflexive evangelical technologies of the self encourage her to narrativize her divided subjectivity through the binary moral language of sin and holiness, and to become most conscious of her habits, thoughts, and desires that are at odds with what she perceives God as asking of her.

Nietzsche saw the affirmation of multiplicity and plurality in life as the essence of the tragic (as well as essentially joyful): we cannot make everything an object of affirmation; we cannot say Yes to all (Deleuze 1983; Nietzsche 1999). And Simmel, influenced by Nietzsche, also theorized culture as essentially tragic, as the human cannot possibly respond to the 'overladening of our lives with a thousand superfluous things from which we are unable to free ourselves' (1997d: 75). The modes of intersubjectivity of the St John's congregants can also be seen as ultimately tragic. These individuals both acknowledge multiplicity and the plurality of forces at work within the self while also—*contra* Nietzsche—longing for a resolution of these tensions, to be able to say Yes over and above all else to God, a reconciliation they know is ultimately impossible in the everyday conditions of social life.

While I have explored here some of the specificities of the forms of intersubjectivity implied within conservative evangelicalism, these questions of the material and intersubjective formation of moral motivation and desire are also relevant to other religious and non-religious lifeworlds. Does the formation of ethical subjectivity necessarily entail a division of the subject, as he or she imagines the way a world could be, memorably expressed by Emerson: 'I know that the world I converse with in the cities and in the farms, is not the world I *think*' (cited in Cavell 2004: 1). This captures a central idea within the history of Christianity: that of 'the human being regarding his existence from two standpoints, and through which human nature can be seen as divided, or double' (Cavell 2004: 1). But this, as Cavell notes, is not limited to Christianity. If ethical subjectivity involves a division of the subject within herself, then how, when, and where does this division take place? What are the discursive, material, and intersubjective processes and forms of attachment implicated in this within other lifeworlds? And what forms of exclusion and othering are bound up with these modes of attachment? Marx's diagnosis that, with Protestantism, there was 'no longer a question of the struggle of the layman with the priest outside himself, but rather of his struggle with his own inner priest, with his priestly nature' holds for conservative evangelicals today. And drawing attention to the forms of relationality implied in particular modes of subjective division helps deepen understanding of the affective interconnections of self and social collectivity in this process further. In the story told here, I have shown the centrality of shame, guilt, and doubt in the process of subjective division for conservative evangelicals in London, but we might ask what other emotional affects are involved in processes of subjective division taking place in other religious and non-religious lifeworlds?

Focusing on how members of St John's perceive God as addressing and binding the whole church in an intimate love relationship reveals the limitations they place on individual agency, even as they are individuated through their sense of a responsibility to respond to a divine address. This opens up how people hold differing ideas of agency and subjection together in the contemporary world. American Protestant fundamentalism has been seen, as Turner writes, as a 'sustained struggle against the expressive revolution . . . a struggle between two conceptions of the self – the Kantian ascetic and disciplined self, and the expressive-affective mobile self', the former emerging from Protestant asceticism and the latter a 'distortion of the expressive self of the conversionist sects of the eighteenth and nineteenth centuries' (2011: 81). Yet focusing on the differing ways evangelicals relate to the personality of God and on their relations with each other reveals how, although there is a discursive privileging of the rational and ascetic, also expressed (and often lingering below the surface of narrativity) is an emotional eroticism of desire for communion with God. Evangelicals' desire for coherence and order within themselves and social life, bound up with their focus on the transcendent coherence of God, is related to an understanding of a rightly ordered society as structured through modes of obedience and submission to hierarchical authority, manifested in relations between humans and God, and in the spheres of church, home, and family life. This emphasis on submission to authority leads evangelicals to experience this heteronomous moral orientation as running counter to modern ideals of autonomy. This is, however, deeply rooted in central narratives of Western Christianity, as expressed for example in Augustine's depiction of the two cities:

> [The] two cities were created by two kinds of love: the earthly city was created by self-love reaching the point of contempt for God, the Heavenly city by the love of God carried as far as contempt of self. In fact, the earthly city glories in itself, the Heavenly City glories in the Lord . . . In the former, the lust for domination lords it over its princes as over the nations it subjugates; in the other both those put in authority and those subject to them serve one another in love, the rulers by their counsel, the subjects by their obedience. The one city loves its own strength shown in its powerful leaders; the other says to its God, 'I will love you, my Lord, my strength.'
>
> (Augustine 1984: 593)

Yet although this moral imagining of a coherently ordered social, relational, and subjective order expressed in the City of God is—as evangelicals experience—ultimately impossible to realize amid the messiness and fragmentation of modern life, this nevertheless shapes their 'moral ambitions' for themselves to journey towards that City (Elisha 2011).

Their ambitions to be 'aliens and strangers', distinctive from those around them, and the shaping of this moral ambition through their focus on the personality of God, and their desire to 'witness' to others, can be compared with Nietzsche's expression of moral perfectionist sentiments:

> How can your life, the individual life, receive the highest value, the deepest significance? How can it be least squandered? Certainly only by your living for the good of the rarest and most valuable exemplars, and not for the good of the majority, that is to say those who, taken individually, are the least valuable exemplars . . . for culture is the child of each individual's self-knowledge and dissatisfaction with himself. Anyone who believes in culture is thereby saying: 'I see above me something higher and more human than I am; let everyone help me to attain it; as I will help everyone who knows and suffers as I do.'
>
> (cited in Cavell 2004)

Many thinkers—including Nietzsche, Sennett, and others—have however criticized the impulse to turn towards the transcendent and look for images of coherence as ultimately futile, denying acknowledgement of both the joys and the inevitable disappointments of both contemporary social life and the human condition. As Oliver Burkeman puts it in his provocative critique of particular kinds of 'positive thinking' and 'self-help' cultures, *The Antidote*, 'perhaps the most valuable of all talents is to be able *not* to seek resolution; to notice the craving for completeness or certainty or comfort, and *not* to feel compelled to follow where it leads' (2012: 206). Yet while Burkeman argues that seeking certainty and completion is a flawed quest, as they will always ultimately elude us, although such cravings may *not* lead us to be happy, as he argues, they may have other subjective, social, and political effects that invite further sociological attention. And the desire for completeness and certainty can—as the lives of members of St John's show—simultaneously, somewhat paradoxically, be held together with the acknowledgement of the impossibility of resolution.

Perhaps, as Cavell argues, visions of and arguments about the good city—what he calls 'an imagination of justice'—are important, and utopian moments in moral thinking, transcendental elements, may in the end be 'indispensable in the motivation for a moral existence' (p. 18). Reflecting on the imaginings of and desire for a transcendent City of God formed through participation at St John's—and the difficulty of maintaining this—I wonder about the roles that different religious cultures play today in shaping particular experiences of either hope or disappointment in the contemporary social order, and the role these play in moral and political motivation and action. How do the temporal logics, memories, and dreams implicated in these cultures shape both the everyday realities and stories people tell about their engagements with others? The particular orientation towards the future encouraged at St John's can be seen as part of a broader evangelical logic of engagement with the world, where the world is understood as in need of salvation creating an impulse of responsibility to work towards that salvation. Maybe this utopian imagination written into the narrative of two cities—however differently it is articulated—is ultimately, inevitably tragic, because the utopian ethic of love inscribed in the Kingdom of God will perhaps always be at odds with the violence, injustices, and exclusions of the immanent political order, and it therefore encourages disappointment in this. But it can also at the same time offer individuals grounds for comfort and consolation, and perhaps also a particular kind of moral seriousness and motivation that is often missing in wider contemporary social and political life. If the conditions of culture, indeed of life, in all its multiplicities, complexities, intensities, conflicts, and beauty, are ultimately tragic, then how particular forms of life are a means of responding to this, and how these shape the ways in which we connect with and separate from others, are questions not only for scholars of religion, but for all of us, to address.

Bibliography

Alpha. 2010. 'The Alpha Course Script 1: Who is Jesus?', *Alpha International*, <http://www.hinckleybb.co.uk/downloads/ALPHA.pdf> (accessed 11 December 2014).

AlSayyad, Nezar and Mejgan Massoumi (eds). 2011. *The Fundamentalist City? Religiosity and the Remaking of Urban Space*, London: Routledge.

Anderson, Johan, Robert M. Vanderbeck, Gill Valentine, Kevin Ward, and Joanna Sadgrove, 2011. 'New York encounters: religion, sexuality, and the city'. *Environment and Planning A* 43: 618–33.

Arcade Fire. Not dated. 'Neon Bible', *Arcade Fire*, <http://www.arcadefire.net/lyrics/neon/> (accessed 8 August 2012).

Asad, Talal. 1993. *Genealogies of Religion: Discipline and Reasons of Power in Christianity and Islam*, Baltimore, MD: The Johns Hopkins University Press.

Augustine. 1961. *Confessions*, trans. R. S. Pine-Coffin, London: Penguin.

Augustine. 1984. *Concerning the City of God against the Pagans*, trans. Henry Bettenson, London: Penguin.

Austin-Broos, Diane J. 1997. *Jamaica Genesis: Religion and the Politics of Moral Orders*, Chicago: University of Chicago Press.

Badiou, Alain. 2003. *Saint Paul: The Foundation of Universalism*, trans. Ray Brassier, Stanford: Stanford University Press.

Baudelaire, Charles. 1995. *The Painter of Modern Life and Other Essays*, ed. and trans. J. Mayne, London: Phaidon.

Bauman, Zygmunt. 2000. *Liquid Modernity*, Cambridge: Polity Press.

BBC News. 2012. 'Banned gay bus ad group looks at legal action against TfL', *BBC News*, 13 April 2012, <http://www.bbc.co.uk/news/uk-england-london-17706866> (accessed 18 April 2012).

Beaumont, Justin and Chris Baker (eds). 2011. *Postsecular Cities: Space, Theory and Practice*, London: Continuum.

Bebbington, David. 1989. *Evangelicalism in Modern Britain: A History from the 1930s to the 1980s*, Abingdon: Routledge.

Beck, Ulrich. 2005. *Power in the Global Age*, Cambridge: Polity Press.

Beckett, Samuel. 2006. *Waiting for Godot: En attendant Godot*, London: Faber & Faber.

Beckford, James A. 2003. *Social Theory and Religion*, Cambridge: Cambridge University Press.

Bell, Daniel. 1978. *The Cultural Contradictions of Capitalism*, New York: Basic Books.

Bender, Courtney, 2012. 'Practicing Religions'. In *The Cambridge Companion to Religious Studies*, ed. Robert A. Orsi, 273–95, New York: Cambridge University Press.

Benjamin, Walter. 1999. *Illuminations*, London: Pimlico.

Berger, Peter. 1969. *The Sacred Canopy: Elements of a Sociological Theory of Religion*, New York: Anchor Books.

Berger, Peter, B. Berger, and H. Kellner. 1974. *The Homeless Mind: Modernization and Consciousness*, New York: Vintage.

Berman, Marshall. 1983. *All That Is Solid Melts into Air*, London: Verso.

Bialecki, Jon. 2008. 'Between Stewardship and Sacrifice: Agency and Economy in a Southern California Charismatic Church'. *Journal of the Royal Anthropological Institute* 14(2): 372–90.

Bialecki, Jon. 2009. 'Disjuncture, Continental Philosophy's New "Political Paul," and the Question of Progressive Christianity in a Southern California Third Wave Church'. *American Ethnologist* 36(1): 110–23.

Bialecki, Jon. 2011. 'No Caller ID for the Soul: Demonization, Charisms and the Unstable Subject of Protestant Language Ideology'. *Anthropological Quarterly* 84(3): 679–704.

Bielo, James S. 2009. *Words upon the Word: An Ethnography of Evangelical Group Bible Study*, New York: New York University Press.

Bielo, James S. 2011a. *Emerging Evangelicals: Faith, Modernity and the Desire for Authenticity*, New York: New York University Press.

Bielo, James S. 2011b. 'City of Man, City of God: The Re-Urbanization of American Evangelicals'. *City and Society* 23 (Special Issue 1): 2–23.

Bourdieu, Pierre. 1984. *Distinction: A Social Critique of the Judgement of Taste*, London: Routledge.

Bourdieu, Pierre. 1990. *The Logic of Practice*, trans. Richard Nice, Cambridge: Polity Press.

Bourdieu, Pierre and Loïc Wacquant. 1992. *An Invitation to Reflexive Sociology*, Chicago: University of Chicago Press.

Brierley, Peter (ed.) 2006a. *Religious Trends Number 6*, London: Christian Research.

Brierley, Peter. 2006b. *Pulling Out of the Nosedive: A Contemporary Picture of Church-going*, London: Christian Research.

Brown, Callum G. 2009. *The Death of Christian Britain: Understanding Secularisation*, 2nd ed. Abingdon: Routledge.

Bruce, Steve. 2002. *God is Dead: Secularization in the West*, Oxford: Blackwell.

Bryant, Levi, Nick Srnicek, and Graham Harman. 2011. 'Introduction'. In *The Speculative Turn: Continental Materialism and Realism*, ed. Levi Bryant, Nick Srnicek, and Graham Harman, 1–18, Melbourne: Re-Press.

Buck-Morss, Susan. 1991. *The Dialectics of Seeing*, Cambridge, MA: The MIT Press.

Burchardt, Marian and Irene Becci. 2013. 'Introduction: Religion Takes Place: Producing Urban Locality'. In *Topographies of Faith: Religion in Urban Spaces*, ed. Irene Becci, Marian Burchardt, and José Casanova, 1–21, Leiden: Brill.

Burkeman, Oliver. 2012. *The Antidote: Happiness for People Who Can't Stand Positive Thinking*, Edinburgh: Canongate.

Butler, Jon. 1990. *Awash in a Sea of Faith: Christianizing the American People*, Cambridge, MA: Harvard University Press.

Butler, Judith. 1990. *Gender Trouble: Feminism and the Subversion of Identity*, New York: Routledge.

Butler, Judith. 2005. *Giving an Account of Oneself*, New York: Fordham University Press.

Butler, Judith. 2009. *Frames of War*, London: Verso.

Campbell, Elaine. 2010. 'Narcissism as Ethical Practice? Foucault, Askesis and an Ethics of Becoming'. *Cultural Sociology* 4(1): 23–44.

Cannell, Fenella. 2006. 'Introduction: The Anthropology of Christianity'. In *The Anthropology of Christianity*, ed. Fenella Cannell, Durham, NC: Duke University Press.

Carrette, Jeremy R. 2000. *Foucault and Religion: Spiritual Corporality and Political Spirituality*, London: Routledge.

Casanova, José. 1994. *Public Religions in the Modern World*, Chicago: University of Chicago Press.

Casanova, José. 2013. 'Religious Associations, Religious Innovations and Denominational Identities in Contemporary Global Cities'. In *Topographies of Faith: Religion in Urban Spaces*, ed. Irene Becci, Marian Burchardt, and José Casanova, 113–27, Leiden: Brill.

Cavell, Stanley. 2004. *Cities of Words: Pedagogical Letters on a Register of the Moral Life*, Cambridge, MA: Harvard University Press.

Chapman, Mark, Shuruq Naguib, and Linda Woodhead. 2012. 'God-change'. In *Religion and Change in Modern Britain*, ed. Linda Woodhead and Rebecca Catto, 173–95, London: Routledge.

Chester, Tim. 2010a. 'A Vision for the City', *Reaching The Unreached*, 10 October 2010, <http://www.reachingtheunreached.org.uk/cultural/a-vision-for-the-city/> (accessed 30 June 2012).

Chester, Tim. 2010b. 'Tim Keller on the Middle Class Culture of Conservative Evangelicalism', *Reaching The Unreached*, 18 October 2010, <http://www.reachingtheunreached.org.uk/category/church/> (accessed 17 March 2011).

Christian Action Research and Education. 2010. 'Who We Are', *Christian Action Research and Education*, <http://www.care.org.uk/about/who-we-are> (accessed 25 July 2012).

Christian Concern. 2011. 'Launch of Equalities and Conscience Petition', *Christian Concern*, 10 March 2011, <http://www.christianconcern.com/our-concerns/social/launch-of-equalities-and-conscience-petition> (accessed 24 April 2012).

Christian Concern. Not dated a. 'Not Ashamed: About', *Not Ashamed*, <http://www.notashamed.org.uk/about.php> (accessed 13 January 2012).

Christian Concern. Not dated b. 'About Christian Concern', *Christian Concern*, <http://www.christianconcern.com/about> (accessed 25 July 2012).

Christian Concern. Not dated c. 'Not Ashamed: Read the Declaration', *Not Ashamed*, <http://www.notashamed.org.uk/read.php> (accessed 13 June 2012).

Church Society. 2003. 'Thirty Nine Articles: Articles 1-5', *Church Society*, <http://www.churchsociety.org/issues_new/doctrine/39a/iss_doctrine_39A_Arts01-05.asp> (accessed 10 August 2012).

Church Times. 2013. 'Welby: Church needs to avoid drifting to divorce'. *Church Times*, 30 August 2013, <http://www.churchtimes.co.uk/articles/2013/30-august/news/uk/welby-church-needs-to-avoid-drifting-to-divorce> (accessed 11 September 2013).

Coalition for Marriage. 2012. 'Coalition for Marriage: About Us', *Coalition for Marriage*, <http://c4m.org.uk/> (accessed 24 April 2012).

Coleman, Simon. 1996. 'Words as Things: Language, Aesthetics and the Objectification of Protestant Evangelicalism'. Journal of Material Culture 1(1): 107–28.

Coleman, Simon. 2000. *The Globalisation of Charismatic Christianity: Spreading the Gospel of Prosperity*, Cambridge: Cambridge University Press.

Coleman, Simon. 2006. 'Materializing the Self: Words and Gifts in the Construction of Charismatic Protestant Identity'. In *The Anthropology of Christianity*, ed. Fenella Cannell, 163–84, Durham, NC: Duke University Press.

Coleman, Simon. 2009. 'The Protestant Ethic and the Spirit of Urbanism'. In *When God Comes to Town: Religious Traditions in Urban Contexts*, edited by R. Pinxten and L. Dikomitis, 33–44, New York: Berghahn.

Coleman, Simon. 2010. 'An Anthropological Apologetics'. *South Atlantic Quarterly* 109(4): 791–810.

Coleman, Simon. 2011. ' "Right Now!" Historiopraxy and the Embodiment of Charismatic Temporalities'. *Ethnos* 76(4): 426–47.

Comaroff, Jean. 2010. 'The Politics of Conviction: Faith on the Neo-Liberal Frontier'. In *Contemporary Religiosities: Emergent Socialities and the Post-Nation-State*, ed. Bruce Kapferer, Kari Telle and Annelin Eriksen, 17–38, New York: Berghahn.

Comaroff, John and Jean Comaroff. 1992. *Ethnography and the Historical Imagination*, Boulder, CO: Westview Press.

Cox, Harvey. 1965. *The Secular City: Secularization and Urbanization in Theological Perspective*, London: SCM.

Craib, Ian. 1994. *The Importance of Disappointment*, London: Routledge.

Crapanzano, Vincent. 2000. *Serving the Word: Literalism in America from the Pulpit to the Bench*, New York: The New Press.

Csordas, Thomas J. 2012. *Language, Charisma and Creativity: Ritual Life in the Catholic Renewal*, Basingstoke: Palgrave Macmillan.

Cupitt, Don. 1984. *The Sea of Faith*, London: BBC Books.

Daily Mail. 2012. 'Heavy-handed courts are persecuting Christians and driving them underground, says Lord Carey', *Daily Mail*, 14 April 2012, <http://www.dailymail.co.uk/news/article-2129593/Heavy-handed-courts-persecuting-Christians-driving-underground-says-Carey.html#ixzz22CsZtZZT> (accessed 24 April 2012).

De Certeau, Michel. 1984. *The Practice of Everyday Life*, Berkeley: University of California Press.

De Certeau, Michel. 1985. 'What We Do When We Believe'. In *On Signs*, ed. Marshall Blonsky, 192–202, Oxford: Basil Blackwell.

De Certeau, Michel. 1992. *The Mystic Fable*, vol. 1: *The Sixteenth and Seventeenth Centuries*, trans. Michael B. Smith, Chicago: University of Chicago Press.

Deleuze, Gilles. 1983. *Nietzsche and Philosophy*, trans. Hugh Tomlinson, London: Athlone Press.

Deleuze, Gilles and Félix Guattari. 2004. *A Thousand Plateaus: Capitalism and Schizophrenia*, trans. Brian Massumi, London: Continuum.

Dorling, Daniel. 2011. *Injustice: Why Social Inequality Persists*, Bristol: Policy Press.

Eagleton, Terry. 1990. *The Ideology of the Aesthetic*, Oxford: Basil Blackwell.

Elias, Norbert. 1994. *The Civilizing Process*, trans. Edmund Jephcott, Malden, MA: Blackwell.

Eliot, T. S. 1974. *Collected Poems 1909–1962*, London: Faber & Faber.

Elisha, Omri. 2008. 'Faith beyond Belief: Evangelical Protestant Conceptions of Faith and the Resonance of Anti-Humanism'. *Social Analysis* 52(1): 56–78.

Elisha, Omri. 2011. *Moral Ambition: Mobilization and Social Outreach in Evangelical Megachurches*, Berkeley: University of California Press.

Engelke, Matthew. 2007. *A Problem of Presence: Beyond Scripture in an African Church*, Berkeley: University of California Press.

Engelke, Matthew. 2010a. 'Strategic Secularism: Bible Advocacy in England'. In *Contemporary Religiosities: Emergent Socialities and the Post-Nation State*, ed. Bruce Kapferer, Kari Telle, and Annelin Eriksen, 39–221, New York, Berghahn Books.

Engelke, Matthew. 2010b. 'Number and the imagination of global Christianity; or, mediation and immediacy in the work of Alain Badiou'. *South Atlantic Quarterly* 109(4): 811–29.

Engelke, Matthew. 2011. 'The Semiotics of Relevance: Campaigning for the Bible in Greater Manchester'. *Anthropological Quarterly* 84(3): 705–36.

Engelke, Matthew. 2012. 'Angels in Swindon: Public Religion and Ambient Faith in England'. *American Ethnologist* 39(1): 155–70.

Engelke, Matthew. 2013. *God's Agents: Biblical Publicity in Contemporary England*, Berkeley: University of California Press.

Erzen, Tanya. 2006. *Straight to Jesus: Sexual and Christian Conversions in the Ex-Gay Movement*, Berkeley: University of California Press.

Featherstone, Mike. 1995. *Undoing Culture: Globalization, Postmodernism and Identity*, London: Sage.

Finke, Roger and Rodney Stark. 2005. *The Churching of America 1776–2005: Winners and Losers in our Religious Economy*, New Brunswick, NJ: Rutgers University Press.

Fitzgerald, Timothy. 2000. *The Ideology of Religious Studies*, New York: Oxford University Press.

Foucault, Michel. 1978. *The History of Sexuality*, vol. 1: *The Will to Knowledge*, trans. Robert Hurley, London: Penguin.

Foucault, Michel. 1979. *Discipline and Punish: The Birth of the Prison*, trans. Alan Sheridan, London: Penguin.

Foucault, Michel. 1982. 'Subject and Power'. In *Michel Foucault: Beyond Structuralism and Hermeneutics*, ed. H. L. Dreyfus and P. Rabinow, 208–26, 2nd ed. Chicago: Chicago University Press.

Foucault, Michel. 1985. *The History of Sexuality*, vol. 2: *The Use of Pleasure*, trans. Robert Hurley, London: Penguin.

Foucault, Michel. 1988. 'Technologies of the Self'. In *Technologies of the Self: A Seminar with Michel Foucault*, ed. Luther H. Martin, Huck Gutman, and Patrick H. Hutton, 16–49, Amherst: University of Massachusetts Press.

Frisby, David. 1986. *Fragments of Modernity: Theories of Modernity in the Work of Simmel, Kracauer and Benjamin*, Cambridge, MA: The MIT Press.

Frisby, David. 2002. *Georg Simmel*, revised edition, London: Routledge.

Frisby, David. 2004. 'Preface'. In *The Philosophy of Money*, ed. David Frisby, trans. Tom Bottomore and David Frisby, xv–xlvi, 3rd ed., London: Routledge.

Frykholm, Amy. 2004. *Rapture Culture: Left Behind in Evangelical America*, Oxford: Oxford University Press.

GAFCON. 2009. *Being Faithful: The Shape of Historic Anglicanism Today*, London: Latimer Trust.

Giddens, Anthony. 1990. *The Consequences of Modernity*, Cambridge: Polity.

Goffman, Erving. 1971. *Relations in Public: Microstudies of the Public Order*, London: Allen Lane.

Gordon, Colin. 1987. 'The Soul of the Citizen: Max Weber and Michel Foucault on Rationality and Government'. In *Max Weber, Rationality and Modernity*, ed. Sam Whimster and Scott Lash, 293–316, London: Routledge.

Griffith, R. Marie. 2004. *Born Again Bodies: Flesh and Spirit in American Christianity*, Berkeley: University of California Press.

Guardian. 2012a. 'Anti-gay adverts pulled from bus campaign by Boris Johnson', *Guardian*, 12 April 2012, <http://www.guardian.co.uk/world/2012/apr/12/anti-gay-adverts-boris-johnson> (accessed 18 April 2012).

Guardian. 2012b. 'Conservative Christians are becoming more confident in the political arena', *Guardian*, 12 April 2012, <http://www.guardian.co.uk/world/2012/apr/12/con servative-christians-confident-political-arena?intcmp=239> (accessed 18 April 2012).

Guest, Mathew. 2007. *Evangelical Identity and Contemporary Culture: A Congregational Study in Innovation*, Milton Keynes: Paternoster.

Gunnemann, Jon P. 2005. 'Property and Sacred Ordering in Global Civil Society'. In *Religion in Global Civil Society*, ed. Mark Juergensmeyer, 91–115, Oxford: Oxford University Press.

Habermas, Jürgen. 1989. *The Structural Transformation of the Public Sphere: An Inquiry into a Category of Bourgeois Society*, trans. Thomas Burger, Cambridge: Polity Press.

Habermas, Jürgen. 2008. 'Notes on a Post-Secular Society'. *New Perspective Quarterly* 25(4): 17–29.

Hall, David D. (ed.) 1997. *Lived Religion in America: Towards a History of Practice*, Princeton: Princeton University Press.

Hall, David D. 2006. *The Faithful Shepherd: A History of the New England Ministry in the Seventeenth Century*, Cambridge, MA: Harvard University Press.

Harding, Susan Friend. 2000. *The Book of Jerry Falwell: Fundamentalist Language and Politics*, Princeton: Princeton University Press.

Harvey, David. 1989. *The Condition of Postmodernity: An Enquiry into the Origins of Cultural Change*, Oxford: Basil Blackwell.

Hatch, Nathan. 1989. *The Democratization of American Christianity*, New Haven: Yale University Press.

Heelas, Paul and Linda Woodhead, with Benjamin Seel, Bronislaw Szerszynski, and Karin Tusting. 2005. *The Spiritual Revolution: Why Religion is Giving Way to Spirituality*, Oxford: Blackwell.

Hirschkind, Charles. 2001. 'The Ethics of Listening: Cassette-Sermon Audition in Contemporary Egypt'. *American Ethnologist* 28(3): 623–49.

Hirschkind, Charles. 2006. *The Ethical Soundscape: Cassette Sermons and Islamic Counterpublics*, New York: Columbia University Press.

Hunter, James Davison. 1983. *American Evangelicalism: Conservative Religion and the Quandary of Modernity*, New Brunswick, NJ: Rutgers University Press.

Iannaccone, Laurence, R. 1994. 'Why Strict Churches are Strong'. *American Journal of Sociology* 99(5): 1180–211.

Keane, Webb. 2004. 'Language and Religion'. In *A Companion to Linguistic Anthropology*, ed. Alessandro Duranti, 431–48, Oxford: Blackwell.

Keane, Webb. 2006. 'Anxious Transcendence'. In *The Anthropology of Christianity*, ed. Fenella Cannell, 308–23, Durham, NC: Duke University Press.

Keane, Webb. 2007. *Christian Moderns: Freedom and Fetish in the Mission Encounter*, Berkeley: University of California Press.

Keane, Webb. 2010. 'Minds, Surfaces, and Reasons in the Anthropology of Ethics'. In *Ordinary Ethics: Anthropology, Language, and Action*, ed. Michael Lambek, 64–83, New York: Fordham University Press.

Kelley, Dean. 1972. *Why Conservative Churches are Growing*, New York: Harper & Row.

Kermode, Frank. 2000. *The Sense of an Ending*, New York: Oxford University Press.

Knott, Kim. 2010. 'Religion, Space and Place: The Spatial Turn in Research on Religion'. *Religion and Society* 1: 29–43.

Laidlaw, James. 2002. 'For an Anthropology of Ethics and Freedom'. *Journal of the Royal Anthropological Institute* 8(2): 311–32.

Lambek, Michael. 2002. 'The Anthropology of Religion and the Quarrel between Poetry and Philosophy'. *Current Anthropology* 41(3): 309–20.

Lambek, Michael. 2010. 'Introduction'. In *Ordinary Ethics: Anthropology, Language, and Action*, edited by Michael Lambek, 1–36, New York: Fordham University Press.

Lash, Scott and Jon Urry. 1994. *Economies of Signs and Space*, London: Sage Publications.

Latour, Bruno. 1993. *We Have Never Been Modern*, trans. Catherine Porter, Cambridge, MA: Harvard University Press.

Latour, Bruno. 2004. 'Why Has Critique Run out of Steam? From Matters of Fact to Matters of Concern'. *Critical Inquiry* 30: 225–48.

Latour, Bruno. 2005. *Reassembling the Social: An Introduction to Actor-Network-Theory*, Oxford and New York: Oxford University Press.

Latour, Bruno. 2010. *On the Modern Cult of the Factish Gods*, Durham, NC: Duke University Press.

Latour, Bruno. 2011. 'Reflections on Etienne Souriau's *Les différents modes d'existence*'. In *The Speculative Turn: Continental Materialism and Realism*, ed. Levi Bryant, Nick Srnicek and Graham Harman, trans. Stephen Muecke, 304–33, Melbourne: Re-Press.

Latour, Bruno. 2013. *An Inquiry into Modes of Existence*, trans. C. Porter, Cambridge, MA: Harvard University Press.

Levin, David Michael (ed.). 1993. *Modernity and the Hegemony of Vision*, Berkeley: University of California Press.

Levinas, Emmanuel. 1987. *Collected Philosophical Papers*, trans. A. Lingis, Dordrecht, Martinus Nijhoff.

Levine, Donald N. 1971. 'Introduction'. In *On Individuality and Social Forms*, ed. Donald N. Levine, ix–lxv, Chicago: University of Chicago Press.

Luhr, Eileen. 2009. *Witnessing Suburbia: Conservatives and Christian Youth Culture*, Berkeley: University of California Press.

Luhrmann, Tanya. 2004. 'Metakinesis: How God Becomes Intimate in Contemporary U.S. Christianity'. *American Anthropologist* 106(3): 518–28.

Luhrmann, Tanya. 2012. *When God Talks Back: Understanding the American Evangelical Relationship with God*, New York: Vintage.

Luhrmann, Tanya, Howard Nusbaum, and Ronald Thisted. 2010. 'The Absorption Hypothesis: Learning to Hear God in Evangelical Christianity'. *American Anthropologist* 112(1): 66–78.

Lynch, Gordon. 2012. 'Living with Two Cultural Turns'. In *Social Research After the Cultural Turn*, ed. Sasha Roseneil and Stephen Frosh, 73–92, London: Palgrave Macmillan.

Lynch, Michael. 2000. 'Against Reflexivity as an Academic Virtue and Source of Privileged Knowledge'. *Theory, Culture and Society* 17(3): 26–54.

McCarthy Brown, Karen. 1999. 'Staying Grounded in a High-Rise Building: Ecological Dissonance and Ritual Accommodation in Haitian Voudou'. In *Gods of the City*, ed. Robert A. Orsi, 79–102, Bloomington: Indiana University Press.

McCutcheon, Russell T. 1997. *Manufacturing Religion: The Discourse on Sui Generis Religion and the Politics of Nostalgia*, Oxford: Oxford University Press.

McDannell, Colleen. 1995. *Material Christianity: Religion and Popular Culture in America*, New Haven: Yale University Press.

McGrath, Alister E. 1994. *Christian Theology: An Introduction*, Oxford: Blackwell.

McGuire, Meredith B. 2002. 'New-Old Directions in the Social Scientific Study of Religion: Ethnography, Phenomenology, and the Human Body'. In *Personal Knowledge and Beyond: Reshaping the Ethnography of Religion*, ed. James V. Spickard, Shawn Landres, and Meredith B. McGuire, 195–211, New York: New York University Press.

McGuire, Meredith B. 2008. *Lived Religion: Faith and Practice in Everyday Life*, Oxford: Oxford University Press.

MacIntyre, Alasdair. 2007. *After Virtue: A Study in Moral Theory*, 3rd edition. London: Bristol Classical Press.

Martin, David. 2005. *On Secularization: Towards a Revised General Theory*, Aldershot: Ashgate.

Marx, Karl. 1975. *Early Writings*, trans. Rodney Livingstone and Gregor Benton, London: Penguin Books.

Marx, Karl. 1988. *The Communist Manifesto*, trans. Frederic L. Bender, New York: W.W. Norton.

Massey, Doreen. 1999. 'Cities in the World'. In *City Worlds*, ed. Doreen Massy, John Allen, and Steve Pile, 100–36, London: Routledge.

Massumi, Brian. 2002. *Parables for the Virtual: Movement, Affect, Sensation*, Durham, NC: Duke University Press.

Mauss, Marcel. 1990. *The Gift: The Form and Reason for Exchange in Archaic Societies*, trans. W. D. Halls, New York: Norton.

Mauss, Marcel. 2006. 'Techniques of the Body'. In *Techniques, Technology and Civilisation*, ed. Nathan Schlanger, 77–95, New York: Berghahn Books.

McKinnon, Andrew M., Marta Trzebiatowska, and Christopher Craig Brittain. 2011. 'Bourdieu, Capital and Conflict in a Religious Field: The Case of the "Homosexuality" Conflict in the Anglican Communion'. *Journal of Contemporary Religion* 26(3): 355–70.

McLeod, Hugh. 1974. *Class and Religion in the Late Victorian City*, London: Croom Helm.

McLeod, Hugh. 1996. *Piety and Poverty: Working-class Religion in Berlin, London and New York 1870–1914*, New York: Holmes and Meier.

Mead, George Herbert. 1962. *Mind, Self and Society: From the Standpoint of a Social Behaviourist*, Chicago: University of Chicago Press.

Mellor, Philip A. and Chris Shilling. 1997. *Re-forming the Body: Religion, Community and Modernity*, London: Sage.

Mellor, Philip A. and Chris Shilling. 2010. 'Body Pedagogics and the Religious Habitus: A New Direction for the Sociological Study of Religion'. *Religion* 40: 27–38.

Merleau-Ponty, Maurice. 2002. *Phenomenology of Perception*, trans. Colin Smith, London: Routledge.

Meyer, Birgit. 2008. 'Religious Sensations: Why Media, Aesthetics and Power Matter in the Study of Contemporary Religion'. In *Religion Beyond A Concept*, ed. Hent De Vries, 704–23, New York: Fordham University Press.

Meyer, Birgit. 2010. 'Aesthetics of Persuasion: Global Christianity and Pentecostalism's Sensational Forms'. *South Atlantic Quarterly* 109(4): 741–63.

Miles, Jack. 1996. *God: A Biography*, New York: Vintage Books.

Miller, Daniel. 1987. *Material Culture and Mass Consumption*, Oxford: Blackwell.

Mitchell, W. J. T. 2005. *What Do Pictures Want? The Lives and Loves of Images*, Chicago: University of Chicago Press.

Morgan, David. 2010. 'Introduction'. In *Religion and Material Culture*, ed. David Morgan, 1–17, London: Routledge.

Morgan, David. 2012. *The Embodied Eye: Religious Visual Culture and the Social Life of Feeling*, Berkeley: University of California Press.

Nietzsche, Friedrich. 1999. *The Birth of Tragedy and Other Writings*, ed. Raymond Geuss and Ronald Spiers. Cambridge: Cambridge University Press.

Noll, Mark. 1994. *The Scandal of the Evangelical Mind*, Michigan: William B. Eerdmans.

O'Neill, Kevin Lewis. 2010a. *City of God: Christian Citizenship in Postwar Guatemala*, Berkeley: University of California Press.

O'Neill, Kevin Lewis. 2010b. 'I Want More of You: The Politics of Christian Eroticism in Postwar Guatemala'. *Comparative Studies in History and Society* 52: 131–56.

Orsi, Robert A. 1999. 'Introduction'. In *Gods of the City*, ed. Robert A. Orsi, 1–78, Bloomington: Indiana University Press.

Orsi, Robert A. 2005. *Between Heaven and Earth: The Religious Worlds People Make and the Scholars who Study Them*, Princeton: Princeton University Press.

Orsi, Robert A. 2012. 'The Problem of the Holy'. In *The Cambridge Companion to Religious Studies*, ed. Robert A. Orsi, 84–105, New York: Cambridge University Press.

Pardo, Italo and Giuliana B. Prato. 2012. 'Introduction: The Contemporary Significance of Anthropology in the City'. In *Anthropology in the City: Methodology and Theory*, ed. I. Pardo and G.B. Prato, 1–28, Farnham: Ashgate.

Pew Forum. 2010. 'U.S. Religious Landscape Survey: Affiliations', *The Pew Forum on Religion and Public Life*, <http://religions.pewforum.org/affiliations> (accessed 16 August 2012).

Pinxten, Rik and Lisa Dikomitis (eds). 2009. *When God Comes to Town: Religious Traditions in Urban Contexts*, New York: Berghahn Books.

Poewe, Karla (ed.) 1994. *Charismatic Christianity as a Global Culture*, Columbia, SC: University of South Carolina Press.

Porterfield, Amanda. 2012. *Conceived in Doubt: Religion and Politics in the New American Nation*, Chicago: University of Chicago Press.

Postman, Neil. 1985. *Amusing Ourselves to Death*, London: Methuen.

Prasad, Leela. 2012. 'Constituting Ethical Subjectivities'. In *The Cambridge Companion to Religious Studies*, ed. Robert A. Orsi, 360–79, New York: Cambridge University Press.

Preddy and Hall v Bull and Bull. 2011. Bristol County Court, 18 January 2011, <http://www.judiciary.gov.uk/wp-content/uploads/JCO/Documents/Judgments/bull-v-hall-and-preddy.pdf> (accessed 11 December 2014).

Putnam, Robert. 2000. *Bowling Alone*, New York: Simon and Schuster.

Pyyhtinen, Olli. 2010. *Simmel and 'The Social'*, Basingstoke: Palgrave Macmillan.

Richard Dawkins Foundation for Reason and Science. Not dated. 'Mission Statement for the US Foundation', *Richard Dawkins Foundation for Reason and Science*, <http://richarddawkins.net/pages/mission> (accessed 7 August 2012).

Ricoeur, Paul. 1992. *Oneself as Another*, trans. Kathleen Blamey, Chicago: University of Chicago Press.

Riesman, David. 2001. *The Lonely Crowd*, New Haven: Yale University Press.

Riis, Ole and Linda Woodhead. 2010. *A Sociology of Religious Emotion*, Oxford: Oxford University Press.

Robbins, Joel. 2004. *Becoming Sinners: Christianity and Moral Torment in a Papua New Guinea Society*, Berkeley: University of California Press.

Robbins, Joel. 2010. 'Anthropology, Pentecostalism, and the New Paul: Conversion, Event, and Social Transformation'. *South Atlantic Quarterly* 109(4): 633–52.

Robbins, Joel. 2012. 'On becoming ethical subjects: freedom, constraint, and the anthropology of morality', Anthropology of This Century, <http:%20http://aotcpress.com/articles/ethical-subjects-freedom-constraint-anthropology-morality/#sthash.KE1yZOsu.dpuf> (accessed 16 July 2013).

Rose, Nikolas. 1990. *Governing the Soul: The Shaping of the Private Self*. London: Routledge.

Rose, Nikolas. 1996. 'Identity, Genealogy and History'. In *Questions of Cultural Identity*, ed. Stuart Hall and Paul du Gay, 128–50, London: Sage.

Roose, Kevin. 2009. *The Unlikely Disciple: A Sinner's Semester at America's Holiest University*, New York: Grand Central Publishing.

Sadgrove, Joanna, Robert M. Vanderbeck, Kevin Ward, Gill Valentine, and Johan Andersson. 2010. 'Constructing the boundaries of Anglican orthodoxy: an analysis of the Global Anglican Future Conference (GAFCON)'. *Religion* 40(3): 193–206.

Sassen, Saskia. 2001. *The Global City: New York, London, Tokyo*. 2nd ed. Princeton: Princeton University Press.

Sassen, Saskia. 2010. 'The City: Its return as a lens for social theory'. *City, Culture and Society* 1: 3–11.

Schmidt, Leigh Eric. 2000. *Hearing Things: Religion, Illusion and the American Enlightenment*, Cambridge, MA: Harvard University Press.

Sennett, Richard. 1990. *The Conscience of the Eye: The Design and Social Life of Cities*, London: Faber & Faber.

Sennett, Richard. 1998. *The Corrosion of Character*, New York: W.W. Norton & Company.

Sennett, Richard. 2002a. *The Fall of Public Man*, London: Penguin.

Sennett, Richard. 2002b. *Flesh and Stone: The Body and the City in Western Civilization*, London: Penguin.

Sennett, Richard. 2012. *Together: The Rituals, Pleasures and Politics of Cooperation*, London: Penguin.

Sheldon, Ruth. 2013. 'Exploring Student Engagement with Israel-Palestine within UK Universities'. PhD thesis, Canterbury: University of Kent.

Shilling, Chris. 1993. *The Body and Social Theory*, London: Sage.

Shilling, Chris. 2005. *The Body in Culture, Technology and Society*, London: Sage.

Shilling, Chris and Philip A. Mellor. 2010. 'Sociology and the Problem of Eroticism'. *Sociology* 44(3): 435–52.

Shilling, Chris and Philip A. Mellor. 2013. 'Making Things Sacred: Retheorising the Nature and Function of Sacrifice in Modernity'. *Journal of Classical Sociology* 13(3): 319–37.

Simmel, Georg. 1971a. 'The Stranger'. In *On Individuality and Social Forms*, ed. Donald N. Levine, 143–9, Chicago: University of Chicago Press.

Simmel, Georg. 1971b. 'The Metropolis and Mental Life'. In *On Individuality and Social Forms*, ed. Donald N. Levine, 324–39, Chicago: University of Chicago Press.

Simmel, Georg. 1997a. 'Bridge and Door'. In *Simmel on Culture*, ed. David Frisby and Mike Featherstone, 170–4, London: Sage.

Simmel, Georg. 1997b. 'Money in Modern Culture'. In *Simmel on Culture*, ed. David Frisby and Mike Featherstone, 243–55, London: Sage.

Simmel, Georg. 1997c. 'The Conflict of Modern Culture'. In *Simmel on Culture*, ed. David Frisby and Mike Featherstone, 75–90, London: Sage.

Simmel, Georg. 1997d. 'The Concept and Tragedy of Culture'. In *Simmel on Culture*, ed. David Frisby and Mike Featherstone, 55–75, London: Sage.

Simmel, Georg. 1997e. 'Religion and the Contradictions of Life'. In *Essays on Religion*, ed. Horst Jürgen Helle, 36–44, New Haven: Yale University Press.

Simmel, Georg. 1997f. 'The Crisis of Culture'. In *Simmel on Culture*, ed. David Frisby and Mike Featherstone, 90–101, London: Sage.

Simmel, Georg. 1997g. 'The Philosophy of Fashion'. In *Simmel on Culture*, ed. David Frisby and Mike Featherstone, 187–206, London: Sage.

Simmel, Georg. 1997h. 'The Personality of God'. In *Essays on Religion*, ed. Horst Jürgen Helle, 45–62, New Haven: Yale University Press.

Simmel, Georg. 2004. *The Philosophy of Money*, ed. David Frisby, trans. Tom Bottomore and David Frisby, 3rd ed. London: Routledge.

Singh, Bhrigupati. 2014. 'How Concepts Make the World Look Different: Affirmative and Negative Genealogies of Thought'. In *The Ground Between: Anthropologists Engage Philosophy*, ed. Veena Das, Michael D. Jackson, Arthur Kleinman, and Bhrigupati Singh, Durham, NC: Duke University Press.

Smith, Christian. 1998. *American Evangelicalism: Embattled and Thriving*, Chicago: University of Chicago Press.

Smith, Christian. 2000. *Christian America: What Evangelicals Really Want?*, Berkeley: University of California Press.

Sovereign Grace Worship. 2003. 'His Forever', *Sovereign Grace Ministries*, <http://www.sovereigngracestore.com/Product/M4155-07-51/His_Forever.aspx> (accessed 12 August 2012).

Stark, Rodney and Roger Finke. 2000. *Acts of Faith: Exploring the Human Side of Religion*, Berkeley: University of California Press.

Strhan, Anna. 2011. 'Religious Language as Poetry: Heidegger's Challenge'. *Heythrop Journal* 52(6): 926–38.

Strhan, Anna. 2012. *Levinas, Subjectivity, Education: Towards an Ethics of Radical Responsibility*, Chichester: Wiley-Blackwell.

Strhan, Anna. 2013. 'Christianity and the City: Simmel, Space and Urban Subjectivities'. *Religion and Society: Advances in Research* 4: 125–49.

Strhan, Anna. 2014. 'English Evangelicals, Equality and the City.' In *Globalized Religion and Sexuality Identity*, ed. Heather Shipley, Leiden: Brill.

Taylor, Charles. 2007. *A Secular Age*, Cambridge, MA: Harvard University Press.

Thrift, Nigel. 2008. *Non-Representational Theory: Space, Politics Affect*, London: Routledge.

Thurow, Lester C. 1996. *The Future of Capitalism: How Today's Economic Forces Shape Tomorrow's World*, London: Nicholas Brealey.

Tonkiss, Fran. 2005. *Space, the City and Social Theory: Social Relations and Urban Forms*, Cambridge: Polity Press.

Turner, Bryan S. 1983. *Religion and Social Theory*, London: Heinemann Educational.

Turner, Bryan S. 1986. 'Simmel, Rationalisation and the Sociology of Money'. *The Sociological Review* 34(1): 93–114.

Turner, Bryan S. 2011. *Religion and Modern Society: Citizenship, Secularisation and the State*. Cambridge: Cambridge University Press.

Tweed, Thomas. 2006. *Crossing and Dwelling: A Theory of Religion*, Cambridge: MA, Harvard University Press.

Urry, John. 2007. *Mobilities*, Cambridge: Polity Press.

Valentine, Gill. 2008. 'Living with Difference: Reflections on Geographies of Encounter'. *Progress in Human Geography* 32: 323–37.

Vasquez, Manuel A. 2011. *More than Belief: A Materialist Theory of Religion*, New York: Oxford University Press.

Vertovec, Steven. 2001. 'Religion and Diaspora'. ESRC Transnational Communities Research Programme *Working Papers* 01-01, <http:www.transcomm.ox.ac.uk> (accessed 13 May 2013).

Wacquant, Loïc. 2004a. *Body and Soul: Notebooks of an Apprentice Boxer*, New York: Oxford University Press.

Wacquant, Loïc. 2004b. 'Following Pierre Bourdieu into the field', *Ethnography* 5(4): 387–414.

Waghorne, Joanne Punzo. 1999. 'The Hindu Gods in a Split-Level World: The Sri-Siva Vishnu Temple in Suburban Washington, D.C.', in *Gods of the City*, ed. Robert A. Orsi, 103–30, Bloomington: Indiana University Press.

Walker Bynum, Caroline. 2013. *Resurrection of the Body*, New York: Columbia University Press.

Ward, Graham. 2000. *Cities of God*, London: Routledge.

Ward, Graham. 2009. *The Politics of Discipleship*, London: SCM Press.

Ward, Pete. 1997. *Growing Up Evangelical: Youthwork and the Making of a Subculture*, London: SPCK.

Warner, Rob. 2007. *Reinventing English Evangelicalism, 1966–2001*, Milton Keynes: Paternoster Press.

Weber, Max. 1948. 'Religious Rejections of the World and their Directions'. In *From Max Weber: Essays in Sociology*, ed. H. H. Gerth and C. Wright Mills, 323–59, London, Routledge and Kegan Paul.

Weber, Max. 2001. *The Protestant Ethic and the Spirit of Capitalism*, trans. Talcott Parsons, London: Routledge.

Webster, Joe. 2008. 'Establishing the "Truth" of the Matter: Confessional Reflexivity as Introspection and Avowal'. *Psychology and Society* 1(1): 65–76.

Wilford, Justin G. 2012. *Sacred Subdivisions: The Postsuburban Transformation of American Evangelicalism*, New York: New York University Press.

Wilkins, Amy C. 2008. *Wannabes, Goths and Christians: The Boundaries of Sex, Style, and Status*, Chicago: University of Chicago Press.

Winkett, Lucy. 2010. *Our Sound is our Wound*, London: Continuum.

Wood, Maxwell Thomas. 2011. 'Penal Substitution in the Construction of British Evangelical Identity: Controversies in the Doctrine of Atonement in the Mid-2000s', PhD Thesis, Durham University, *Durham E-Theses*, <http://etheses.dur.ac.uk/3260/> (accessed 12 August 2012).

Woodhead, Linda. 2012. 'Introduction'. In *Religion and Change in Modern Britain*, ed. Linda Woodhead and Rebecca Catto, 1–33, London: Routledge.

Yeats, W. B. 1992. *Collected Poems*, London: Vintage.

Zigon, Jarrett. 2007. 'Moral Breakdown and the Ethical Demand: A Theoretical Framework for an Anthropology of Moralities'. *Anthropological Theory* 7(2): 131–50.

Zito, Angela. 2008. 'Culture'. In *Key Words in Religion, Media and Culture*, ed. David Morgan, 69–82, New York: Routledge.

Zuckerman, Phil. 2011. 'Why Evangelicals Hate Jesus', *The Huffington Post*, 3 March 2011, <http://www.huffingtonpost.com/phil-zuckerman/why-evangelicals-hate-jes_b_830237.html> (accessed 25 August 2011).

Index

Footnotes are indicated by the page number followed by 'n' and the note number.